Black Cloud

Other Books by Eliot Kleinberg

Pioneers in Paradise: West Palm Beach, the First 100 Years
(with Jan Tuckwood)

Florida Fun Facts

Historical Traveler's Guide to Florida

Weird Florida

War in Paradise: Stories of Florida in World War II

Our Century (with the staff of the *Palm Beach Post*)

Black Cloud

The Great Florida Hurricane of 1928

Eliot Kleinberg

CARROLL & GRAF PUBLISHERS

NEW YORK

BLACK CLOUD
THE GREAT FLORIDA HURRICANE OF 1928

Carroll & Graf Publishers
An Imprint of Avalon Publishing Group Inc.
161 William St., 16th Floor
New York, NY 10038

First Carroll & Graf edition 2003

Epigraph quote from *Their Eyes Were Watching God* by Zora Neale Hurston, copyright © 1937 by Harper & Row Publishers, Inc. Renewed 1965 by John C. Hurston and Joel Hurston. Reprinted by permission of HarperCollins Publishers Inc.

Library of Congress Cataloging-in-Publication Data is available.

ISBN: 0-7867-1146-9

Printed in the United States of America
Interior design by Shona McCarthy
Distributed by Publishers Group West

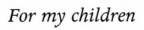

For my children

It woke up old Okechobee and the monster began to roll in his bed.

—Zora Neale Hurston, *Their Eyes Were Watching God*

Contents

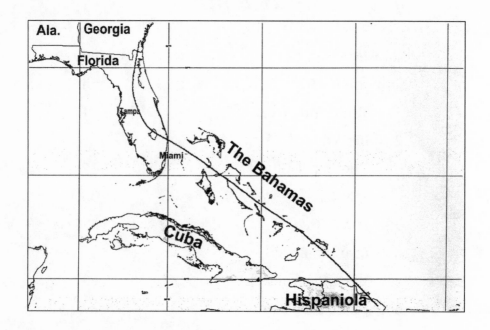

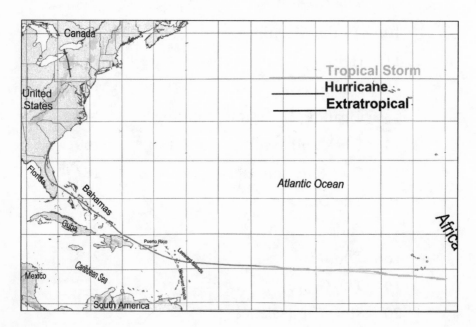

Storm track maps

Map courtesy of the National Hurricane Center

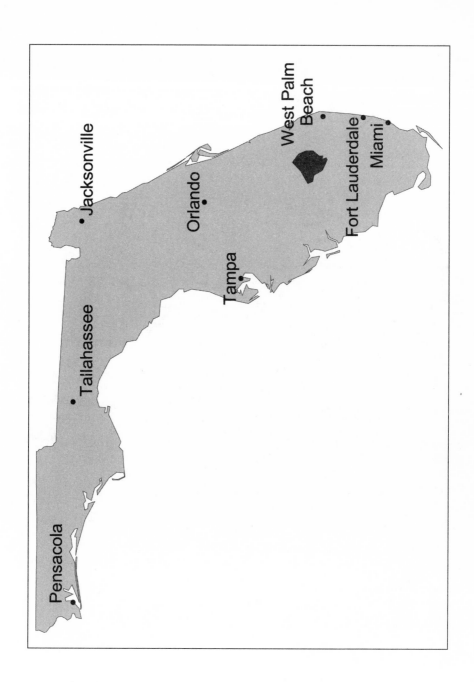

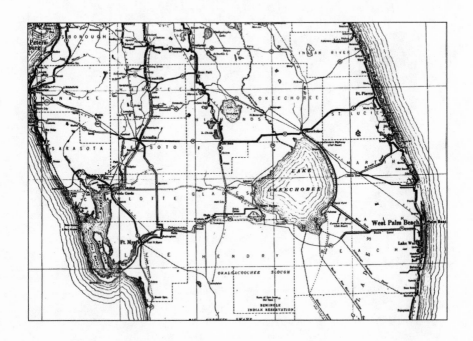

Road map circa 1926, courtesy of
the Florida Department of Transportation

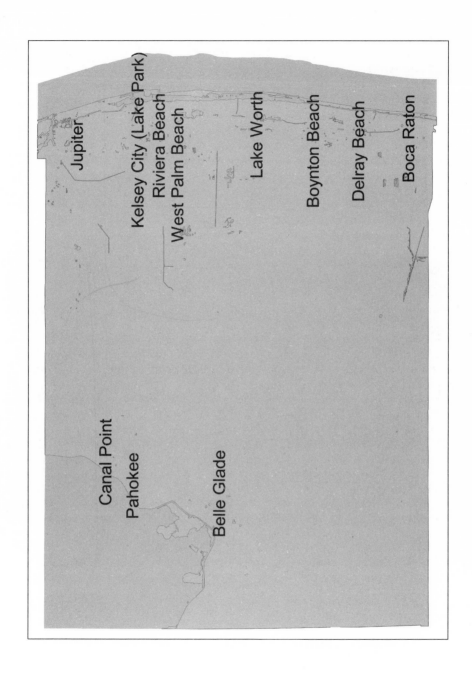

Local Map, with Lake Okeechobee in northwest corner
U.S. Census/Christine Stapleton, *Palm Beach Post*

The bracelet caught Festus Stallings's eye. It was on another of the corpses, all of them bloated and discolored from days in standing water and merciless sun that stole their identities and reduced them to lost debris. Stallings reached and closed his hand around the bauble. It was on the arm of a little girl. A month earlier, she had proudly shown him the bracelet, a gift for her second birthday. He grabbed her by that arm, lifted her up, and added her to the pile of death. The fire whooshed. The workers stepped back, staggered by the burst of heat and the smell of gasoline and burning flesh. A thick, oily, cloud of smoke rose. It rose above the muck, above the bent sugarcane and tattered vegetable stalks, above the scattered sticks that had once been homes, above the great lake. Into the Florida sky.

It was a black cloud.

September 1928

It is a great lake; so big that standing at its shore is like standing at an ocean. For centuries, no white man saw it, and today it is hidden not by mystery but by a towering dike. Native Americans named it "big water." Even today, locals refer to it simply as "the lake."

Along its southeastern shore lie a number of farm towns. One is Belle Glade. Along its main street, in front of its library, stands a sculpture, motionless and silent. A man, a woman, and a boy are running. The woman carries an infant in her arms. As they look over their shoulders, they raise their arms in a feeble attempt to ward off an unseen wall of water. Below the statue, a concrete relief shows houses, people, vegetation, and animals swirling helplessly in water. You can't hear the deafening rush of wind, the pounding rain, the screams.

About 35 miles to the east, in West Palm Beach, is Tamarind Avenue, one of the city's roughest streets. It's a place that often appears in the same sentence with TV news-talk such as "drug deal gone bad" and "drive-by shooting." At the corner of Tamarind and 25th Street is a field surrounded by a chain-link fence. For three-fourths of a century, no marker noted the fact that nearly seven hundred people lay entombed under the street. Second-class citizens in life, they became truly invisible in death. They are the faceless dead of the great storm of 1928.

Seventy-five years later, to say that the storm is still the deadliest weather event to strike Florida and the eastern United States does it a disservice. Nothing even comes close. Hurricane Andrew, the storm that defined hurricanes for most people living today, flattened much of one of America's largest metropolitan areas. But it killed only 15 people. The 1928 storm's official death toll is 1,836. And that number, assigned by the American Red Cross and state health officials in the weeks following the disaster, is almost certainly low. Too many people were hurriedly put into mass graves, stacked in piles and burned, or found as piles of bones years later in the fields. Historians suggest that 2,500 to 3,000 is a more realistic number. The volume of death was so staggering to the pioneer region that after a while, people just stopped counting.

In summer 2003 the National Hurricane Center made plans to change that official count to 2,500—not as a result of any new evidence, but reflecting a need to have a more accurate number in time for the storm's seventy-fifth anniversary. The storm would then be officially classified as the second deadliest disaster in American history, behind only the Galveston Hurricane of 1900, which killed between 6,000 and 12,000 people, and passing the Johnstown, Pennsylvania, flood of 1889, which killed 2,209.

Besides the Florida deaths, the 1928 storm also killed at least 312—perhaps up to 1,600—in Puerto Rico, an American possession. If you figure the higher death appraisals of the 1928 storm and include those lost in Puerto Rico, the grim scoreboard of dead on U.S. soil surpasses 4,500; add deaths on other Caribbean islands, and it exceeds 6,800.

Twin hurricanes of 1893 are said to have killed 2,000 each in the United States, but those are only estimates. The 1928 storm killed more than the 1906 San Francisco earthquake (about 700), more than the sinking of the *Titanic* (1,503), and probably more than the estimated 3,000 who died on September 11, 2001.

The hurricane may have also accounted for the most deaths of black people in a single day in U.S. history. One has to wonder: Had the storm drowned 3,000 white businessmen in downtown West Palm Beach, or smashed a black-tie affair on ritzy Palm Beach, instead of killing mostly black migrant workers from the Caribbean in the vegetable fields of Florida's interior, might it have received more attention over the years?

Palm Beach County, one of the largest in the eastern United States, is home to one of the world's great enclaves of wealth and society. Its glittering ocean draws tourists from around the globe. But a half-hour drive to the west takes you to another world, one of dirt roads, tractors, and never-ending farm fields. Today, as in the 1920s, the people who work there do some of the country's toughest work and live in some of its poorest towns.

In the early decades of the twentieth century, South Florida was a shining gem, attracting investors and snowbirds who wanted a piece of the cities of gold lying in the warm sun. They poured their money into the region with such abandon that opportunistic salesmen made fortunes buying and selling the same property over and over. Those sellers and buyers and dreamers created a frenzy which would fling them even deeper into the Great Depression that was about to end the partying.

Once, the great Everglades flowed to the sea from Lake Okeechobee, the largest lake in the South. Then people decided that if they drained that useless swamp, the muck that was exposed would provide the richest farming soil in America. They were right. But they didn't know—or didn't care to know—the environmental catastrophe they were helping set into motion.

Farmers came seeking their fortune in the black soil. They planted fruit and vegetable crops and, eventually, 700,000 acres of sugarcane, supplying one-fourth of the nation's output. In the hardscrabble towns of the Deep South and the desperately impoverished islands of the Caribbean, people looked to Florida. They weren't investing in waterfront lots or strolling tony shops. They were the poorest of the poor, struggling to meet their most basic needs under the burden of grinding poverty and the constant fear that comes from oppression.

So they came, in rusty buses or creaking ships, leaving their families behind for what they believed was the best chance to feed them. They lived in tent cities or shantytowns. And every day, in the blistering South Florida sun, they gathered the winter vegetables that brought color to a gray winter's day or chopped the green cane that brought sweetness to households across the land. Many white farmers also toiled, and many of them also had little to their names. Towns sprang up to serve the farms. Canals and roads were built that moved produce to grocers and mills across the land.

Always there was the lake. It gave those who settled around it water for their homes and crops and livestock, and fish for their tables and packinghouses. Shaped like a giant frying pan, only 20 feet deep at most, it appeared generous and benign.

But there was the water.

At first, there wasn't anything to keep it from seeping out of the lake and into the countryside. So the government put together a berm of mud, dirt, and rock around it. In most places, it was about six feet high. It was just enough to protect the farms and villages—as long as it didn't rain too hard, too fast, and as long as the wind didn't slosh the water out of the shallow lake and up against that flimsy dike. In 1926, it did, and six hundred people died. But no one changed anything about the dike. Besides, how much damage could a hurricane do forty miles inland?

Two years later, everyone would find out.

Tamarind Avenue

At 3 A.M. on a February day in 1919, a young soldier stepped off a train, still in his doughboy's uniform. He had traveled down the coast of what was still, in many places, the last frontier on the eastern seaboard. His ride had gone through a city of big business, a bustling center of real estate frenzy, with hotels and shops springing up almost daily: West Palm Beach.

The train had crossed a bridge from mainland West Palm Beach and run out of track on one of the most exclusive island communities in America, Palm Beach, and in front of one of the ritziest hotels in America: Henry Flagler's Royal Poinciana.

Carmen Salvatore didn't know how to get to Pahokee, where his bride of two years and a new life awaited. But as he eyed the sumptuous furnishings of the hotel lobby, he just knew it wasn't here.

Carmen was all of twenty-two years old.

The young man walked into the lobby and up to a weary night clerk.

"How do I get to Pahokee?" he asked.

The clerk was puzzled. "Never heard of it."

With nothing to do and nowhere to go until dawn, he walked across the bridge back to the mainland, to Clematis Street, the main east-west street of downtown West Palm Beach. As a policeman eyed him, he pretended to window-shop. Finally, with morning arriving, he walked to Howard Park, about a mile southwest of the waterfront. At the park was a small lake. It was a turning basin for fishing boats coming in from Lake Okeechobee with their catches.

Some folks who had come in from Pahokee realized who he was. After all, his wife had recently been walking a mile down the ridge to meet every mail boat from the coast. Now, he hitched a ride with one of the fishermen. Before he left, he bought a pound of cooked bacon to munch on during what he thought might be a ride of just a few hours back up the canal to Pahokee. After all, it was only 35 miles. But it took ten hours. The townsfolk had come to meet the mail boat, as they always did, and they saw Carmen Salvatore, first person in the town to return from the Great War. Carmen scanned the crowd. Then he saw Ella. She'd climbed onto a makeshift raft to meet his boat. Holding Carmen, Jr., she leaped from it and into his arms.

By 1928, the Salvatores would have four young children and a home just a few feet from the muck dike that surrounded Lake Okeechobee.

As Carmen had stood looking into those West Palm Beach shop windows in the dead of night on his first night back from the Great War, $5\frac{1}{2}$-year-old Clothilda Miller slept not far from those Clematis Street shops. They might as well have been on Mars. Today's Florida is by all accounts the most assimilated and most un-southern of the southern states. Now it is a hodgepodge of New Yorkers, Midwesterners, Southerners, and immigrants from the Caribbean and all over the world. But in the 1920s, South Florida was still part of the Deep South.

Three-quarters of a century later, Clothilda tells her family's story from memory. Whatever records, photographs, or items of value that existed the night of September 16, 1928, were swept away with the family home. Only in recent years did a relative come across the certificate from her parents' wedding on March 31, 1907, at the Holy Trinity Episcopal Church in West Palm Beach. Clothilda's family were "Conchs." The name, from a shelled delicacy famed in the islands, refers to black immigrants from the Bahamas looking for a better life on the mainland. Isaac A. Miller had come from Bannerman Town in Eleuthera. His wife, Frances J. Moxcy Miller, came from Nassau, the capital. They had six children: Lena, Nolan, Frances, Clothilda, Samuel, and Tunis. Clothilda was born in November 1913.

In segregated Florida, the Millers could not live just anywhere.

Isaac built a wooden home for his family on a plot at 13th Street and Henrietta Avenue, in the heart of West Palm Beach's black neighborhood. Frances did laundry for a Palm Beach family. Isaac, a tall man, rode the bicycle-rickshaw combinations popular among Palm Beach's "snowbirds," the rich Northerners who spent their winters in Palm Beach. The contraptions, powered by black drivers, were later disparagingly called "Afromobiles. " He also toiled on crews building roads across booming South Florida. He made about $12 a week. Every day, when he got home, he would put down his bag, ask the children about school, lead them in prayer, and work with them on their ABCs and numbers. Then everyone would sit down for family dinner. He was also a layman at his church, and it was his job to ring the bell on Sunday. Services were at 7:00 A.M., followed by Sunday School at 9:00 A.M. and another service at 11:00 A.M.

If they were what would be considered poor, the children didn't know any better. They didn't have luxuries or a big house and they slept two or three to a bed. But dinner was usually ham, liver, or lamb, with rice or macaroni, and everyone ate. They had a pet dog, and the girls loved their delicate china baby dolls. They had no radio, but they did have a wind-up record player, and the scratchy sounds of jazz drifted through the home as the children danced playfully.

In 1928, Clothilda was fourteen and a student at Industrial High School, the local segregated school for blacks. She went from 8:00 to 3:00. On Monday and Tuesday, and again on Thursday and Friday, she watched the children of a white dressmaker after school.

Not far from the Miller home, along Tamarind Avenue, lay an unofficial cemetery for the blacks of West Palm Beach. Soon it would be a very crowded place.

In the fall of 1928, Clothilda's father decided to go into business with Ernest Rolle, the brother of his wife Frances. Already living in the Glades were Frances's sister, Susan Wells, and Wells's children, Emmy and Elbert. Susan Wells had been there less than a year. Isaac and his brother-in-law Ernest would start a farm in a now-vanished settlement still marked by a sign near State Road 715 and the Hillsboro Canal, just west of the Belle Glade city limits. It was called Chosen.

Not far from Clothilda's West Palm Beach home was the home of Coot Simpson.

Big Water

Before everything else there had always been the lake.

It covers 730 square miles, making it three-fourths the size of Rhode Island. At 33 miles long and 30 miles wide, from the shore, you cannot see the other side. It is so big that it stands out even on world maps and pictures from space as a giant hole in a peninsula stabbing from North America toward the tropics. It is the third-largest freshwater lake completely within U.S. borders, behind only Lake Michigan (22,300 square miles) and Lake Iliamna in Alaska (1,150). As an outdoor attraction, the lake outdraws the Grand Canyon, Yosemite, and Yellowstone. Five times more people visit it each year than nearby Everglades National Park.

Its surface can rise as much as two inches a night, when it stops evaporating and rivers and creeks continue feeding it. It can drop back down that much in the heat of the day. It holds enough water to give 300 gallons to every living person on earth. But it is shallow: 21 feet at its deepest point and 6 to 10 feet in most spots. Place it in a swampy peninsula squeezed between two seas and add tropical temperatures, and you get an unusual meteorological machine that makes for capricious weather. More than one fisherman or pleasure boater has been lost to storms that raced down from the north or in from either coast, whipping up the waves as they would in the ocean. Seminoles named it Okeechobee: Big Water.

Early European explorers talked of a mysterious, uncharted "Lagoon of the Holy Spirit." Early-nineteenth-century coastal settlers lived within 60 miles of the lake, yet doubted its existence. It was war that exposed the big lake to the romance of the American public. "Manifest Destiny" had always been presumed to be east to west, but of course it went north and south as well. From 1835 to 1842, America fought one of its most unpopular conflicts: the Second Seminole War. At the time, Florida had been part of the United States only since 1821—after three centuries of Spanish rule—and had only 34,700 residents. Soldiers trekked through swamp and mud and three died of disease for every one who died in battle. But the military had walked the lake's banks. Regardless, as late as the 1870s, one New York newspaper described a cavernous lake lined with 150-foot cliffs, stalked by spiders as long as a child's arm. It was not explored officially, all the way around, until the early 1880s. By then explorers had mapped the origins of the Nile, and it had been three-quarters of a century since Lewis and Clark had canoed from St. Louis to Oregon.

If a theme runs through the history of Florida, it is this: Everything's great, and someone comes along to mess it up. A coarser phrase is often substituted for "mess."

It is a circuitous route from Vicksburg, Mississippi, to the shiny mansions of Palm Beach and the sprawling crop fields along Lake Okeechobee. Where Interstate 20 crosses the Mississippi River, a railroad line parallels it. In the Civil War, the expressway wasn't there, but the railroad was. When a forty-seven-day Union siege finally broke the proud southern city on the cliffs, the North controlled the middle Mississippi. It had also cut that rail line linking the eastern Confederacy to Louisiana, already boxed in by the Union blockade of New Orleans, and its more vital neighbor, Texas. Texas was the only Confederate state with a land border—with Mexico—and a siphon for commerce in and out. Historians now agree the Confederacy was financially broken and starved out as much as it was defeated in battle.

But Texas was also the breakaway nation's prime supplier of beef, timber, cotton, pork, salt, and other supplies. So the Confederacy turned to a new source for those supplies: Florida. As a result, by the end of the war, Florida was as economically devastated as any of the most war-ravaged southern states.

Occupying soldiers wrote home in amazement of the balmy breezes and lush foliage. State leaders sensed a chance for recovery in tourism. This, leaders saw, was a way out of financial disaster. Then someone asked, "Could we do even better if we got people to move here?"

The problem in the late 1800s was that Florida had only 269,000 people. And the only Florida really open to tourists and potential immigrants was in the northern half. Most of the peninsula was still a dark continent. It had to be tamed.

Florida's weather patterns are cyclical. It may have two moderate droughts, then an extremely wet season, then a period of historic rainfall deficit. Its rainy season, between May and November, accounts for half the calendar year, but three-quarters of the rainfall. It is the time of those "frog strangler" deluges that seem to boil up out of nowhere and dump rain straight down and in such a torrent that it is as if God opened a spigot full blast and tightened it shut just as suddenly.

But even heavy rainfall has limited value when it goes directly into the lake. Much of that water evaporates or works its way out to sea.

The more critical rain falls along the Kissimmee River Valley, a 5,300-square-mile floodplain. Water rushes to the center and into the Kissimmee River. There it slowly works its way down to the lake in a steady flow instead of a wasteful dump from the skies.

Once, the Kissimmee River flowed 103 miles to the north shore of the big lake in a twisting route. All the storm runoff, old vegetation, topsoil, and animal waste that drained into it filtered out as it wound its way toward the lake. In the twentieth century, all that changed.

In 1881, state officials desperate for cash had found a redeemer in Hamilton Disston. Born in August 1844 into the Disston and Sons family of Philadelphia, makers of saws and other tools, Hamilton was only thirty-four when his father died in 1878 and he inherited the business. He had come to Florida for frequent fishing trips and had met Henry Sanford, who founded the town north of Orlando that bears his name.

In 1881, Disston made a deal. He bought four million acres, a 6,250-square-mile chunk of central Florida larger than Connecticut. Today it stretches from Sanford to Orlando to Kissimmee and includes Walt Disney World. It accounts for 11 percent of the state's total land area, and its value today is staggering. For all that land, the saw prince paid an unimaginable 25 cents an acre.

For his $1 million investment, Disston saw hidden promise in central Florida's rich muck. He also believed he could create several recreational waterways that would draw fishermen, pleasure boaters, and tourists.

Disston's immediate goal was to create one major waterway across and down the state. It was the predecessor to the Cross Florida Barge Canal, a disastrous shortcut across the northern peninsula that would be abandoned in 1971, leaving long scars across the land. Disston's dredges cut channels that connected several Central Florida lakes. Men blasted cliffs and deepened creeks and straightened parts of the Kissimmee River.

The Caloosahatchee, a river ("hatchee" is Seminole for "river") which flowed west to the Gulf of Mexico at Fort Myers, began only three miles west of Lake Okeechobee. It seemed to beg for a canal that would span that last three-mile link and connect the big lake to the rest of the world. Disston did it.

By the mid-1880s, the young entrepreneur had created a continuous waterway from central Florida down to Lake Okeechobee and out to the Gulf of Mexico. Boats could now carry people, livestock, and winter crops from Kissimmee to Fort Myers and to the rest of the world. In this time before automobiles became the primary mode of transportation, industry now had a water highway. Environmentalists either kept quiet or were ignored in the rush of optimism.

The *New Orleans Times Democrat* financed a group of explorers who sailed down the Kissimmee, into Lake Okeechobee, through the canal and into the Caloosahatchee and down to Fort Myers. The November 1882 trek of nearly 500 miles took fourteen days. The public was captivated. And soon after completing his project, Disston announced proudly that his canals had dropped Lake Okeechobee's level a foot and a half and the threat of flooding was gone forever. What had really happened? There had been a dry cycle.

A national economic panic in 1893 wiped out the Disston family fortune, and Hamilton killed himself three years later in his native Philadelphia at the age of fifty-one. He had actually received only 1.6

million acres and had permanently drained only 50,000. His heavily mortgaged properties, including the rest of the Florida land that he'd bought for a song, were sold off.

It would be less than a decade before a new champion of drainage emerged. Napoleon Bonaparte Broward, whose name would later adorn a South Florida county, had the charisma and cunning of his emperor namesake and the robust stance and fat mustache of Teddy Roosevelt, a man Broward helped make. Young Napoleon worked in a log camp and on a farm and was a steamboat hand and Newfoundland fisherman. He piloted a steamboat on North Florida's St. Johns River, ran a lumberyard, and developed a phosphate mine, all by the time he was in his forties. When a tidy war was manufactured to the south in Cuba, Broward used his steam tug, the *Three Friends,* to run guns past the Spanish naval blockade to the rebels.

A decade later, in 1907, then-Florida Governor Broward found himself with then-President Roosevelt on a Mississippi River steamboat near Memphis. "Have you still got the *Three Friends*?" the former Rough Rider asked. Broward did. "Well. You ought to be mighty proud of her. If it had not been for the *Three Friends*, you would not be governor now." Broward replied, "You ought to be proud of her yourself, because if it had not been for her you would not be president."

It was no coincidence that the two were on the mighty Mississippi. Roosevelt was inspecting drainage projects, and Broward was championing a big one. He had become governor five years into the new century with new promise for Florida. Although tourism and migration had pulled the state out of its post–Civil War financial straits, it still held only a little more than 500,000 people. But it was on the move. Broward had been elected in no small part based on one of his key campaign promises: to drain the Everglades.

As early as 1848, three years after Florida achieved statehood, U.S. Treasury Secretary Buckingham Smith had declared the Everglades could be "reclaimed" by digging canals. Stephen R. Mallory, then the collector of customs at Key West and later Confederate Secretary of the Navy in the Civil War, had called that idea "totally out of the question." But that didn't stop Napoleon Broward. A half century later, he was proposing all that was needed to turn what he considered a worthless swamp into rich farm-land was to "knock a hole in the wall of coral and let a body of water obey a natural law and seek the level of the sea."

Within a year of his election, dredges were cutting canals from the lake to the ocean, and the water was draining out to sea. Broward was an unsuccessful candidate for the U.S. Senate in 1908 while governor, then won the office two years later. But he died in Jacksonville on October 1, 1910, before taking office. His successor as governor, Albert W. Gilchrist, continued the drainage projects.

Even as the new century was heralding dramatic schemes to engi-neer the land and water, early critics were starting to say that this might not be a good idea. They were drowned out by the pistons of progress and the din of prosperity. Decades later, environmental groups would decry the draining as one of the world's great environmental catastro-phes, claiming that it swallowed Florida's natural beauty, ruined a great drainage and filtering system, and forever altered the area's rainmaking machine.

The first commerce along the lake came from within it. Commercial fishing began at the beginning of the twentieth century, some two decades before farming began to dominate. It was mostly catfish, which many locals didn't consider good eating. Sometimes they were repack-aged as something else and sent to unsuspecting customers around the country who would never know the difference between a can of real salmon and one that actually contained catfish. In the early 1920s, com-mercial fishermen were hit by a double whammy. First, a drought reduced lake levels. Then sports fishermen began complaining that their commercial counterparts were depleting the lake. A state law passed in 1925 banned net fishing in fresh water. Clever fishing-industry leaders got a law passed that declared the big lake to be salt water, since it con-tained such saltwater denizens as mullet and tarpon.

Steamboat traffic was also popular along the lake until railroads and highways reduced travel time around it. Soon the primary business was farming. During the 1910s, below-normal rainfall reduced the floods and encouraged intensive settlement. The new canals, new railroads, new roads, new farming techniques, and allure of Florida's real estate boom all added to the rush. Between 1920 and 1927, the numbers of farmed acres and inhabitants both doubled, to 46,000 acres and 92,000 farmers, workers, merchants, homemakers, and children.

In 1917 the West Palm Beach Canal opened, linking Lake Okeechobee to the coast for commerce. William J. "Fingy" Conners, a Buffalo, New York, publisher and part-time Palm Beach resident, spent $2 million of his own money to carve a private 52-mile toll road from West Palm Beach to the lake. It opened on June 25, 1925. He charged travelers three cents per mile. By 1928, the Florida East Coast Railway had a line from Okeechobee down the east side of the lake to Belle Glade. The Atlantic Coast Line Railroad ran from Fort Myers to Moore Haven, at the lake's southwest corner, and down to Clewiston.

And on April 9, 1928, Belle Glade incorporated as a city. It had fewer than 500 residents. All of Florida had perhaps a million people, but that was double what it had been two decades earlier.

Nearby, settlers had founded Chosen, about a mile from downtown Belle Glade. One story says it was named by a Virginia preacher, eyeing its rich soil and temperate weather and declaring that this was indeed a chosen land. Another version says when a post office went in, someone just picked the name and it stuck.

Dreamy developers envisioned Clewiston, on the lake's southwest shore, growing into a metropolis of 100,000. The great Florida empire-builder Henry Flagler looked to the lake's north shore and settled the town of Okeechobee. He saw it as a great railroad crossroads, the Chicago of the South. Port Mayaca, a tiny settlement on the northeast corner, would be like the exotic Miami suburb of Coral Gables, with a sandy beach, yacht basin, and artificial lakes and inlets called Sapphire and Emerald. When Florida's real estate boom collapsed, a good two to three years before the stock-market crash, those dreams all vanished as well.

But the farms kept coming. Farmers and business leaders bragged the muck was black gold, rich as manure. Truckloads of it were freighted north to Chicago during the 1920s Florida land boom, put in store windows, and used to raise huge flowers and vegetables, all meant to lure people south. But it didn't take long to figure out that the soil was fertile only near the lake; one mile out, its nutrient content plummeted.

Anything grown there would need lots of fertilizer. And it didn't take long to discover that when the muck was exposed to the elements, it would dry up and blow away. In the early 1920s, the federal government opened the Everglades Experimental Station to deal with the rich but unpredictable muck farmlands. That station was placed southeast of the lake, east of Belle Glade. In 1924, in front of the building, a pole was driven down to the bedrock. It showed the muck was nine feet deep. By the end of the twentieth century, it had shrunk to three feet. In other parts of the Glades, it had already blown away down to the limestone that is Florida's bedrock.

Early on, the primary crops were winter vegetables. In 1920 the federal government set up a sugarcane research station at Canal Point. In 1922 farmers first tried planting cane. The first mill started up the following year in Canal Point. Soon others sprang up. But by 1928, sugar was still a minor crop in the Glades.

Pahokee is now a shriveled and depressed town. But at the time, it was the third-most-populous settlement in Palm Beach County. Carmen Salvatore had settled there, on the lake's east shore, on a piece of property hard against the low earthen dike.

Carmen had spent the first five years of his life in Italy before his parents brought him to the New World in the second year of a promising new century. In 1910, when he was fourteen and growing up in New Jersey, the newspapers he tossed onto front porches carried screaming headlines about Halley's comet. Some people believed the earth would go through the comet's tail and civilization would be wiped out. Hysterical people sold their homes, their furniture, and their clothes, then donned robes and crawled into the mountains to meet their maker. Even Salvatore's superstitious mother worried about a deadly catastrophe. But Carmen Salvatore didn't experience one. At least, not this time.

Later, his family says, Carmen grew into a rough-living, short-tempered, cocky city tough not afraid to get into a scuffle. He decided he had to get out of New Jersey or he'd end up dead all too soon. In 1914 the teen took a wood-burning boat down the East Coast to Jacksonville, and then a twenty-two-hour train ride—no food or toilet aboard—to Miami. There, he cut stone for the magnificent mansion that International Harvester farm equipment heir James Deering was building on Biscayne Bay; an estate Deering would call Vizcaya. During its two years of construction, 1,000 men, one in ten Miamians at the time, helped build the landmark. They included Carmen Salvatore.

In December 1917, Carmen married Ella Woodard. He was twenty-two. She was just sixteen. He had met her at the ocean in Miami Beach. She was born in October 1901 and raised in Central Florida, the daughter of a Georgia farmer who came from a long line of plantation operators. She was almost as tall as her husband and, her family says, just as strong. A striking, statuesque woman with dark hair and sharp hazel eyes, she could bring down a rabbit with a rifle to feed her family.

Soon after they married, Carmen went to a Miami enlistment station and signed up to fight in Europe. He told his family he considered it his duty. He left Ella behind, pregnant with Carmen, Jr. In France, Carmen served in the artillery. He would always remember the rain and the mud and the cold. But he got out unhurt. He rode a ship to New York, visited old friends in New Jersey, and boarded a train for Florida. Back home, Ella's father had fallen for the lure of rich farm fields rising from the swamp deep in the interior that lay north and west of Miami. That was where Carmen's future lay as well.

Carmen was one of the first to use muck soil to grow bell peppers, eggplants, and other vegetables. He built his home next to a sprawling cypress tree that would survive him and many calamities and stand tall into the twenty-first century. He was one of the first people in town to own and drive a car.

Carmen liked to say a farmer was a jack-of-all-trades: one day a plowman, the next a carpenter, then a ditchdigger, a dove hunter, a fisherman. He made money but just as quickly lost it to strikes, market conditions and, of course, storms.

Pahokee had initially welcomed Salvatore as a World War I hero. But he was a Yankee, an Eye-talian and Catholic, and that didn't go down well in the Deep South of the 1920s. For his first two months in Pahokee, he let the comments slide. Finally, on the porch of McNab's general store, the local deputy, Alvin Jones, made one ethnic crack too many. Salvatore split the lawman's lip and broke his glasses. The justice of the peace, who was a friend of Jones, set up his bench under a banyan tree and fined Salvatore $50 and costs. He didn't even let Salvatore call witnesses. So Carmen went to West Palm Beach and persuaded the sheriff to order a new trial there. Bootleggers who belonged to the Ku Klux Klan decided that tar and feathers might cut through the judicial proceedings. Salvatore knew they were coming and climbed into his big cypress tree with a double-barreled shotgun. But after a lengthy argument among the Klansmen over who would be the first to open Carmen's front gate and enter his yard, they left.

Later, Salvatore grew fed up with locals who, during Prohibition, brought 55-gallon drums of moonshine to the center of town, near the hand pump and horse trough, where they filled Nehi bottles and sold them to locals. He got tired of stepping over unconscious drunks on the way to church on Sunday mornings. So when no one was looking, he poured out the contents of a drum belonging to Horace Redding, a local merchant. The hooch was worth $500—more than $5,000 today. Redding suspected Salvatore and threatened to "shoot his brains out" if he could ever prove it. Salvatore believed him. He was afraid of Redding right up to September 1928.

In the 1920s, the long stretch of open land between the farmland and the coast made them into separate worlds. The coast was full of people who never got dirt under their fingernails. To them, the interior was an unknown place full of faceless blacks and poor, uneducated whites. Dreamers had envisioned a patchwork of small farms worked by white families. What was emerging was a collection of larger farms owned by big business and worked by black migrants from the Deep South or the Caribbean. The black man was the perfect answer to the labor-intensive enterprise of farming the black gold. In the early twentieth century, blacks were "in their place." They had been kept poor—and not just financially. They had been deprived of education, opportunity, or any kind of sense of rooted community. Many had come down to work on Henry Flagler's railroad and communities had been set up for them—always on the west, or inland, side of the tracks. But as many as 5,000 migrant workers are believed to come from the impoverished islands of the Caribbean.

Labor rights were not part of the equation. If a worker was

unhappy, there were many others willing to work. Workers lived in community houses, some of them provided by the growers. Some lived in rickety shacks or shanties thrown together with scrap wood. Some pitched tents. Some lay down at the end of the day on the side of the road or under a stand of trees.

Blacks were believed to account for at least half of the more than 8,000 people living in the towns around the big lake. But it was impossible to get an exact number. Migrants from the South or the islands came in, worked, got paid, and went back to their families. There was no paperwork. Pay was in cash. Many workers were known to their bosses only by a first name. If someone died, it might not be counted if no relative was looking for him.

By 1928, the state's plan to further drain and reclaim the Everglades for farming had collapsed. The Everglades Drainage District was deep in debt, work had stopped, and landowners were refusing to pay the drainage taxes. Congress was being heavily lobbied to pay for flood control. But the federal government was loath to open that door. In April 1928, the chief of the U.S. Army Corps of Engineers reported to Congress that, until the state and local interests exhausted their money, Washington should not take that step.

At the beginning of the twentieth century, water simply flowed unimpeded from the lake's south shore in a sheet, into the Everglades. From there, it moved gently across that wide river of grass to the end of the peninsula and into Florida Bay. For the early settlers and farmers, that simply would not do. So between 1923 and 1925, the state built a 47-mile-long dike of earth. It was about five feet high. Twice in the next three years, it would be shown as useless as a dam made of tissue paper.

In the early 1920s, commissioners of the Everglades Drainage District, founded in 1913, decided to build a more permanent dike around Lake Okeechobee. The plan was for work to start on the dike in 1927. It would be 110 to 130 feet wide at the base and 20 feet wide at the crest and stand 27 feet above sea level. They concluded that such a levee would resist hurricane-driven surge from the lake. But the legislature didn't get around to approving the money for it. The $20 million bond issue was tied up by a lawsuit from Dade County, which complained it would be contributing 80 percent of the money but receiving only 20 percent of the benefits.

"It is indeed unfortunate that through almost trivial and in some cases, prejudiced legislation, plans for the construction of works essential to the safety of life and the protection of property can be thwarted or so long delayed," Fred Cotten Elliot would write bitterly in an October 5, 1928 letter printed in newspapers.

Elliot was a dapper fellow with a neat mustache who for more than a half century would be one of the omnipresent figures in both the historic drainage of the interior and the battle to harness the great lake. The Glades and the lake would consume much of his life as well.

Elliot was a rare breed of Floridian: a native. Born in Tallahassee in 1878, the year Hamilton Disston became a millionaire, he came out of Virginia Military Institute in 1901. He finished one academic spot ahead of George C. Marshall, the man who would become chief of staff of the U.S. Army during World War II and architect of the rebuilding of postwar Europe. Elliot went to New York to work on its subway system. Miserable in the big city, he worked at mining companies in Mexico and then Arizona, where he was injured in an accident and returned to Florida. He spent three years in his own engineering business. In 1911 he took a temporary job as an assistant engineer. A year later, when the state's chief engineer quit amid controversy, Elliot, then only thirty-four, started a job he would hold for more than four decades.

In many ways, Elliot was a visionary. He designed and built the canals that led from the lake and helped drain the swamps. And he envisioned a series of reservoirs around the drained Everglades—a plan that would be abandoned as too expensive, but which is now in use.

At the edge of the sugarcane fields, about two miles east of Belle Glade and Lake Okeechobee and about 40 miles inland from the coast, the University of Florida's Everglades Research and Education Center had opened in 1921. In September 1928, a small staff was performing extensive soil and crop work. They had been making plans to expand the work when a storm struck the area on August 8. While it brought no serious wind damage, it did dump heavy rains on the fields, soaking the muck and hampering research efforts. Conditions were just about returning to normal by the middle of September.

Lawrence E. Will had come to the Glades in 1913, when he was only twenty, to clear sawgrass for agriculture at the first farming settlement, Okeelanta. He and four other men had founded the settlement, which in the decades to follow would fade into the sugar fields. While associated with a land-sales company, he had played a role—his precise extent is still unclear—in production of a flawed 1911 report favoring Everglades drainage. Its publication set off a congressional investigation.

Will went to fight in World War I and returned to skipper passenger and freight boats from the lake down the feeder canals to the coast. He settled in Belle Glade in 1927 and opened a combination car dealership, auto-parts store, and service station.

William Henry and Mattie Mae Boots had moved to the lake in 1916 from Arizona, where their son Vernie had been born in December 1913. The baby was delivered by his father, as were all his siblings. Relatives had been killed in the great 1900 Galveston hurricane, so the Bootses sought refuge from big water in Arizona. But then they decided to try their luck around the big lake in Florida, figuring the fates would never visit two catastrophic hurricanes upon the same family.

The Bootses grew beans, potatoes, and cabbage in an area called Sebring Farms, in Lake Harbor, at the south shore of Lake Okeechobee. But even Florida is sometimes visited by cold snaps strong enough to kill tender vegetables. That first year, the beans were lost in a freeze.

The Bootses returned to Arizona, but couldn't overcome the desert and its irrigation problems; in 1925 they turned around and went back to Florida, back to the lake. Boots, then not even a teenager, worked with his much-older half brother for an outfit that hauled produce to the railhead at Clewiston, near the lake's southwest shore. He was already settling into the Deep South dialect still found in some old-timers; all his life, he would say "Mia-muh" and "hurrikin."

The Bootses lived on a boat called the *Estero*. It had been owned by the Koreshans, an obscure religious group based in Estero, near Fort Myers. Later in 1925 they moved to a home on the farm once owned by the Sebring family. The Sebrings had surrendered to the freezes and the high water from the lake and headed about 40 miles northwest of Lake Okeechobee to establish the town that would bear their name. The Bootses farmed the rich muck soil around their home, growing potatoes, tomatoes, beans, and peas. The cold was always there, threatening the crops each year; the Bootses and their four sons would place paper cups over tomatoes to protect them from the wind.

Boots's dad also worked dragging dirt to the unpaved road from South Bay to the Hendry County line, near Clewiston. The road was being converted to a new highway, U.S. 27. Land was being piled up to raise the road out of the water. When the dirt road was smooth, cars would race by at 60 mph. When the road had been turned to soup by rains, the Bootses would find people who had been bogged for twenty-four hours or more and feasted on by mosquitoes. They would tie a rope to their tractor and pull the cars out. Sometimes they earned more from that than the county was paying to level the road.

At the time, there were only two ways out of the Glades—if you were one of the few with cars. One was north along the lake to Indiantown and east to the coast or north to Tampa or Orlando. The other was north along the lake, then southeast and east on Conners Highway to the coast. U.S. 27 was being built south and west of the lake. Workers had already dug canals for the purpose of dumping the removed dirt onto the land and building up the roadbed to keep the new highway out of the floodplain. But the first asphalt had not been laid yet.

That meant if a hurricane came across from the coast toward the southeast corner of the lake, people who had waited too long to leave would be trapped.

Two extremely wet rainy seasons in a row, 1926 and 1927, had raised the lake's water level. But more than 3,000 farmers flourished in ways that had not been seen in the decade or so since farming had started in earnest in the Glades. The year 1928 promised a bumper winter vegetable crop. Prosperity had drawn people to South Florida. It had drawn Carmen Salvatore from the war to Pahokee, and Clothilda Miller's family from the Bahamas to West Palm Beach. And down from Georgia had come Coot Simpson.

It was September 1928.

The Black Cloud

September 1928

". . . a tropical disturbance of considerable intensity."

June, too soon. July, stand by. August, look out you must.
September, remember. October, all over.

—Mariners' rhyme

The world's great Atlantic hurricanes are apocalyptic machines that move across water, feed off water, push water from ocean to shore and out of giant lakes, and make water a weapon of death. But they start as swirling dust in the arid heart of the Sahara, one of the driest places on earth. No one sees their birth.

The northwest part of Africa, jutting into the Atlantic like the handle of a jug, is home to the Sahara, the world's largest desert, nearly equal in size to the continental United States. Temperatures can push 110 or more, and the world record—132—was set there.

Some 2,500 miles to the east of the Atlantic coast, rising as a physical barrier between the desert and the rich Nile River deltas of Egypt and Sudan, are the Tibesti Mountains in Chad. Cooler wind crossing them makes its way toward the Sahara. In the desert, vapors rise off the ground. The hot vapors, and warm air coming in from where the "jug handle" has a southern shore on the Gulf of Guinea, slam into the cooler mountain winds and form clouds and thunderstorms. In one summer, as many as one hundred such storms can make their way west across the continent toward the Atlantic Ocean.

In a 500-mile swath between the desert and the western shore lies the Sahel, an Arabic word for shore. Here was once a giant swamp to rival the Everglades. By the twenty-first century, thousands of years of climate changes and overconsumption—overfarming, overgrazing, over-logging—had left it an expanse of dried clay and dead trees. Someday the Sahara will take it over altogether and it will all be desert.

The seeming contradiction of great storms growing from dry desert has not been lost on weather researchers. They have concluded that in years of great drought over the Sahara, there have been more and more powerful storms. A University of Miami study traced half the dust over Miami as Saharan sand. Perhaps one day forecasters will be able to look at a satellite image and point to the desert thunderstorm that will be the next great killer hurricane.

Soon the storms are over Senegal, then off the coast of Cape Verde: the green cape. The Senegalese regard the sea as a god that dispenses life and death. It gives them fish and a livelihood, but its waves take their men and send storms that kill people an ocean away. In 1999 the *South Florida Sun Sentinel* sent a reporter and photographer to the Senegal coast. They reported that elders chant supplications and toss a concoction of wine, grain, milk, and water into the waves; priests cut a cow's neck and let it bleed into the surf, then throw its limbs into the waters; and people bang on drums and throw money into the water. They do all this in hopes of appeasing the fickle, exacting sea and obtaining a quiet summer. It doesn't always work. In September 2002, a ferry carrying more than 1,000 people sank in a gale off Senegal's coast, killing most of the passengers and crew.

Most storms die aborning. But sometimes a swirl of wind crosses the coast with just the right ingredients for its survival: the temperature of water and air, the saltiness of the sea, the influence of other winds and atmospheric features.

The Black Cloud

In the southern Caribbean, so close to the equator, water temperatures stay above 80 degrees year-round. Any storms that form during the bookend months of the storm season, which runs from June 1 to November 30, will be born here. Situated in a giant "C" stretching from Florida around Mexico to northeast South America, the storms have little time to strengthen before they strike somewhere.

Some hurricanes form farther north in the Atlantic, when the spring thaw is just finishing up or the first crisp days of autumn are already starting. The ocean water is too cool to give the storms much nurture, so they fall short of becoming historic monsters.

But as the summer beats through July and August, eyes turn to Africa. The sun bears down on the stretch of ocean and land between the Equator and the Tropic of Cancer, and land, air and water get hotter and hotter. And once a storm has left the African coast and is over the waves, warm water exacerbates it, like gasoline poured on a flame.

The storm moves off Cape Verde and moves at or near the Cape Verde Islands, an archipelago about 400 miles off the coast. Colonized by Portugal in the fifteenth century, they became an independent country in 1975. Once they were a way station for the movement of Africa slaves on the "Middle Passage" to America. Their name still sparks fear, but now for a far different reason. The people along the coast who are most vulnerable to tropical storms know the term "Cape Verde" because the deadliest and most powerful hurricanes are first spotted over these chunks of ash and salt and volcanic rock and are called "Cape Verde storms."

From the Cape Verde Islands, it is 2,500 miles to Barbados, at the eastern edge of the New World. Until the late-nineteenth century, that would be the first place anyone would ever notice a hurricane.

For centuries, storms were more the province of folklore than science. Their name came from the Carib Indians of the West Indies. Historians believe "huracan" was probably derived from the Mayan storm god, Hunraken; or the Quiche god of thunder and lightning, hurakan; or other Caribbean Indian terms for evil spirit and big wind.

In the 1930s, the Works Progress Administration sent writers across America, into big towns and down country roads. These writers often didn't let the facts get in the way of a good story. If someone said it, they wrote it down. The *WPA Guide to Florida* said that Seminoles are the first to flee a storm, citing the blooming of the sawgrass: It says "an atmospheric condition" causes the pollen to bloom on sawgrass several days before a hurricane's arrival, giving the natives a warning of the impending storm. The book also quoted one colorful old-timer who'd managed to survive various storms. He said of one, "One day, the wind blowed so hard, it blowed a well up out of the ground; blowed so hard, it blowed a crooked road straight. Another time it blowed an' blowed, an' scattered the days of the week so bad Sunday didn't get around 'til late Tuesday mo'nin.'"

Christopher Columbus ran into a hurricane and lost many of his sailors. Ship's logs describe hundreds of hurricanes in the five centuries that followed. Storms eight days apart in August 1530 leveled Porto Rico. A hurricane in 1588 killed 500 men at sea. The greatest killer is still the hurricane of October 1780, which is credited with killing 22,000 people. It tore up Caribbean islands in October of that year and sank 300 ships, many of them British warships fighting the rebels in the American colonies. Some accounts suggest the loss of ships, equipment, and men contributed to England's humiliating loss to the upstart colonists.

Hurricanes have struck Florida for eons. If not for a hurricane, the oldest continuously inhabited city in North America would be not St. Augustine but Pensacola, on the far west edge of Florida's Panhandle. A Spanish expedition founded it in 1559, six years before St. Augustine, but days later the fleet was smashed by a hurricane and soon Pensacola was abandoned for another century and a half. In 1562, French ships sent to bolster the fledgling colony at Fort Caroline, near Jacksonville, were lost in a storm and Spain maintained a hold on Florida that would last another two and a half centuries. A September 22, 1599 hurricane flooded the struggling settlement of St. Augustine, and it was almost abandoned. Quaker businessman Jonathan Dickinson was shipwrecked in 1696 near Jupiter Island in a storm—possibly a hurricane—and his journal of his two-month struggle to reach St. Augustine is the first detailed account of the region. The July 31, 1715 hurricane sent eleven Spanish ships and more than 700 souls to the bottom of what would later be named the Treasure Coast for the millions in gold, silver, and jewels that those ships took down with them. A June 1733 hurricane in the Keys struck a dozen Spanish ships heading from Havana back to Cadiz, sinking all but one of them. The remains of one of the eleven, the *San Pedro*, are in 20 feet of water off Indian Key. They are now an official state underwater historic site. Two hurricanes and a yellow-fever epidemic forced the Panhandle town of St. Joseph, where Florida's constitution was written in 1838, right out of existence. And an 1851 hurricane damaged the new statehouse for Florida, then a state for only six years.

While Florida's modern history dates back five hundred years, longer than any other place in North America, most of it has occurred in this century. And along with each major development, a hurricane has usually trailed close behind.

While North Carolina and Texas come to mind, it is by far Florida which hurricanes punish the most. Of 158 hurricanes to strike the United States from 1900 to 1996, 57—more than one-third—struck Florida. Texas was second with 36, and North Carolina third, with 25. A lot can be attributed to Florida's 1,350-mile coastline, which alone accounts for more than one third of the total 3,700-mile coast from the Texas-Mexico border to the tip of Maine. But divide Florida into four sections, and the southeast coast alone accounts for 26 hurricanes, about one of every six of those 158 storms.

Break that down to just the 64 major hurricanes—of Category Three or higher on the Saffir-Simpson Hurricane Scale with top sustained winds of at least 111 mph—and it's 15 for Texas, 11 for North Carolina, and a whopping 24 for Florida. The state's southeast coast alone had 11 major hurricanes.

If the region that would later become Palm Beach County experienced catastrophic storms before the beginning of the twentieth century, few white people were there to note it. The 1830 census figures list all of 517 white people living in the southern half of the Florida peninsula. The earliest settlers had come in 1842, 21 pioneers who signed the Armed Occupation Act and were awarded 160 acres each. They were gone in three decades. Local history really began when the Jupiter Lighthouse was built in 1860 and a few families set up a colony around it. The

1880 census lists 257 white people in Dade County, which then stretched about 150 miles from the upper Florida Keys to Stuart.

The first possible hurricane recorded for that region was in 1876. It leveled the fledgling settlement that would later become Palm Beach. Pioneer Marion Dimick Geer had come to the area with her family that year. In a memoir twenty years later, she told of two storms that year, one before their arrival and one after. The first one, she was told, had dumped a bounty of goods onto the beach: pins, needles, money, a cook-stove, trunks of clothes, even a sawmill. She wrote that the second one "scattered our goods hither and yon. Table, stove, chairs, and bureau were blown about and dropped far and near, which was not in accor-dance with our ideas of the gentle zephyrs we had been told fanned the cheeks of those who lived in this favored region."

A hurricane struck the Miami settlement in 1891. And from August to October 1894, West Palm Beach got three more storms—some possibly hurricanes—which killed at least two and damaged boats and wharves.

A 1903 storm did extensive damage to downtown West Palm Beach, which by then had been an incorporated city for nine years and had already been struck by two terrible fires. Local numerologists said they knew the reason behind all the catastrophes: The town's name had an unlucky thirteen letters.

When the 1903 storm struck on September 11 and 12, the *Weekly Lake Worth News* reported top sustained winds were 90 miles an hour. "With the increasing wind, roofs began to tear up and scatter in sections over the streets and yards," it reported. "Chimneys came tumbling down, throwing bricks in all directions; houses were lifted from their foundations, or blown down completely." The newspaper itself lost its tin roof, "stripped into ribbons and hurled into the street," and water got into the building; "This is the first issue of the *News* ever printed with the employees standing in water almost over [their] shoes, and rain coming on them from above."

Its competitor, the *Tropical Sun*, fared far worse; it lost its roof and some walls and machinery was drenched and floors flooded. The glass front "went in with a crash," the *Sun* reported September 16. "The rooftop was hurled up against the bank building."

The Black Cloud

No one in West Palm Beach was killed in that storm. But nine men died when the British steamer *Inchulva* sank off the coast of Delray Beach, about 20 miles to the south. The 400-foot steamer, with a crew of only twenty-eight Irish sailors—seven had deserted at Galveston—was sailing from that Texas port with 7,000 tons of wheat, 150 tons of lumber, 180 bales of cotton, and a batch of cottonseed. As the ship struggled north in the storm, its cargo shifted and the stern broke off. Six men were washed overboard. A rope was thrown and four tried to get back to the ship, but a jagged edge of the torn stern cut the rope. The four, along with their two fellows and two men still on the ship, were lost to the waves. The remaining crew huddled in the front of the ship. Without their bearings, they feared the jolting ship had become trapped on a shoal some 15 miles from land and would break apart any minute. Sunrise revealed the wreck only 200 yards offshore. The crew was rescued and taken to the nearby Orange Grove House of Refuge. The wreck is now a popular diving spot.

On October 17, 1906, the steamship *St. Lucie* left Miami for the Keys, where workers were building Henry Flagler's ambitious railroad to Key West, which would begin operating six years later. About 3:00 the next morning, as the steamer headed south, it ran straight into a hurricane. The storm had crossed Key West and moved into the Gulf of Mexico, but suddenly reversed course. Skipper Steve Bravo sought shelter at Elliott Key, south of Miami Beach, but soon the ship was breaking up. The crew prepared to loose the lifeboats, but then the winds died. But that was only the eye.

It would not be the first time, or the last, that the center of calm around which the giant cyclone circulates would fool someone into thinking the hurricane had passed.

When the storm returned, the two lifeboats were slammed ashore and the men clung to mangroves in the winds. Soon the ship was torn apart and only a few pieces of wood remained. For days, the fate of the *St. Lucie* was a mystery, until a steamer arrived in Miami and deposited 58 exhausted survivors. Another 25 were on a second ship. An estimated 130 had perished.

But none of those early-twentieth-century storms stopped the momentum of Florida's growth. Decades of tourism and settlement had set up the state for an unprecedented real estate boom. In a frenzy of demand, property values doubled and tripled, if only on paper. Newspaper ads and brochures showed palm trees waving in a gentle breeze. They didn't show the fronds being whipped by hurricanes.

In 1920 the population of West Palm Beach was 8,659. Seven years later, it had quadrupled. Towns and cities sprang up all up and down the coast. At the height of the boom, 1924–1925, some lots in Palm Beach County jumped in value from $250 to $50,000. Oceanfront land was going for $1,000 a linear foot. As many as ten trains a day were arriving in West Palm Beach, disgorging both buyers and sellers in an orgy of promiscuous capitalism. Developers trotted grandiose, and often unrealized, schemes. Hobe Sound, north of Jupiter, would be renamed "Picture City" and become the Hollywood of the East. Olympia Beach, a multimillion dollar resort, would rise up at Stuart. Neither ever happened. But down the road, the new town of Boca Raton offered its first lots to people bused down from Palm Beach; the first offering sold for $2.1 million.

On July 26, 1925, the *Miami News* published a Sunday edition that at the time was the fattest newspaper in world history. It weighed 7½ pounds and boasted 22 sections and 504 pages. Much of it was advertisements, sometimes covering multiple pages that trumpeted one real estate development after another. It was a heady time. But by 1926, the boom was already showing its first strains. Railroads and ships couldn't get building materials from northern plants to Florida fast enough. The government was cracking down on con artists. The stock market was shaky.

In the fall of 1926, the University of Miami was preparing to open its doors in Coral Gables. Not far away, the Biltmore Hotel had opened the previous January with a gala dinner dance for 1,500. On the morning of September 16, hotel owner George Merrick, the man who had built Coral Gables, dropped 2,000 letters, announcing his winter season, into the mail. The previous day, the *Miami Herald* had reported a hurricane was somewhere out there in the Caribbean, but was not expected to hit Florida. South Florida's 300,000 residents went about their business. They had experienced a minor hurricane two months earlier.

Skies in Florida were blue and breezes were light, and there were none of the red skies or swells that, in this time before satellites, were often the only harbingers of an approaching storm. Except for a report from Nassau, weather forecasters were getting little information about the storm.

The morning of September 17, 1926, the *Miami Herald* carried a 4-inch-long front-page story that said the storm would miss Florida. But the afternoon *Miami News* reported storm warnings had been instituted at noon and "destructive winds" were expected that night. At the U.S. Weather Bureau's Miami office, chief meteorologist Richard W. Gray nervously watched his barometer drop. The faster the drop, the more powerful the approaching storm. A change of even one-tenth of an inch is significant. The first full-time weather office in Florida had opened in Miami in 1911, and Gray had been its only chief so far. At 11:30 P.M., he hoisted the hurricane warning flags. But the flags were late; squalls were already coming ashore.

Over the next twelve hours, the storm pounded Miami. It ripped buildings, brought torrential rains, and washed boats ashore. The next morning, a wind meter atop a Miami Beach hospital recorded a five-minute sustained wind speed of 123 mph before it was blown away. The storm surge sank or beached at least 150 boats and ships. Downtown Miami's waterfront was flooded for two to three blocks inland from Biscayne Bay. Up to five feet of water stood in homes, shops, and hotel lobbies. The Miami River overflowed. And storm winds weren't limited to Miami. In Fort Lauderdale, 3,500 buildings were damaged, and the Broward County Courthouse lost its roof. A gust lasting less than 30 seconds demolished a naval radio station at the Jupiter Lighthouse, 80 miles north of Miami.

The greatest killer may have been ignorance. When the eye arrived, about 6:00 A.M. on September 18, thousands of people emerged from shelter to see the carnage and kneel in gratitude for having survived a storm they presumed was over. Cars began crossing from Miami Beach across Biscayne Bay to Miami. Gray shouted to the street from the Weather Bureau doorway, "The storm's not over! We're in the lull! Get back to safety! The worst is yet to come!" At 6:45 A.M., the second half of the storm arrived, more vicious than the first. People who had run into the streets were cut to pieces by flying debris, and the cars heading from Miami Beach were washed into the bay. Houses already damaged finally collapsed. Jane Wood—the mother of U.S. Attorney General Janet Reno—was a young child struggling to get back home in the high winds. She reached down and snatched a snapper swimming in the street; the fish became the family's dinner.

"The intensity of the storm and the wreckage that it left cannot be adequately described," Gray wrote in a report. The storm had damaged or destroyed every building in Miami's business district. Miami Beach's hotels and casinos were battered and surrounded by standing water.

"I have just come through Hell," L. F. Reardon of Coral Gables later wrote in a landmark memoir, *The Great 1926 Hurricane and Disaster*. "I must set this down for I'm not sure how long my reason will last. My God, but I'm tired."

Reardon wrote with gripping detail of how he and his family huddled for hours from the storm's fury. "Will this cursed storm never abate or is it determined to decimate us and our beautiful city?" Reardon recalled thinking as the storm's second half began pounding the area. Later, as he made his way to downtown Miami, "signs of desolation that met our eyes were heart-rending. Whole sides of apartment blocks had been torn away, disclosing semi-naked men and women moving dazedly about the ruins of their homes. Houses, stores, and shops lay sprawled. How many dead are under them? Everybody was looking for a drink of water—and there was none to be had."

While the 1926 hurricane had not been the deadliest, most powerful, or even most costly (in actual dollars) to hit Florida, it still impresses meteorologists seventy-five years later. It was the most powerful storm to strike Miami proper. Its top winds were estimated at 150 mph, just short of the catastrophic Category Five, highest position on the Saffir-Simpson Hurricane Scale. Winds averaged 76.2 mph for 24 hours—the longest period on record for any area to experience hurricane-force winds. And never before had officials recorded an Atlantic hurricane with winds higher than 100 mph for more than an hour. The hurricane may have been as strong as Andrew and, unlike Andrew, which made landfall in southern Miami-Dade County, it hit much closer to downtown Miami. Considering downtown Miami's worth now, hurricane researchers believe that if the 1926 storm struck today, the damage costs would be about $80 billion—three times those of Andrew.

The University of Miami opened on October 17, 1926, only two days late, with 560 students, but during the next two decades it struggled through the Great Depression and came close to folding, at one point filing for bankruptcy protection. When the school's football team took to the field for the first time in the fall of 1926, a team member suggested a nickname inspired by the great storm; the Hurricanes. The team adopted as its mascot the ibis, the bird that according to folklore is the first to return after a hurricane passes.

For years, northern industry and newspapers had railed against Miami for siphoning away their people and money. Now, all that animosity turned to sympathy—at least publicly. "Newspapers which, previous to the disaster, were launching the most scatching [scathing] attacks at Florida are now publishing some of the finest editorials ever written about the state," Walter Rose, chairman of the Florida Real Estate Commission, said on October 18, 1926. But newspapers were also running stories that inflated the death toll to 1,000 and suggested South Florida had been leveled. South Florida business leaders worked overtime to downplay the damage. But that just caused drops in donations.

"I predict that Miami will make a world come-back," Mayor E. C. Romfh wrote. "It is the same people who have created the fastest growing city in America who are now turning their energies and enthusiasm to the work of reconstruction in Miami." But the storm was the knockout punch for a city already on rubbery knees. The Florida East Coast Railway offered free rides out, and many took advantage. Workers leveled unfinished homes, and real estate prices plummeted to a penny on the dollar.

Another storm on October 20 just missed Miami after killing 650 people in Cuba. But everyone now knew about Florida and hurricanes, and newspapers across America declared South Florida dead and buried. By 1928, seven West Palm Beach banks had closed. The boom that had been up and running in the early and mid-1920s was now in big trouble.

For South Florida, the 1926 storm had been a large nail in its coffin—perhaps the final one.

But the storm hadn't limited its damage to the southeast coast. It had shot west across the peninsula, with the winds of its outer bands driving water out of Lake Okeechobee's southern end and into Moore Haven, then a town of 1,200 protected only by a 6-foot muck dike along the lake's western shore. The town had received a terse telegram from the Miami weather office on September 17, saying only that a storm was striking there.

"The first break in the dike occurred about three quarters of a mile east of town," Lawrence E. Will wrote in *Okeechobee Hurricane and the Hoover Dike*. "That was soon followed by other breaks. In town the water which had started to come in slowly now began to come in great waves, rising over streets, over floors and then up and still higher."

The water is believed to have risen as high as 17 feet. It tore concrete blocks from the Glades County Courthouse, then under construction; blocks were found in muck years later during the widening of nearby U.S. 27 to four lanes. Some people saved themselves by climbing to the second-floor projection room of the town's movie theater, scrambling out the window, and crossing the street, hand-over-hand, while hanging on to a rope that had been tied between buildings.

The storm went on to damage the historic Gamble Mansion in Bradenton, on the southwest coast, before crossing the Gulf of Mexico and making a second landfall near Mobile, Alabama. Pensacola experienced twenty hours of hurricane-force winds and much of its waterfront was shattered. The storm moved west through Mississippi and Louisiana before breaking up in Texas.

Survivors of the Moore Haven attack were moved to Sebring, about 60 miles to the north. Martial law was declared in Moore Haven and the National Guard moved in. Unidentified dead were buried in a mass grave in the county cemetery in nearby Ortona. Others were found months later. Official reports place the number of deaths in Florida at 243 to 373, with 150 dead in Moore Haven, most by drowning. But many believe closer to 300 died in Moore Haven alone. Three weeks after the storm, up to three feet of water still stood in some streets.

The Everglades Drainage District met in Tallahassee nine days later and resolved to immediately start rebuilding the dike at Moore Haven. But now, people were worrying that if the government didn't build a higher, stronger dike to replace this obviously inadequate one, the next storm would be more catastrophic.

It didn't take long for the criticism to start flying. Local interests said the state should have protected Moore Haven by draining water from the swollen lake through the St. Lucie and Caloosahatchee canals, which stretch east and west, respectively, to the coasts. The editor of the *Everglades News* had specifically pleaded with drainage officials to lower the lake days before the storm struck. The state later retorted that the storm was "an act of God" and the drainage district was in the business of reclaiming swampland, not controlling floods. Engineers also said that lowering the lake might not have saved any lives in Moore Haven, but it would have flooded a far wider area. State engineer F. C. Elliot was not a popular man in the Glades. He would say years later that critics in Moore Haven were so hostile after the 1926 storm there were moments he feared for his safety.

Almost two years later, groups decided to hold a memorial service for the victims of the 1926 storm, especially the hundreds killed in Moore Haven. It was an unprecedented death toll for Florida, one that they figured wouldn't likely be matched. The service was set for the end of September 1928.

One agency had not waited for politics after the 1926 storm: the American Red Cross. The law of averages said there was a better chance of pigs flying than of two catastrophic storms striking so close to each other in short order. But the agency decided, on the side of caution, to write up an action plan anyway. They did mock drills and wrote up maps of hypothetical storms striking the area.

Just up the road from West Palm Beach, Massachusetts restaurateur Harry Kelsey had incorporated his dream town of Kelsey City on November 16, 1923. The town, which would later become Lake Park, was touted as the state's first planned community. Kelsey had bought the land in 1919 and envisioned a metropolis of 100,000. He brought down his wife and children, pitched a tent on the Intracoastal Waterway and auctioned lots. At his peak, Kelsey owned 120,000 acres and 14 miles of oceanfront between Miami and Jupiter. But by February 1925, Kelsey's ads in the *Palm Beach Times* had a desperate sound to them: "We are obliged to sell our close-in acreage and waterfront properties to supply cash for the $2,000,000 development program at Kelsey City during 1925."

Charles Branch worked for Kelsey. In the spring of 1928, one of the company mechanics, Robert White, stopped by. White wanted advice. He'd decided to build a 12-by-12-foot storm shelter in the side of a sand dune near his home. His coworkers razzed him mercilessly for what they saw as his paranoia.

The 1928 season started busily. Burned by the 1926 storm, the state kept Lake Okeechobee's level down at 13.3 feet. One storm, on August 7–11, had come in low, crossed Haiti's jutting southwest hook, paralleled Florida's Gulf Coast and come ashore in the state's armpit, staggering through Georgia and the Carolinas. And one on August 12–16 crossed the middle Antilles, passed south of Jamaica, and fizzled off the Yucatán.

But it was the first storm of the season that had caught the attention of South Floridians.

First spotted on August 5, about 500 miles southeast of Palm Beach, it came ashore early on August 8, between Stuart and Fort Pierce, with top winds reported at 80 mph—barely hurricane strength—and moved west toward the Orlando area. It tore through key citrus-growing regions and destroyed the equivalent of 8 million boxfuls out of the 20 million ripening on trees. Losses were estimated at $18 million.

In three days, 13.16 inches of rain drenched the Kissimmee River Valley. The Associated Press reported a sheet of water 25 miles across in places covered the swamp areas west of Fort Pierce and around the lake's eastern and northern shores. The report said many families were marooned, a great swath of vegetable and citrus groves was under water, and bridges were washed out. Fish swam in the streets of Okeechobee, the cattle town and railhead at the lake's northern end. Taylor Creek, one of rivers that feed into the big lake, "became a mighty river overnight," the report said.

In all, 47.5 inches of rain had fallen on South Florida in August and

September alone. It was an amount equal to the average total for an entire year. Total rainfall for the year, through September 30, would be 88 inches.

Perhaps most ominously, the drainage canals around the lake were filling rapidly, and this one rainstorm had brought the lake up as much as 2½ feet. It was now at about 16½ feet above sea level, about 1½ feet above what the War Department considered desirable. On top of that, the St. Lucie Canal, which drains toward the Atlantic Ocean at Stuart, had developed a 50,000 cubic-foot sandbar at Indiantown, about nine miles east of the lake. That sandbar acted as a dam, slowing the flow of water out of the lake.

On Wednesday, September 12, the front page of the *Palm Beach Post* carried stories about reporters who had gathered in Schenectady, New York to watch the first-ever broadcast of a play in a new medium called television. Palm Beach County's agricultural agent, S. W. Hiatt, just returned from the Iowa State Fair, said the Florida farm-product booth, which he had managed, had been a big success. He said many people expressed interest in visiting Florida, or even relocating. Palm Beach County's small Jewish population prepared for the start that Friday night of the Jewish New Year. The Lake Worth Ladies' Bible Class had had an "enjoyable meeting and picnic." In New York, Babe Ruth had hit his forty-ninth home run of the season; at the time, he accounted for nearly one of every nine American League dingers. Back home, the baseball City League and Glades League planned a series of playoffs for Sunday, September 16.

The forecast called for partly cloudy skies with local thunder-showers Wednesday and Thursday. At the very bottom of the page was a 41-word Associated Press story out of Washington. It said a "tropical disturbance of considerable intensity" had formed in the open Atlantic and would likely pass over the Lesser Antilles on Wednesday. The head-line read, "Storm Warning."

The storm was 2,200 miles from Florida.

The Islands

". . . the drums were rolled."

On Thursday, September 13, in Kelsey City, mechanic Robert White, who had built his own storm shelter at his home, stopped at the office of supervisor Charles Branch. He wanted to know if Branch had heard about a storm that was in the Leewards.

The Leeward Islands, fifteen large ones and many tiny ones, arc away and down from Porto Rico. Pronounced "LOO-word," with a romantic maritime flair, their name is itself a bit of marketing; the lee side of a boat is the side sheltered from the wind. Just to the south, the Windward Islands form the lower arc, swinging back to the west and down almost to South America. They comprise five main islands plus a chain of smaller ones. Because of their position, they are more exposed to winds from the northeast, thus their name.

These fragile pearls are the easternmost bodies in the central Atlantic and the first stop for any storm crossing the vast bathtub of warm water between the continents. Their small size makes them improbable targets. But it leaves their inhabitants with no place to run. And because they lie from north to south, a large hurricane angling northwest toward Florida can tear through them.

On the morning of September 10, the *S.S. Commack* was in the middle of the Atlantic Ocean, at latitude 17 north and longitude 48.15 west, about 600 miles east of a line stretching north from Barbados into the open sea. The crew reported the wind was blowing from the northeast at Force 7. They were measuring on the old Beaufort Wind Speed Estimation Scale. Force 7 was 32 to 38 mph. The crew took the measurements and radioed them to the U.S. Weather Bureau.

For the first time, men had encountered the great storm of 1928. In fact, it was the most easterly report ever made of a hurricane at that time. In the 1920s, the world had no satellites or hurricane-research jets or views from space. People judged storms only by what they could see of them on the horizon. Over the next eight days, weather officials would track the storm as it crossed more than 5,000 miles from the Caribbean to Canada and killed perhaps as many as 7,000 people.

At 2:00 P.M., about 280 miles to the south, at latitude 14 north and longitude 51 west, the crew of the *Clearwater* measured winds of Force 5 —19 to 24 mph—and reported that their barometer had dropped 0.1 inch in just two hours. Later, the *Clarissa*, 70 miles to the south at 13 north, 51 west, recorded Force 6—25 to 31 mph.

The three alliterative merchant ships, almost lined up on a southwesterly line, provided all the evidence weather officials needed to conclude that a hurricane was 600 miles east-northeast of Barbados and heading due west.

The storm then became the responsibility of Alexander J. Mitchell. Born in Alabama during the Civil War, in November 1861, he had apprenticed at weather stations across the South and took over the Jacksonville station in 1895. At the time, forecasting had improved dramatically but was still primitive compared to the science it would evolve into by the end of the twentieth century.

Early on September 11, he issued his first advisory about the storm, announcing that at 8:00 P.M. on September 10, a "tropical disturbance" was at about latitude 15 north, longitude 50 west, and moving west to west-northwest. That placed it 1,600 miles from Florida—as far as southeast Florida is from Denver. Even if it aimed straight at Florida, it was still some five days away.

The Islands

On the morning of September 11, the merchant ship *Inanda,* at 17 north, 56 west, reported a northwest wind of Force 10, or 55 to 63 mph. The storm's sustained winds were now about 10 mph below official hurricane strength.

By 8:00 P.M., the wind changed direction at Bridgetown, capital of the British colony of Barbados, a tiny island that sticks into the ocean just east of the arc formed by the Windwards. Barbados is less than 250 miles north of the Serpent's Mouth, a strait named by Christopher Columbus just north of the Orinoco River delta in Venezuela, on the northern coast of South America. That meant the storm had cut right though the central Atlantic on almost a straight line.

At that hour, Mitchell's advisory described a "tropical disturbance of considerable intensity." It suggested that on the morning of Wednesday, September 12, the center of the storm would likely pass north of the largest of the Windward Islands: the French possession of Martinique.

The first victim of the storm of 1928, however, was not Martinique, but its British neighbor, Dominica, about 30 miles away. At 754 square kilometers—about 290 square miles—Dominica is about four times the size of Washington, D.C. and is less than half the size of Lake Okeechobee. Its highlight is 441-foot Mount Diablatins. The storm struck about 8:00 A.M. on September 12. The seawall was smashed, crops were destroyed, and at least one death was reported.

Its neighbor, Martinique, "lay south of the center of the hurricane and sufficiently removed there from to avoid the disastrous consequences that these storms usually entail," Walter S. Reineck, the American consul at Martinique, reported in a September 17 note which had taken three weeks to be read in Washington. The secret dispatches to the State Department from U.S. diplomats stationed in the tropical paradises—not declassified until the 1960s—start with the stilted diplomatic language of the time, "I have the honor to report that . . ." Considering the grim nature of the dispatches, the wording is a bit silly. And the reports provide scathing insight into the colonial attitude toward the local population.

On the island's northwest coast, houses were washed into the ocean, "but these were negro huts of no particular value," Reineck wrote. He said most of the damage was among fruit trees, especially lime trees, cocoa trees, and sugarcane. But, the "obedient servant" assured his supervisors, there was enough cane to afford a full complement of the island's precious export: rum. Reineck said deaths were limited to three or four. All were apparently sailors who had tried to swim from small boats or help other people in the water. Newspapers reported as many as twenty boats foundered off the island.

At Pointe à Pitre, the largest city in Guadeloupe, C. Holman B. Williams was at his office about 2:00 P.M. on Tuesday, September 11, when he had a visitor. Williams was director of the French colony's agricultural station, and the visitor was the manager of the West India and Panama Telegraph Company. The man told Williams there was "a certain amount of anxiety in the British colonies" about the approaching storm. Williams's barometer was falling, but slowly, so he wasn't alarmed. But by 7:00 P.M., a radio report from Martinique said "a disturbance" was to the east and closing. The sugar factories had all closed for the day, and no one would be there to receive a message.

Guadeloupe, a French colony of 230,000, had an especially grim history with hurricanes. A September 1776 hurricane had killed some 6,000 people in Pointe à Pitre Bay.

After Williams received another alarming message, this one from San Juan, Porto Rico, he decided to go to the mayor. Remarkably, the mayor hadn't yet read a message from the island's governor asking him to warn the population any way he could. The darkening skies were growling with thunder. Lightning moved among the clouds. At 9:00 P.M., "the drums were rolled and the population advised to take every precaution."

The wind gusts began at 3:00 A.M. on Wednesday, September 12. On Williams's barometer, the pressure started moving down rapidly. At 7:00 A.M., the post office opened and warnings were sent to the sugar factories. But they never got them. The telephone and telegraph lines were already down. "Up to 9 A.M., the sky remained overcast but quiet," Williams wrote to the U.S. National Weather Bureau. Despite the growing winds, the shops stayed open, some to 10:00 A.M. and some later. Williams wasn't going to wait. At 10:00 A.M., he moved his family from his home, which had no heavy doors, to the adjacent agricultural station, which had a flat roof and iron doors. The air pressure continued to drop.

Now Williams went down to the wharf and found ships having problems. Branches were falling from trees, and by 11:30 A.M., roofs, doors, windows and balconies were breaking off and falling into the street.

Williams's barometric recordings show the pressure bottoming out at 1:30 P.M. at 27.75 inches, compared to a normal reading of about 30 inches. At the Saintes, tiny islands about 22 miles southwest of Pointe à Pitre, the director of a bacteriological laboratory recorded a reading of 27.45. Williams said his low reading stayed that way for an hour, during which there was a slight calm which became a dead calm between 2:00 and 2:30 P.M. Williams said he could see the sun almost coming through the clouds. That, of course, would have been the eye. And that meant the worst was yet to come.

At 2:30 P.M., the barometer began to rise and the wind returned, now from the south. It would continue until midnight. The shift to the south brought a storm surge bearing down on the city. "Despite the excellent protection offered by the coral reefs," the storm barreled into the city's harbor, Williams wrote. Many of the deaths on the island occurred there. The level rose to 12 feet above the high-water mark and dragged boats and barges onto the city streets—one near a bandstand, one near the post office, one next to the building where Williams waited out the storm.

At 5:30 P.M., Williams reported, he and an associate traveled the 60 yards to Williams's home and were "thrown down by the wind" as they dodged flying debris. Williams estimates the winds blew at hurricane force for sixteen hours and reached more than 150 mph. He doesn't say if that was sustained or in gusts. He said that at one factory, pieces of iron weighing more than 250 pounds were torn off and thrown 50 yards. Williams said some people believed there were also earthquakes, but said he didn't feel any at his station.

For the most part, scientists see no link between earthquakes and hurricanes. But in October 1990, when Hurricane Klaus sideswiped the West Indies arc for four days, at least seven earthquakes occurred on the ocean floor. Researchers suggest that changes in the atmosphere trigger the temblors.

Based on the destruction and barometer readings taken from private stations around the island, Williams conjectured the storm's center was 14 miles wide, and it moved at about 14 mph.

Among those killed: Horace Descamps, editor of a local newspaper and the correspondent for the Associated Press, and M. Bain, assistant administrator of the colony. Early on in the storm, at 7:00 A.M. on September 12, about 16 miles east of the capital in the town of St. François, the *Albotros*, a small merchant vessel loaded with eighty casks of rum, had foundered. Five local men fought to save the ship, but drowned, as did her crew.

On September 20, eight days after the storm, American consul William H. Hunt wrote Secretary of State Frank Kellogg a grim report of the island's destruction and Hunt's own ordeal. He called the storm the worst ever to strike Guadeloupe's two islands: Basse-Terre (low land), the main island of Guadeloupe, and Grand-Terre (large land). He said it had killed some 900 people and perhaps double that and virtually the entire surviving population was without shelter.

Hunt said the storm struck Pointe à Pitre "with unprecedented suddenness" between 10:00 and 11:00 A.M. on September 12, an hour before the U.S. Weather Bureau's official landfall of noon. Hunt said the storm wrecked homes, trees, power lines, and sailboats. By 6:00 A.M. on September 13, he wrote, "Pointe à Pitre was a perfect picture of a city that had been dynamited during the preceding night." He said only the city's police station, built of reinforced concrete, survived the wind. Hunt's own home had not. The winds tore off the building's galvanized iron roof and tore apart the partition between offices. At Hunt's living quarters, originally built for offices, all of his furniture, clothes, and personal effects were drenched and ruined. He told his supervisors at the State Department they'd have to build him a new place, since few buildings were still standing and there was nothing to rent. According to news reports on September 19, three-quarters of Guadeloupe's residents were homeless. Two steamships left Martinique with supplies for their island neighbor.

Hunt reported that the storm destroyed the islands' coffee and banana crops and half the sugarcane crop and leveled most of the farm buildings and barracks. The distilleries that produced the island's liquor were damaged or destroyed.

Hunt said he spent the next several days in bed with malaria and the flu "with nothing to shelter me except two doors, which were blown down during the cyclone, placed over my bed and covered with an old carpet to protect me from the rain pouring through the uncovered roof, practically every day or night."

Hunt had reported that the mayor of Pointe à Pitre was appealing to the American Red Cross for help. While the agency prepared to cable $10,000 to Hunt, a note from someone in the State Department's division of western European affairs—it's signed only in unintelligible initials— warned of the dangers of trusting that kind of money to black people.

"In view of the rottenness of local politics on the island it might be inadvisable to hand such a large sum as ten thousand dollars to the local political gentry who range from cafe au lait to cafe noir in complexion," the bureaucrat wrote. He added, "The governor of the island, a white Frenchman from continental France, would seem to be the appropriate person to handle the money. According to the Consul's latest report he is a man of integrity and long service in the colonial career."

Being a little more diplomatic, Secretary of State Kellogg only warned Hunt, "You should be careful to turn it over to the most responsible officially constituted relief organization on the island."

But the proud French, in the form of their Red Cross, finally declined the money from their American counterparts, expressing their "deep appreciation" but saying they had things in control.

In December 1928, the French embassy would write Kellogg, asking if the weather bureau would include Guadeloupe and Martinique in its forecasts. "If so, how many hours in advance could the forecasting be made," ambassador Paul Claudel asked. "Furthermore, what steps should be taken by the Colonies of Guadeloupe and Martinique to avail themselves of those forecasts?"

C. F. Marvin, chief of the Weather Bureau, wrote back that the Weather Bureau broadcast warnings via telegram and radio and cooperated with counterparts in Cuba and Jamaica. He said he would be happy to relay warnings to the French islands, and began doing just that the following summer. But, in this age before satellites and reconnaissance flights, Marvin wrote that the bureau had to depend on ships at sea to report storm sightings and readings.

"Unfortunately few ship reports are received from these areas," he wrote, "and consequently, the islands . . . frequently can be given little advance warning."

At the island of Antigua, northeast of Guadeloupe, a doctor's home and the "poor house" were among the buildings destroyed. Hundreds of homes were reported smashed. Government offices, schools and a hospital were damaged.

Montserrat is a tiny bean-shaped, British-controlled island of only 39 square miles. It was named by Columbus for a mountain in Spain. Montserrat's position puts it in the path of hurricanes. Since records were kept, it had been struck by 41, about one every $8\frac{1}{2}$ years. The century was less than three decades old, but already Montserrat had been struck by no fewer than ten, half of them severe. In 1924, a hurricane had struck the island's north and east areas, The nearby islands of Guadeloupe and Dominica had rushed in relief. Montserrat's residents had repaired quickly and suggested their government mandate concrete buildings and perhaps provide loans and grants. Nothing came of it.

Four years later, the island was expecting a good harvest, cotton pests were under control, and there was talk of a power plant, an ice plant, and even a newspaper. A brutal heat wave enveloped the island. But word was coming from the United States that a storm of "considerable intensity" was threatening. At St. George's Hill, signals were sounded. Commissioner Major Herbert Walter Peebles visited several areas of the island, urging people to board up. For ten hours, the storm ravaged the tiny island, with Plymouth, the capital on the island's south side, taking a direct hit. All its government and commercial buildings were damaged or destroyed. Salem, to the northwest, was all but flattened. At least 42 died, and more than 600 houses were destroyed. The poor, in frail structures, were hardest hit.

At 8:30 P.M. on September 12, a weather advisory from Washington used the word "hurricane" for the first time. It said the storm would pass south of the Virgin Islands and Porto Rico Thursday and be over southern Haiti Thursday night, September 13.

The Islands

At 10:00 A.M. Thursday, an advisory by Mitchell declared, "This is a dangerous storm." But he said it would likely pass south of the Mona Passage, between the Dominican Republic and Porto Rico, on Thursday evening and move south of the city of Santo Domingo, capital of the Dominican Republic, on Friday morning.

Back in West Palm Beach, the *Palm Beach Post*, in reporting this newest advisory on its September 13 front page, had reported there was every indication the storm would move into the Gulf of Mexico, taking it away from Florida, and "no fear was voiced by weather-wise persons that this section would feel the effect of the storm." The story, now in its second day of coverage in the *Post*, was still receiving only modest play, at the bottom of the front page.

Kelsey City mechanic Robert White stopped to tell supervisor Charles Branch that the storm was still in the Atlantic. Branch got in his car and drove up to the Coast Guard station in Jupiter. The commander told him all the ships at sea were reporting the huge storm.

Christopher Columbus had named the island of St. Christopher when he landed there in 1493; it was later shortened to St. Kitts. The storm passed that tiny island on Thursday, September 13. Damage was less intense but at least nine deaths were reported, six of them from the collapse of a schoolhouse. Ironically, the storm had a beneficial long-term effect on the quality of housing, especially in slums. Most homes had been built on wood foundations; following the storm, homes on the island had stronger foundations.

At least thirteen died in neighboring Nevis.

In August 1924, young R. Spencer Byron had gone to bed and been awakened in the early hours by his mother. She had survived an 1899 storm and she was waking her son to tell him a hurricane was upon the island. "I danced with joy," he recalled years later. "Mother said seriously, 'You'd better get on your knees and pray.' "

Now it was 1928. Byron noticed the waters of the Caribbean starting to rise around Nevis "and looking very treacherous." While radio warning systems were limited, weather watchers on the island were spreading the word and police moved through the island, telling people to board up their homes or moving those people to safer public buildings. Scouting had recently been introduced to the island and Byron and his brothers, following the code of doing good deeds, spent the afternoon helping people prepare their homes and move to shelter. Some decided Byron's modest wood home was safe enough and he and his father worked to board it up. They ran out of wood and had to break up benches to board up the rest of the windows. His brothers, Theodore and Vincent, went to the home of an ill neighbor and brought him and his elderly mother over in the darkness and increasing rain and wind. Theodore cut his leg in the struggle and it was later learned the old woman had broken two ribs in her dash to safety. One man, Dannie Walwyn, had left his mother's home, apparently to see to some animals, and when he didn't return, the mother wailed, "Dannee! Dannee! Dannee!" Eventually she burst into sobs, moaning, "He's gone. He's gone!" But her son finally showed up unhurt.

The people in Byron's home heard the wind howl, felt the home shift on its supports, and heard the roof creak as the wind struggled to separate it from the building. A nearby home slid down a hill atop the rain-softened earth. The group began to sing the hymn "Simply Trusting Every Day" and prayed for protection. Byron's mother provided food and hot drinks industriously. After the storm passed, a boat arrived bearing scouts from nearby Antigua to help, Byron would recall.

After Nevis, the storm passed across the Anegada Passage, separating the Leeward and Windward Islands from the U.S. and British Virgin Islands and Porto Rico.

Late on Thursday the merchant ship *Matura,* out of Trinidad and headed for Brooklyn, stood at a dock in St. Croix, largest of the U.S. Virgin Islands. The waterfront was modest, protected only by a small offshore breakwater that protected the harbor from the effects of wave action. The *Matura* boasted a crew of 69 and 13 passengers. On this morning, Captain John H. Hendrickson was watching as 60 stevedores sweated and struggled to load sugar into his ship from two giant barges alongside it. Hendrickson looked at his barometer. It was dropping. And dropping. Soon it was at 27.5 inches.

"A tremendous wind struck us," Hendrickson told the *New York Times*. The crew wrestled the ship away from the dock just before the barges broke loose and slammed into the shore. A sea anchor was dropped, but it did little good. All that night and for two days, waves "as high as the Woolworth Building" rocked the ship. Officers guessed the winds reached 150 mph. As the crew scrambled to close hatches, water crashed across the deck and into the radio house, where operators desperately transmitted warnings to land to be forwarded to the weather office in Porto Rico. With no sun, moon, or stars overhead for two days, the operator could give only an approximate position of the ship, about 10 miles southwest of the harbor. But Hendrickson wanted to at least get that message out so searchers would have a starting point if the *Matura* went down.

Twice the radio antenna blew down, and twice operators were able to rig it in the driving winds. Two hatches were smashed and several feet of iron railing vanished. Cooks couldn't get a fire going in the galley. It didn't matter; everyone was too seasick to eat.

Late on Friday, September 14, conditions settled enough for the *Matura* to try to return to harbor. But with waves breaking over the city and flooding the streets, seas were still too high. The ship waited until Saturday. Then it resumed the loading of the sugar before leaving for Brooklyn, where it would arrive, two days late, on Friday, September 21. Before leaving St. Croix, the crew had waited for a family of five that had booked passage. But they finally left when someone said it was believed the family had been killed.

The Red Cross later determined that virtually everyone on the island of 11,000 had suffered some kind of loss. The agency said 143 buildings were flattened by the storm. The Red Cross sent by ship 125 square feet of galvanized corrugated iron sheets, 100,000 board feet of roof sheeting, and 140,000 board feet of assorted lumber. The agency decided food, clothing and medical supplies weren't a concern on St. Croix.

On September 17, an amateur radio operator at St. Thomas wired that St. Croix reported five dead, hundreds injured, and damage "in the hundreds of thousands." A sugar factory was destroyed. The head of the Red Cross local chapter said later that day there were six dead and that boats had sunk in the harbor at Christiansted. She said winds had been as strong as 100 mph, and rain fell steadily for two days.

Now it was St. Thomas's turn. At 50 miles north of the storm's center, winds were recorded at 90 mph. A newly built breakwater was destroyed. A navy yard and commercial warehouses were in ruins, and several barges sank. The adjacent island of St. John reported minimal damage.

As many as 700,000 were reported homeless in the Virgin Islands. A Red Cross official who had traveled there from Porto Rico on September 21 said that building material from the mainland was desperately needed.

In those tiny islands of the Atlantic, the unnamed storm had already killed more than 1,000 people and caused millions of dollars in damages. The islands it smashed had offered little to weaken it and the warm waters it passed through continued to give it strength. Now it was heading for a larger target: Porto Rico. And soon it would have a name: San Felipe.

Back in West Palm Beach, winds were light to moderate, with scattered showers.

The storm was 1,100 miles from Florida.

Porto Rico

September 13–14, 1928

The Feast of San Felipe

For centuries, hurricanes had no names. In the Caribbean, with a Catholic tradition brought by European settlers, major storms that struck on a saint's feast day were named for that saint. On September 13, 1876, a storm had smashed Porto Rico. It was named "San Felipe" for St. Philip. In September 1928, it was again the time of St. Philip.

Porto Rico is a rectangular island roughly 100 miles by 35 miles, with a land area of about 3,300 square miles, making it about three-fourths the size of Jamaica. When America took possession after the Spanish-American War in the spring and summer of 1898, it renamed the island Porto Rico. Congress would change it back in 1932. In 1928, the island had 2 million residents; Florida, sixteen times the size, had only about 1.3 million.

Porto Rico was also home of the U.S. Weather Bureau's strategic office in the capital of San Juan. The office worked with colleges in Porto Rico and the mainland as well as forty different climate agencies, publishing daily rainfall data from 600 stations in the islands, Central America and parts of South America. And, for every place east of the Dominican

Republic, it was responsible for tracking and forecasting hurricanes. For years, director Oliver Fassig had complained that it was difficult enough for the critically important bureau to do such daunting work in a structure built to both properly monitor and withstand severe weather. Instead, his makeshift operation was set up in a converted garage.

On Tuesday morning, September 11, Fassig came to his office. He scanned the morning weather map; it was clear of storms. But he had a message from Washington. It was the first advisory on the storm. By 3:00 P.M., reports were coming in from St. Lucia and Barbados that winds were shifting direction, a sign that a storm was approaching. Around that time, the radio station in Ensenada, in Porto Rico's southwest corner, intercepted a message to Barbados from the *Inanda*. Fassig wrote that the ship reported "a storm of considerable intensity was raging over the Atlantic about 300 miles east of the Leeward Islands."

Those, Fassig reported, "were the first indications" of the storm's approach. But he said the ship's report was incomplete, and so it was impossible to locate the storm's center.

Fassig's office put out a radio broadcast every two hours, starting on Tuesday night. When the director learned that the storm had passed Dominica Wednesday afternoon, he followed historical assumptions that storms in the area moved north-northwest at 12 to 13 mph and predicted it would probably pass south of the island Wednesday night or Thursday morning. The office distributed warnings to the island's seventy-five police districts as well as other agencies. But by Wednesday morning, reports from other islands still suggested a path south of Porto Rico. "While no dangerous winds are expected over Porto Rico precautions should be taken," said the advisory Fassig issued.

But by 6:00 P.M. Wednesday, Fassig got alarming news. The storm was centered more north than had earlier been estimated. It would probably pass right over the Virgin Islands and plow head-on into Porto Rico. Fassig's office immediately scrambled to distribute the new, more urgent advisories and ordered hurricane warnings hoisted at St. Thomas, in the U.S. Virgin Islands, as well as at twelve ports along the Porto Rican coast: "Latest reports show that the storm will pass over the Virgin Islands and Porto Rico tonight and Thursday morning," he wrote. A late forecast from Washington suggested the storm would be over southern Haiti Thursday night, on a westward path that would take it toward Mexico, and spare Florida. "The general course," U.S. Weather Bureau chief Richard Gray said from Miami, "is to the path of recent disturbances which disappeared in the Yucatán Channel."

Gray would be wrong. The storm did not go to the Yucatán to die.

But forecasters were right about Porto Rico. The storm broke over the island's southeast portion early Thursday morning, September 13, Fassig reported. He said its center crossed at Guayama, on the island's southeast corner, and moved west-northwest across the island's breadth, following the path of the San Ciriaco storm of August 8, 1899, which had killed more than 3,000.

At 4:00 A.M., the lights went out at Catano and a lighthouse went dark. The flag at the lighthouse depot came down. Workers raced from building to building trying to put up boards and tie items down, but the wind threw them against walls and onto the ground. A door flew off its hinges.

For perhaps as many as eighteen hours, the storm pounded the island, crawling at 13 miles an hour while it tore apart the countryside. Fassig's office marked the center crossing south of San Juan, which sits on the northeast shore, at 2:30 P.M. on Thursday. Guayama, on the south coast, and Cayey and Aibonito, in the southeast interior, all reported 20 to 30 minutes of calm, indicating the eye had passed over them.

At 11:45 A.M., one of Fassig's wind indicators recorded a top sustained wind speed of 150 and a top gust of 160 mph—then promptly lost one of its wind cups. Fassig calculated that the storm's center was 30 miles away and said "estimates of 200 miles per hour near the center of the storm appear to be not much overdrawn."

Most of the devastating damage to his bureau occurred between 2:30 and 3:30 P.M. The bureau's office building lost its roof. About 2:30 P.M., the nearby shed that housed weathers balloons collapsed and its roof was thrown 50 feet. The 50-foot tower on which weather instruments were mounted held up, but the anemometer cups and cross-arms were plucked off one at a time by the wind. Some pieces were later found at the San Antonio docks one-third mile away. Fassig said workers replaced the wind gauge twice that afternoon.

About twenty-five people from nearby residences hid from the storm in Fassig's home with his wife and cook. About 3:30 P.M., during the height of the storm, the home lost its roof. The huddled occupants decided they had to abandon the home. They made their way 500 feet to the Baptist mission building.

The storm passed over the Central Cordillera mountain range and exited between Aguadilla and Isabela, on the island's northwest corner.

In Ponce, on the central south coast, winds reached 60 mph about 11:00 A.M. and the eye apparently passed between 3:00 P.M. and 5:00 P.M. Nafael Rio, a broker, later sent the weather bureau a printout that showed the lowest barometric reading at about 5:00 P.M. Winds then picked up again, reaching a maximum of 80 mph, and blew until daybreak. Ponce officials reported many buildings demolished, ten dead and 700 homeless. Initial reports said the Ponce area's coffee crop, the best in 10 years and much of it already presold in Europe, was wiped out. It was valued at $15 million—$147 million today.

In Coamo, northeast of Ponce and inland, switchboard operator Felicita Cartagena stayed at her post, relaying information until she was killed. She was one of nine who died in the town. In Guayama, east of Ponce along the coast, people ran into a church being built; the walls collapsed, killing fourteen.

The storm destroyed many of the island's lighthouses and tore the roof off the headquarters of J. R. Monteiro, the lighthouse district superintendent. For two hours, "it did not seem as if anything would stand its force or any life would survive," Monteiro wrote for the *Lighthouse Service Bulletin*.

Stations reported more than two feet of rain fell over the interior of the island on September 13 and 14—the most in three decades—with about 10 inches measured along the coast. Readings were hard to come by; Fassig estimated most rain gauges overturned, including the one at his office, and high winds made it impossible to measure more than 50 to 75 percent of the actual rainfall. Adjuntas, in the west-central mountain region, reported 29.6 inches, a figure Fassig himself questioned.

At the governor's palace in San Juan, trees were uprooted, windows and doors blown in, and water flooded the place. The freighter *Helen* was pushed onto the rocks near the San Juan harbor.

The storm had sneaked up on Horace J. Head of Rochester, New York, a passenger on the cruise ship *San Lorenzo*. He had been taking a swim at a hotel pool in San Juan with the ship's radio operator when a gust suddenly sprang up and blew water out of the pool. From the beach 200 yards away, sand peppered the windows and raked Head's eyes. Within fifteen minutes, the gust was gone. Head said all was calm for the next three to four hours. But by Thursday noon, Head was in a "wild nightmare," he told the *New York Times* on his return September 18.

"We could see persons running about in the city, dodging the trees, lumber, stones and big pieces of metal that were being driven about over their heads. Ambulances and doctors were racing about trying to gather up the dead and injured."

Head said he finally found a ride in a car that raced through the countryside. He said the floodwaters washing the red soil from the hills "looked like a river of blood."

Estelle Rice, a passenger on the *San Lorenzo*, watched the storm as the ship rocked at its pier in San Juan. Rice said rain pelted the ship all day and the iron roof of a nearby pier was torn off and thrown onto the *San Lorenzo*'s deck.

"We could see whole houses hurtle past," she told the *London Times* correspondent when the ship arrived in New York. "The terrific roar made any conversation impossible, even though all doors and portholes were closed."

And the ship's captain, a Captain Folker, huddling in a waterfront hotel, watched ships come out of the water and smash onto land, their masts cracking and windows shattering. Folker watched in amazement as two nearby cows continued to graze, seemingly oblivious to the wind and rain.

The advisory issued by Mitchell, in Jacksonville, at 9:30 P.M. on Thursday, said he'd received no reports from Porto Rico but that the storm was probably near the island's southwest corner and would pass over or near Santo Domingo, capital of the Dominican Republic. In

Miami, Gray said if Florida felt any effects from the storm, it would be late Saturday or early Sunday.

The Washington advisory from Mitchell repeated: "This is a dangerous storm."

The *Palm Beach Post*, which had placed the story at the bottom of the front page Wednesday and Thursday, placed it right at the top, front, and center, on Friday, in two stories. One gave the early, horrifying reports out of Porto Rico; the other described the storm's path. The headline of the latter read; "Florida is believed safe from Hurricane now sweeping island." Weather bureau officials were quoted as saying the storm might change course or dissipate before it ever threatened the Florida coast.

But the West Palm Beach chapter of the American Red Cross got going anyway. The Miami storm of two years earlier had mobilized the relief agency's Florida units to a plan of action should another devastating storm come along. Now, with the possibility of a strike within three days, the group began a preparedness committee.

On the morning of Friday, September 14, the storm finally moved off Porto Rico's northwest coast. At 10:14 A.M., Fassig, his weather office and home smashed, was able to get off a telegram to Washington: ". . . Wind estimated 160 miles per hour east at 2:30 P.M. stop. Office force OK residence completely demolished office damaged considerable anemometer down raingauge down other instruments OK. Fassig." A second telegram six minutes later read; "Balloon shed completely destroyed." Fassig would write a week later that no one was hurt but that repairs to the weather office would run $3,500 and take two years to complete. He mailed a layout of the bureau, scribbled with arrows and notes saying "entire roof blown off," "brick walls collapsed," "kitchen gas range and water heater destroyed," and, in one restroom, "nothing but the seat left."

Because the island was so small and the storm ripped across it lengthwise, virtually every part of it suffered. Fassig initially estimated 300 dead and several hundred thousand homeless. He attributed the smaller death toll in this storm, compared to past hurricanes, to the advance warning. Of those who did die, many had been cut to pieces or lost limbs as sheets of zinc flew off roofs and cut through the air like scythes. In Cayey, a woman was found with a child in each arm; all three had been chopped up by the flying sheets of zinc.

In Rio Piedras, just south of San Juan, medical buildings had been all but destroyed; 300 tuberculosis patients were living in the open, and 70 lepers had been concentrated at an administrative building. Nearly 75 percent of San Juan's homes and 40 percent of its commercial buildings had been destroyed. Property and crop losses were estimated at $50 million—$492 million today. The *London Times* provided grim figures on deaths and destruction and patronizingly bemoaned, "They are mostly poor country folk, whose staple food is bananas."

Governor Horace Towner wired President Calvin Coolidge that half the territory's homes were destroyed and 700,000 people were homeless. He sent dispatches to the press, calling the disaster "the most serious the Island has ever suffered."

On Monday, September 17, Coolidge ordered the military to divert two army transport ships, loaded with food, to the island. Plans were made to load a supply ship Tuesday morning in New York with 1.5 million pounds of supplies for swift dispatch to the south by afternoon. The cargo: one-third salt pork and salt codfish, one-third beans and rice, and one-third flour. A commercial steamship delayed its sailing and police blocked traffic on busy New York streets so three carloads of meat could race to the steamer for loading. The first army relief ship, the *St. Mihiel,* arrived in Porto Rico on September 19 with 559 tons of supplies. The second ship arrived the next day. Colonel Henry M. Baker, national director of the American Red Cross, and four staffers arrived by ship as well.

The Red Cross freed up $50,000 and rushed in two million pounds of flour, rice, beans, salt, pork, and equipment for two field hospitals, including 36,000 blankets, 5,000 cots, and nearly 1,000 tents. By the end of September, the agency would also distribute more than 24,000 pieces of clothing and a large supply of medicine.

By the end of the week, officials were saying the best way to rebuild Porto Rico was to put people to work, not hand them charity. Cuba, Colombia, and the Dominican Republic sent money, and the Dominican president ordered fresh fruit and vegetables rushed to his

American neighbor. Merchants who did business with Porto Rico chipped in. Building materials firms rushed supplies. Vaudeville performers put on benefit shows. Pastors in pulpits exhorted their flocks to dig deep. Masonic lodges across the Americas and Caribbean raised nearly $84,000 for the island; $51,000 came from a national fund, and the rest ranged from $15,000 out of the New York chapter to $5 from a lodge right in San Juan.

Mail service resumed, but carriers had a new problem. They kept returning to their post offices with mail addressed to buildings and homes that were no longer where they were supposed to be. The island's health commissioner reported on September 18 that bodies were being buried where they were found, sometimes without identification and with no report made to authorities. The commissioner said hospitals and drugstores had been flattened and the critical medicines in them blown away. By September 24, the number of reported flu cases had risen to about 15,000.

When the *San Lorenzo* had finally left for New York, passenger Horace Head said despite the island's struggle to cope with the disaster, some residents still came down to the dock to smile and wave and shout, "Bon voyage."

On September 20, the magazine *Gráfico* published an "edición especial del Ciclón de San Felipe." On its cover was a photograph of homes reduced to sticks in San Juan's Perla neighborhood. Inside, a "Vision of Ruin": picture after picture showed shattered homes, downed trees, smashed sugarcane wagons, swamped boats, a radio tower draped over a two-story building; wood piled in the street. There were images of smashed walls and exposed interiors at San Juan Stadium and a major factory, and of a building on Avenida Ponce de León with its top floor gone and an entire balcony hanging drunkenly. And, in one blurry picture, a "hero of Perla" held in his arms a child found alive in one of the flattened homes.

Governor Towner was deluged by complaints that mass confusion had delayed relief in the seventy-two hours following the storm. A committee of citizens called on him to declare martial law, requisition food supplies, and draft men for work. The committee said profiteering and looting were unchecked, and disease and famine stalked the island. On Tuesday, September 18, Towner called out 2,000 National Guardsmen to patrol twenty-three towns.

The *Times*, a San Juan paper, criticized Towner in its September 18 issue, quoting Baker as saying that President Calvin Coolidge had called the day after the storm "to take charge of the relief commission to this island . . . thus showing that the President in Washington was so much better informed than our own governor, whose cables to the United States were all filed nearly 96 hours after the storm."

The newspaper also reported price gouging. Food was marked up. Roofing and other construction materials tripled; corrugated zinc went from $2.25 per sheet to $10 and, in some cases, $16. Candles that normally cost two cents rose to a nickel. Looting was rife at first but diminished in the two days after the storm "due to the use of revolvers and pistols . . ."

Federal surveys concluded losses in Porto Rico totaled about $85.3 million, $46.4 million of that to crops alone. These and other surveys gave varying figures for individual crops. The highs were: coffee industry, $21 million; sugarcane, $17.3 million; bananas, $5.7 million; citrus, $2.8 million; coconuts, $1.7 million; tobacco, $1.5 million. The surveys estimated rebuilding costs alone at $7.3 million. Congress approved $11.2 million in aid, $6 million of that in loans to farmers. These figures, in today's dollars, would be almost ten fold.

For centuries, roads had been maintained by the old Spanish custom of "road menders," their homes set two miles apart; each was responsible for two miles of road. With their help, the island's 1,500 miles of roads were cleared within days. And while the storm destroyed some 321 school buildings and damaged 414 others, within three weeks, 90 percent of school operations was back up.

Today, the official death count is 312. The real toll is more likely somewhere between 600 and 1,600. Had the storm dissolved after striking Porto Rico, people would still be talking about the great Porto Rico hurricane in 1928.

But it still hadn't done its worst.

By Thursday afternoon, September 14, the storm, had left Porto

Rico and moved north of Hispaniola, the giant, mountainous island that is home to Haiti and the Dominican Republic. In Porto Plata, on the Dominican Republic's northern coast, some homes lost roofs and ships were damaged. The freighter *Lillian* was driven ashore. Cap-Haïtien, on Haiti's northwest coast, got only heavy rains.

Over the centuries, Hispaniola has suffered for Florida's sake. Many a swirling storm has been ripped to shreds, or caromed harmlessly into the open Atlantic, or both, after slamming into the island's mountains. The mountains are the tallest in the West Indies, reaching as high as the Dominican Republic's Duarte Peak, which rises 10,417 feet, nearly two miles above sea level. They have the effect of a stick in a bicycle wheel's spokes, ripping apart the circulation of the giant cyclone and weakening it.

But it moved too far to the north for Hispaniola to have any effect.

And a map of the storm's path reveals that it didn't make the large curve officials had confidently predicted for several days. In fact, from Porto Rico on, it described an almost-perfect parabola. Had it curved more, it would have stayed well offshore, bringing Florida only heavy coastal swells, and perhaps striking the Carolinas or continuing its curve out to sea and sparing the U.S. east coast altogether. Continuing on a west-northwest route, it would have crossed the 700-mile length of Cuba, weakening or perhaps even breaking up in its long, exhausting journey over land. Or it might have moved into the Gulf of Mexico and threatened either the Yucatán, northeast Mexico, Texas or the upper Gulf Coast.

Instead, it stayed right on the arc.

The storm was 700 miles from Florida.

Bearing Down

September 14–16, 1928

"Recurve not yet indicated"

On Friday, September 14, West Palm Beach residents were making some plans but weren't in a panic. Forecasters and cracker-barrel pundits competed for the best answer to the big question: Will it hit us?

The forecasters were saying no.

At noon Friday there "seemed to be a tendency toward a curve eastward," a wire story said. As in, away from Florida.

Out in the Atlantic, the Turks and Caicos and the Bahamas, scores of flat chunks of rock, stretch like a hurricane alley pointing northwest from Hispaniola right to southeast Florida. In 1928, the thirty islands of the Turks and Caicos were part of the British colony of Jamaica. The Turks had been visited by hurricanes about every twenty years—in 1866, 1888, and 1908. So, when two storms struck in 1926, locals figured they'd met their quota for a while.

Cleo Goodwin, a special observer for the U.S. Weather Bureau, had lost his wife in May 1927 "from the effects of the 1926 hurricane." Now a new storm was ravaging Grand Turk. At 11:50 A.M. on September 14, a U.S. Weather Bureau advisory said the storm would likely pass near

Turks Islands that night. As it approached, Goodwin's workers wanted to keep their radio going for as long as possible, a strategy later credited with saving lives, especially in the outer islands. That meant waiting until the last minute to take down the antenna. But when the radio equipment was finally shut down, no one wanted to go outside and climb the tower. Finally, Lance Corporal William A. Godet volunteered and scampered up the pole in the growing winds.

By midnight and into Saturday, September 15, the wind was up to 120 mph, but it dropped to only about 36 mph within half an hour, an indication that Grand Turk suffered only a glancing blow. About 3:00 A.M., winds blew back up to 60 mph. By dawn, they had subsided.

"The wind was most peculiar in its action," Goodwin wrote, saying it was calm in one spot and strong enough nearby to knock someone down. He said the sand, whipped by the wind and rain, was blinding; Goodwin would write in his letter to weather officials in Washington that his eyes were still sore days later. Goodwin said one building rolled over twice and had to be torn apart to remove it. He said another house was carried over walls and vacant lots and spun around.

Returning to his home after the storm, Goodwin found his carriage house flattened and most of his poultry killed. He did not have kind words for the masses.

"The people here should certainly appreciate the services of the Bureau for the timely warning given them, but I am afraid they are of a class that appreciate nothing and while we were working hard they were home comfortable and then come out after all is over and want to dictate to those that watched diligently," he wrote.

On the morning of September 15, "there was not a vestage [sic] of green to be seen on the Island of Grand Turk, looked [sic] as it if had been swept by forest fire," Goodwin wrote. But a month later, he wrote, rains had restored the island's verdant foliage.

George Frith, a businessman on Grand Turk, wrote on September 16 to say that the storm had passed about nine miles to the south. "Without your reports and warnings, I do not know, and can not even form the remotest idea, of what would happen to these islands," Frith wrote the U.S. weather officials. "The hurricane that raged here all Friday beats all that I know of."

Frith said two of his ships, the *C. Maud Gaskill* and *William A. Naugler,* were loading salt for Canadian ports at Salt Cay when the vessels washed ashore in the storm, but their crews were saved. He didn't mail his letter right away, and in a postscript dated September 18, he wrote, "From news received this A.M. we fear a great loss of life at some of the outer islands."

In fact, the Caicos Islands had suffered great damage, especially among crops, and residents were reported to be starving. Salt, a key product of the islands, was a top casualty: 225,000 bushels were lost. Relief boats were sent out and administrators in Jamaica scrambled to provide financial help.

The greatest tragedy had been at Ambergris Cay, about 12 miles south of South Caicos. There are two different versions of what happened. Goodwin said a sloop on its way to Grand Turk to be registered was lost, with 18 people drowned. But in his official report of the storm, W. E. Tatem, Hurricane Relief Officer for the island colony, said conch fishermen had anchored their boat in a small creek on the cay, but the entire island had become submerged and 17 of the crew of 21 were lost. Eight of the dead left wives.

The storm had passed over the southern part of the Turks Islands and the northwest part of the Caicos, and while the winds were stronger and present longer than in the 1926 storm, the damage was actually less severe. Authorities again gave special praise to the U.S. Weather Bureau for its warning. W. E. Tatem said many buildings had been repaired from the 1926 storm and built better, and the rebuilding limited damage as well. "It might well be said," Tatem wrote, "that our many misfortunes have been followed by bountiful blessings for which we need to be thankful."

A week later, on September 26, a British Royal Navy ship, the *Durban,* would land at Grand Turk and offer relief. It was politely declined by the island's commissioner. But the captain did turn over a ton of potatoes. The captain and some of his officers dined that night at the commissioner's home. Among the captain's party: his lieutenant, the future King George VI of England.

As the storm had marched across the ocean, never wavering from its parabolic path toward South Florida, stories about it had marched up the front page of the *Palm Beach Post*.

Mitchell's advisory from Jacksonville, from 9:00 P.M. on Friday, September 14, as the storm was ripping through the Bahamas, had said the storm was 75 miles southeast of "Turk's Island" and moving northwest about 300 miles a day. He told reporters, "The storm no longer threatens the lower East Coast of Florida."

In Miami, forecaster Richard Gray also stuck to his prediction that the storm would continue to arc.

"The recurving of the storm will take it east of the Bahamas unless it again changes its course," Gray said Friday. "Its present direction of movement makes it improbable that it will affect the east coast of Florida."

Cuban weather officials concurred with Gray. At the Jesuit observatory in Belen, Father Mariano Gutierrez-Lanza said neither Cuba nor Florida should be concerned.

But on Friday evening, the *Post* got a copy of a government weather report that had been picked up by the wireless station in Jupiter. Blaney T. Himes, a retired U.S. Navy hydrographic officer, looked it over. He told the paper Florida's east coast was going to get some or all of the storm. For the first time, the *Post* addressed the possibility that Palm Beach County would be struck.

By Saturday morning, September 15, the headline now read: "Florida May Feel Storm's Path; Present Course Will Bring Hurricane to Lower Coast Sunday." A second story said Saturday would be the critical day. "Tonight will be the longest [latest] it is considered advisable to delay preparations to forestall damage from the wind," the paper wrote.

As is always the case, the paper was still hedging its bets, trying to toe the line the press does even today between giving adequate warning and creating one more "cry wolf" event.

"Giving ironclad forecasts upon the hurricane is practically impossible," the paper wrote. "There is the chance the hurricane might hover in its course, delaying the continuance of its march toward the Florida coast until Monday or Tuesday. Possibilities were apparent last night that the storm might veer to the right and travel northward, which would head it again to sea. Again, it may continue to the Florida coast and strike at a point which it is now too early to determine."

Another story started with this dramatic description about what the storm had done so far: "Borne on a hurricane's back desolation and death rode ruthlessly across the sunny palm-decked islands of the Caribbean today and it was believed that when the debris of the storm's fury settled the specters of famine and disease would be found stalking in its wake."

That Saturday morning, weather official Richard Gray had still said the storm would miss South Florida, although it was now considered a threat to the coasts of northeast Florida and southeast Georgia.

"The location of the tropical disturbance this morning shows it has followed the course indicated by yesterday's report," Gray said. "It will not cause high winds on the lower East Coast of Florida." He predicted top winds at 35 mph.

Just to be safe, Gray, for the first time in the life of the 1928 hurricane, issued storm warnings for the mainland of the United States. They stretched 200 miles from Miami to Titusville, near Cape Canaveral. The advisory predicted winds at the southeast Florida coast would reach gale force during Sunday and by noon, hurricane force winds would be as far west as 79 degrees longitude, or 60 miles off Florida's southeast coast. The warnings sent directly to Miami and West Palm Beach said that "every precaution should be taken [Saturday night] in case hurricane warnings should be found necessary on the east Florida coast."

The advisory finished with a line that, for the first time, nibbled away at the reassurances the storm would miss Florida which the confident Gray had proffered for several days. It said, "Recurve of hurricane's path not yet indicated."

Dr. William J. Buck had not waited.

Buck was believed to be the only doctor anywhere along the southern part of Lake Okeechobee, from Pahokee to Moore Haven. He was a major during World War I and had run the base hospital for the U.S. 82nd Division in Le Mans, France. Buck was among the early settlers of Belle Glade when it incorporated in the spring of 1928. Not content with doctoring, he was also president of the Belle Glade town council and had founded the American Legion's Belle Glade post.

Not satisfied with weather officials' continued reassurances that the storm would miss Florida, Buck had taken his own action on Saturday and Sunday. He sent fellow Legionnaires across the Glades to spread the warning. Some four hundred people jammed into the town's two hotels.

"White and negroes were brought in alike," Buck would say on September 21. "It was a time of terror and there was no discrimination. Our effort was to save lives."

Few would share Buck's position.

In Kelsey City, Charles Branch stopped by to see his mechanic, Robert White. He found White furiously stocking the storm shelter he'd built. He was planning to put thirty people in it. White had laid a map on his table and charted the storm's progress. He placed a ruler on the paper, paralleling the path. It led right to West Palm Beach. The two looked at each other. White told his supervisor that whatever he planned on doing, he'd better do it now. Branch was sufficiently unnerved. He loaded one truck with lumber and the other with men and told them to start boarding up the company's properties. He called his wife and told her to take their son and head for Orlando. She said she wouldn't leave without him. He finally convinced her, insisting he'd follow. Everyone was making plans to leave except Harry Kelsey's son, Ted. He didn't believe the storm would hit, and if it did, he was dying to see what it would be like.

Branch looked up; there wasn't a cloud in the sky.

Noah Kellum Williams, a dairy farmer and Palm Beach County Commissioner from Jupiter, had driven the 20 miles down to West Palm Beach Saturday afternoon. He heard a report that the storm was coming. Men stood around in groups, discussing which buildings might survive and which might come down.

As the barometer fell and a brisk wind brought rains and squalls, people braced windows and secured boats and yachts. But the school year was still set to open Monday. West Palm Beach merchants were preparing for Wednesday's "Dollar Day," when many stores were cutting prices to encourage sales. A car dealer's ad boasted the DeSoto Six, "brilliant and revolutionary in its field," for only $845. A meeting of American Legion posts from Key West to Titusville was still set for Sunday afternoon in Fort Pierce. Thirty-nine Palm Beach County churches had advertised the times of their Sunday services. At First Baptist Church in downtown West Palm Beach, Reverend C. H. Bolton's 11:00 A.M. sermon would be "God's Will for America" and, at 8:00 P.M., "Summer is ended and we are not saved." By 8:00 P.M. Sunday, every person in West Palm Beach, of every religion, would be praying for salvation.

As Saturday's paper was being spread on breakfast tables across South Florida, it became clear to Weather Bureau forecasters that on the morning of Sunday, September 16, the storm would pass near Nassau, the capital of the Bahamas, on New Providence Island, northeast of the much larger Andros Island.

". . . this hurricane is of wide extent and is attended by dangerous and destructive winds," an advisory read.

In Nassau, ships scrambled to find safe harbor.

About noon Saturday, Bahamian officials in Nassau lost communication with Inagua Island, 400 miles southeast. But the island would suffer little damage. San Salvador, where Christopher Columbus is believed to have first landed when he encountered the "New World" in 1492, experienced 110 mph winds; the storm's center was believed to have passed 50 miles to the southwest. Homes and a church were damaged. Another 150 houses were lost on Cat Island.

At about 3:00 P.M., the German steamer *August Leonhardt* was about 250 miles east-southeast of Nassau at 23.10 north, 74.10 west, heading from New York to Porto Columbia, Venezuela.

R. Sievers, the ship's second officer, watched as the barometer dropped to a frightening 27.80 inches and a northeast wind blew at Force 12—more than 75 mph. Then the center passed over the ship and it was enveloped in a calm lasting ten minutes. Now the wind shifted to the south-southeast "with an indescribable force," Sievers wrote. "The force of the wind . . . could only be judged by the noise made by the storm, which reminded me of the New York subway going full speed passing switches."

Rain and spray drove horizontally across the deck and the ship's whistle began to blow eerily in the violent winds. Sievers watched as waves slammed the 2,500-ton freighter and spray shot up to the masthead, about 130 feet above the ocean's surface, leaving salty residue that the crew later cleaned off the ship's antenna and insulators. Hatch tarps, boat ventilators, covers, and anything else that wasn't attached solidly flew off and disappeared in the vicious sea.

"It is impossible to describe the sea and swell," Sievers wrote. "Spray, rain and foam was so dense that we could not see our forecastle head."

Meteorologists guessed that the eye of the storm passed a 65-mile stretch of ocean between Nassau and Harbour Island, at the north end of Eleuthera—the birthplace of Isaac Miller, who was this day on his farm near Belle Glade.

At 10:00 P.M., D. Salter, meteorological recorder for Nassau, measured a northeast wind at 40 mph "and freshing rapidly." It was 55 by midnight, 65 mph by 1:30 A.M., and 75 mph at 2:00 A.M. By 4:00 A.M., it had crossed the 100 mph mark.

But that was just a guess. At 3:30 A.M. Sunday, just after recording a speed of 96 mph, the cups on Salter's anemometer, or wind gauge, had blown away. By 5:00 A.M., he estimated, winds were at 110 to 120 mph, with a driving rain. But by 6:00 A.M., the winds had dropped dramatically. Salter measured a total of 9 inches of rain during the storm's passage.

Just across Nassau's harbor lay Hog Island, once a place where farmers bred pigs to supplement their regular diet of fish and other seafood. It would become the more melodious Paradise Island. The storm had snapped the electric cable to Hog Island, and it shot out a shower of sparks, lighting the night sky.

Several ships sank or were tossed against rocks. The storm also tossed debris through the streets of Nassau, knocked down power and telephone lines, flooded homes, and terrorized residents, many of whom fled their homes for schools and church halls.

At least four churches reported considerable damage. A statue of Christopher Columbus was struck and a piece of the explorer's hat broken off. A bandstand was demolished. Two outhouses at a hospital lost their roofs. A nearly completed pier, built to handle passenger ships, the island's lifeblood, was swept away, leaving only its pilings.

On Bay Street, the city's main street, most buildings suffered significant damage, as did the market wharf and sponge wharf. Nearby, a large piece of roofing struck the city's cathedral and threw open its door, exposing the interior to the storm's winds and floodwaters. A Wesleyan Methodist church that had been damaged in an 1866 storm lost much of its roof, as did a garage where many residents had stored their cars for protection. Remarkably, most of the cars were undamaged. Telegraph service was knocked out at 2:00 A.M. Sunday but was back up by noon Monday. The newspaper also reported "one of the male lunatics escaped" from the city's hospital and hadn't been found.

On Sunday, a ten-year-old girl helping a neighbor fell into a trench on Bay Street and drowned. Her parents reported her missing but she wasn't spotted until Tuesday. Another child had to have a leg amputated after it was broken during the storm.

A golf tournament set to start Sunday morning was postponed for at least a week; the course was still under water. At St. Johns Church, where congregants had been arguing over the fate of the current pastor, the hurricane at least temporarily made that moot, as it leveled the building. The *Nassau Tribune* reported some people looting damaged stores "like a carrion crow swoops down on a fainting victim in the barren wastes of the desert." Government agencies carried away some debris and a contractor hauled off 1,709 truckloads of trash. In the 1926 storm, so many downed trees had been collected that the firewood made from them was still being used now, two years later.

Salter's report to U.S. weather officials concluded the storm had done "considerable damage" to property in Nassau and lesser damage to crops but had caused no deaths, "probably owing to the precaution taken as a result of the numerous early warnings received by wireless telegraphy and made public." Officials also credited the experience of the 1926 storm, saying it had blown away weaker buildings and surviving structures had been rebuilt to be stronger.

J. Frank Points, American Vice Consul in Nassau, called the storm the worst in the Bahamas since the historic 1866 hurricane—even worse than the 1926 storm, which went on to ravage Miami. He said this 1928 storm had done considerable damage throughout the city and to both his residence and that of two assistants, identified only as Miss Gyr and Miss Porter. Rain had rushed into their rooms at about 3:30 A.M., drenching everything before it could be moved. The staff would spend the next few days in swimsuits and raincoats, "for any other clothing that was donned was wet through in five minutes time."

Eleuthera reported that 100 mph winds destroyed 128 homes and damaged 154 and killed one man who was crushed under his house. The Police Court and private warehouses and a wharf were destroyed and many government offices damaged. Virtually every farm on the island was wrecked and the radio station knocked out.

"The years 1866 and 1926 will now be forgotten and 1928 will hold the first place as the year of the worst storm that has ever visited this part of the island of Eleuthera," a *Nassau Guardian* correspondent wrote September 22 from the town of Governor's Harbour.

Harbour Island reported that 95 mph winds unroofed the Church of England building and damaged many other structures but that no one was killed. Six houses fell at Long Cay and 200 people who were at Atwood's Cay to harvest tree bark lost their boats and were stranded. Acklin Island reported forty boats and most crops destroyed.

The islands of Bimini and West End, between Nassau and the Florida coast, also reported damage but no deaths. Bimini's famed "rum row," the waterfront dock where smugglers picked up contraband rum and other liquor for the short run across the Atlantic to the Prohibition-defiant United States, had been smashed by the 1926 storm. Now it was reported to have again sustained heavy losses. The wharf had been damaged and small ships sunk. Nearly every home on the island was reported damaged or destroyed.

Even in faraway Havana, about 350 miles to the west, the storm's outer bands sent water crashing over the sea wall along the famed Malecón promenade. Shipping was virtually stopped.

The Bahamas' national Board of Agriculture would later race shipments of seed corn to the "Out Islands" and cabled elsewhere for tomato seeds.

"No useful purpose can be served by Out Islanders coming to Nassau in search of work. There are enough unemployed people here to feed the labour market for some time to come," the *Nassau Guardian* said in a September 22 editorial. It added for its readers in Nassau proper: "It is no time for sitting down and bemoaning the sadness of one's lot. It is a time for action and when that action takes the form of rebuilding houses and churches it is to be hoped that they will be more securely and safely built than they were so that when the next hurricane strikes these islands the toll of damage may not be so great."

At the end of the month, the Royal Navy ship *Durban,* which had already stopped at Grand Turk, would arrive in Nassau, again bringing its prominent crew member, the future George VI. It was the first visit by a member of the royal family in seven decades.

"Although far from the centre of the Empire and little in contact with the outside world it is encouraging to find that the plight of these islands arouses such interest and such spontaneous offers of assistance from our fellow subjects and neighbors," the *Nassau Guardian's* September 22 editorial read.

In a statement Saturday night, September 15, U.S. weather official Richard Gray had said the advisories for the Florida coast that he had posted earlier in the day were only precautionary. He said the storm "had not changed its northwesterly course." And, he added, "There was no indication Saturday night that dangerous winds will occur in the Miami area. Gray predicted that, by Sunday morning, the storm would be 170 miles east of Miami, and no threat to South Florida. And, in a 9:30 P.M. telegram from the Jesuit observatory in Belen, Cuba, Father Gutierrez-Lanza again said Florida was in no danger for the ensuing twenty-four hours.

But at 6:00 P.M. Saturday in Kelsey City, Charles Branch was planning on the probability of a hit. He sent his workers home to ride out the storm or, if they wanted, prepare to head out of town. Branch himself made plans to join his family in Geneva, northeast of Orlando. One black employee looked at the sky and said, "Is we going to have a storm?"

Branch replied, "Lonnie, when you get home, start praying. And don't stop until it's over."

Even as the winds were dying down in the Bahamas early Sunday, those islands would soon become historical fine print. And any hopes that they could count on a lot of help from their longtime friends in the nearby United States would be dimmed. South Florida soon would not be able even to save itself.

It was Sunday, September 16, 1928.

The storm was moving about 14½ miles an hour—a pace of about 175 miles every 12 hours.

And it was 200 miles from Florida.

West Palm Beach

"The sky turned that peculiar color. And then, Oh Boy!"
About 1:00 A.M., Sunday, September 16, 1928, in Yellowstone National
Park, Frank B. Willits, a longtime resident of the Glades, was awakened
from his sleep. In the dark, he noticed that his friend, Noel McAlister of
South Bay, was stirring. The two had driven their Model T Ford out
west, all the way from Florida. They had no clue what was happening
back home.

Noel sat up. He wanted to go home. He couldn't say why. Willits
couldn't sway him. So the two packed up and started driving back across
the continent.

"Storm Moving Nearer Coast from Islands," the *Palm Beach Post*'s
Sunday headline said. "City Prepares for High Winds Throughout Day."

The paper was deluged with calls. Stores reported the sale of thousands of candles and lamps, despite the danger of fire. Lumber was
snatched up as merchants boarded the plate-glass windows of their shops.
About 2:00 A.M. Sunday, West Palm Beach police were called to a noisy
party at 425 13th Street. It turned out several people there were "excited
about storm, getting ready to motor north."

69

As late as midnight into Sunday, when the *Palm Beach Post* editors were putting the paper to bed, the word from the U.S. Weather Bureau was still "optimistic." But over the next several hours, Richard Gray's optimism slipped away minute by minute.

For the first time, Gray was now saying the storm would strike Florida. He said, however, that it would hit north of the heavily populated region from Miami to West Palm Beach. That stretch, he predicted, would receive winds of no more than 54 mph. The *Post* reported the storm would hit Florida somewhere unless it changed its course—or blew itself out, something that wasn't about to happen.

The *Post* said its offices at 328 Datura Street would be open Sunday and people could call for the latest storm advisories or come to where they would be posted at the Palm Beach Mercantile Company, 260 Clematis Street, and at the King and Brewer insurance firm at the Citizens Bank Building, 105 South Narcissus Avenue. If hurricane warnings were ordered displayed, the paper said, they would fly from the Citizens Bank Building.

That's what the Sunday-morning papers said when they landed in driveways across the West Palm Beach area. But by dawn, Gray had a new set of predictions. Now, at last, in his mind, the prospect of a true disaster had gone from impossible to a long shot to unlikely to a near certainty.

Gray sent the following warning by telegraph to newspapers, radio stations, and anyone else set up to receive weather information: "Hoist hurricane warnings 10:30 A.M. Miami to Daytona, Fla. No report this morning from Nassau. Indications are that hurricane center will reach the Florida coast near Jupiter early to-night [sic]. Emergency. Advise all interests. This hurricane is of wide extent and great severity. Every precaution should be taken against destructive winds and high tides on Florida east coast, especially West Palm Beach to Daytona."

But who heard it? Who read it?

At 10:30, it was too late for the morning newspapers. By the time the afternoon editions hit the streets, storm-force winds would already be blowing. In 1928, perhaps one in forty South Floridians owned a radio. The advent of television was two decades away. Telephones? A rare luxury. The situation among the struggling farmers and the migrant workers in the interior was even worse.

In the afternoon, a rare and chilling symbol began appearing across coastal South Florida. It is a flag: a black square inside a larger red square. Now it is a pennant for the University of Miami Hurricanes football team. There was a time when it was virtually the sole method by which people were told a storm was coming. One flag signified a tropical storm. Two: a hurricane. Flagpoles along the coast had already held a single square. On the afternoon of September 16, a flag with two squares went up each staff.

There is anecdotal evidence that people spread the word the old-fashioned way. Several days after the storm, South Bay businessman Frank Schuster stopped by the Miami office of the U.S. Weather Bureau. He wanted to let Richard Gray know he'd received good advance warning of the storm even out in the Glades—Gray's notes don't say how. But Schuster said the alert had enabled him to save 211 people by making several car trips in that area, with the help of others, "for the purpose of collecting the white residents and moving them to a large barge." Apparently Schuster didn't have time to save black residents.

W. D. Faucette, chief engineer for the Seaboard Air Line Railway Company, wrote from Savannah on December 31, 1928, saying he'd read Mitchell's summary of the storm and was impressed with the account of Schuster's actions. "While I do not know Mr. Schuster and his associates, this is such a splendid act, I presume it has been drawn to the attention of those public authorities to whom such deeds are reported," Faucette wrote. The U.S. Weather Bureau said its Miami officials had taken the time to compliment Schuster on his service.

Also, a weather observer in Moore Haven reported that while the destruction in "the stricken area" was "appalling," he'd asked many residents if they received warnings, "and they all replied in the affirmative." The observer doesn't say what form the warnings took.

Then there's the folklore that Seminoles can mystically sense a storm is on the way by watching sawgrass bloom. Black educator Mary McLeod Bethune repeated a story that Seminoles were seen leaving several days before the storm, saying, "Follow Indian, Indian no fool, going to dry land, big water coming." One has to wonder if the Seminoles, like Schuster, had simply heard by word of mouth that a storm was coming.

At 1:00 P.M. Sunday, the U.S. Weather Bureau sent out an updated alert. It was terrifying. Gray was moving the hour of expected landfall from Sunday night to the afternoon: "Hoist northeast storm warnings north of Punta Gorda to Apalachicola. Hurricane central noon about 26 North, 79 west, moving northwestward. Its center will move inland between Miami and Jupiter probably late this afternoon. Increasing northeast winds along west Florida coast reach gale force Tampa to Apalachicola to-night [sic]."

But by the time of the 1:00 P.M. advisory, winds were already picking up in downtown West Palm Beach.

In the black section of town, fourteen-year-old Clothilda Miller had been hearing the neighborhood gossip about the storm all weekend: It was big. It was little. It was going to turn. Clothilda's father Isaac and his brother-in-law, Ernest Rolle, were 40 miles away, on the small farm they had set up in Chosen, near Belle Glade. Her mother was also out there. She had gone out on Friday to help her sister pack for a planned move back to the coast. She had taken Clothilda's brother, Samuel, then about eleven. Ernest's wife, Anna Belle, had been put in charge of the Miller children while everyone was gone. A Mr. Ewell, who lived diagonally across the street, had offered them his home if the storm became too severe.

In a rarity that Sunday morning, the Millers had not gone to church. The day had a holiday atmosphere. They had cooked a big dinner. Outside, it rained and rained. Lena, one of Clothilda's sisters, asked God to bless the food and keep them safe in the storm. They ate, cleaned up the dishes, and waited.

Beryl Lewis, a writer at the *Palm Beach Post,* had gotten up that morning and prepared to attend Sunday school, then play a game of tennis with Bill Matthews, a colleague at the paper. The wind was up to about 25 mph, with gusts up to 40; not exactly tennis weather. But the sun was shining, and besides, Lewis's own morning paper, which not only informed him during breakfast but paid his salary as well, had said the storm would miss Palm Beach County.

Lewis and Matthews arrived at the church. They went from floor to floor. No one was there. Convinced Sunday school had been canceled, they returned to Matthews's apartment. Pretty soon, the rain began.

Shortly after lunch, Tom Rickards and his family took their maid home, then headed for Rickards's office at the county courthouse. Built in 1916, it was, Rickards believed, the strongest building in Palm Beach County. The family brought a folding cot and bedding for Rickards's grandmother, as well as some sandwiches and coffee. With them was Rickards's young son Tommie. Tom Rickards was the small county's justice of the peace and coroner. Within twenty-four hours, he would be presiding over more than one thousand bodies.

At noon, tile began falling off the Kettler building, at 118½ Myrtle in downtown West Palm Beach, and police blocked the street. Around that time, the mayor called for the police chief and city manager to meet him at the Red Cross headquarters in the American Legion building at 218 Datura Street at 2:00 P.M.

Determined not be caught unprepared, as their island neighbors had been, West Palm Beach area Red Cross officials had late Saturday called for an 11:00 A.M. meeting on Sunday to mobilize for an emergency. About one hundred people gathered and were given assignments: water, food, medical supplies, clothes, transportation. Chapters across the state were doing the same thing so they'd be ready to move quickly into the storm region. About 2:00 P.M., the head of the West Palm Beach Red Cross unit called counterparts in Miami, Tampa and Jacksonville. If he didn't call back in twelve hours, he said, start sending people. Five minutes later, the telephone lines went down.

The Red Cross's national headquarters issued a release saying that money was pouring in to help the wrecked islands and that ministers around the country were issuing pleas from their Sunday-morning pulpits. But, the agency said, it was now starting to gear up for a new threat: Florida.

"Indications that Florida might suffer another catastrophe of terrifying proportions became increasingly certain throughout the day," the agency announced. "With the hurricane moving steadily on a bee line for the east coast of Florida, gathering speed as it progressed and maintaining a wind velocity but little less than when it hurled itself across Porto Rico," the Red Cross was speeding disaster workers to Jacksonville. There, they would prepare themselves to move into South Florida.

National Vice Chairman James L. Fieser was pulled out of a Red Cross conference in West Virginia. He headed south to lead the effort. About noon, he said, "We pray this hurricane may be turned aside before it strikes our shores." But prayer did not deter the storm.

Ruth Stewart, wife of a West Palm Beach dentist and mother of two, had telephoned the *Palm Beach Post* newsroom and was told that the storm would strike 20 miles north of West Palm Beach in the early evening. Then the power and telephone went out at the Stewart home at 420 Independence Road. The Stewarts boarded up openings in the porch and debated fleeing to Miami, but decided it was too late; winds were already starting to lift small pieces of debris into the air.

By 2:00 P.M., Ruth wrote, the storm was "well on."

Ruth had stuffed towels into window frames and doors, but wind-driven rain began to trickle in. It gathered in the spaces between windows and screens and flowed down walls. About 3:00 P.M., a board, apparently from the roof, crashed down on the front porch. The family ran from window to window, nailing in more boards, as they heard window frames crack and weaken. For the next three hours, they mopped the growing flow of water furiously and continued to nail more boards into place. All the time, she wrote, the wind made a constant roar that drowned out the crashes from both their home and adjacent ones, where chimneys were falling and roofs and walls were being ripped from their foundations. The Stewarts debated making a run for it. They gathered their cash and sewed it into their clothes. But Ruth Stewart finally decided against fleeing, fearing she'd never be able to walk and hold on to her small son at the same time.

About 3:00 P.M., the power failed in West Palm Beach. Two hours later, the water stopped running. At 3:20 P.M., police officers fought their way to Okeechobee Boulevard near the waterfront, after receiving a report that a man was dead in his car. The officers found only a man dead drunk and sent him to the jail. Two miles up the road, Taylor's Auto Shop lost its roof.

T. R. Gill, an Associated Press reporter, and J. P. Buchanan, a newsreel photographer for Paramount News, were driving in the storm in Kelsey City. They decided to get into a shed for cover. The moment the car stopped, the shed's roof came down; Gill dove under the car and Buchanan under a nearby vehicle as the walls of the shed crashed down around them. Gill hid in a nearby hedge. He later broke into a home for cover, but its walls came down, too.

Dick Wilson, a bank director and lumber-company executive, was one of those who fled to the Kelsey City town hall. The building's structure included a garage area that housed the fire truck. The people inside couldn't keep the giant doors closed against the wind. They rolled the fire truck against the doors and added their weight and strength. "I think we'd better pray," someone said. When it came Wilson's turn, he said, "Lord, I'm not much on offering prayers and I don't do well with it. But I can promise you this: if you get us out of this, I'll know how to pray next time."

At the courthouse, little Tommie Rickards found as many as 500 people crowding the halls, which were pitched into darkness when the power went out. Children screamed for water, of which there was none, and wailed with fear as the wind howled outside and plaster and glass crashed around them. Rickards collected water from a leak. But when he sipped some, he realized it wasn't rain, but ocean water driven through the air all the way from the beach, more than a mile away.

At 5:00 P.M., the U.S. Weather Bureau began earnestly warning people in other parts of the state that were in the storm's path, specifically a section of the peninsula's west coast, along the Gulf of Mexico, from near Fort Myers to where the peninsula curves into the Panhandle.

"Change to hurricane warning 6 p.m. Punta Rassa to Cedar Keys, Fla., and display northeast storm warnings west of Apalachicola to Mississippi Coast. Hurricane center 4:00 P.M. near coast between Miami and Jupiter, still moving northwestward unless course changes. Hurricane center will reach west coast not far from Tampa Monday morning. Emergency. Advise all interests to take precautions. This hurricane is of great intensity and wide extent."

The advisory had said that at 4:00 P.M., the storm was near the coast. The word "near" was wrong.

Because of the technology of the 1920s—primitive compared to today's satellites and computers—there's a lot of uncertainty about "landfall," the term for the spot where the storm's center, or eye, came ashore. Of course, people began feeling the storm hours before landfall. And, ironically, landfall was the time when the eye passed over and winds subsided to nothing.

Any effort now, seventy-five years later, to pinpoint the exact landfall of the eye is almost a ridiculous exercise. This was a storm that spanned hundreds of miles, tore up 60 miles of coastline, and drowned thousands of people some 40 miles inland. But, for this storm or any, finding that center spot would give researchers then, and now, a starting point to help measure a storm's path and map its power and destruction as it moved across land.

Richard Gray, from the U.S. Weather Bureau in Miami, said on September 17, 1928, the day after the storm struck the Florida coast, that he believed landfall was at Delray Beach and hurricane-force winds were felt from just north of Hollywood to somewhere north of Jupiter—in other words, across two Florida counties covering about 75 miles of coast. Gray said "serious structural damage" from the storm stretched from Gomez, a now-abandoned settlement north of Jupiter in Martin County, to Pompano Beach, a distance of 60 miles. Damage was reported as far north as Vero Beach and as far south as Miami. That means that tropical-storm-force winds, of 39 to 73 mph, were present as much as 130 miles from the center. Gray said the storm spanned 500 miles and brought strong winds to both Key West and Jacksonville. It was the first storm in history to spark official Weather Bureau warnings for the lengths of both Florida coasts.

Later, Gray changed probable landfall to about 11 miles north to Lake Worth, saying the lull appeared longest there. Gray believed the storm's eye was 25 miles across, nearly twice the estimated 13-mile width of the 1926 storm that had struck Miami.

In Jupiter, Bessie Wilson DuBois described hearing the bell at her home and realizing the wind had changed direction. She said nothing about a lull. People report being in the eye from Kelsey City—now Lake Park—to Delray Beach. Presuming a mostly symmetrical eye, Gray would be correct in his estimate that the eye—or center—was 25 miles wide.

While the eye itself has no wind, a hurricane's most powerful winds are in the eye wall, the interior of the storm surrounding the eye.

National Hurricane Center forecaster Brian Jarvinen estimated in 2002 that landfall was near Lake Worth and the eye was 25 to 30 miles across. Jarvinen said the most powerful winds would have been in the eye wall north of Lake Worth—in other words, downtown West Palm Beach. He believed the strongest winds radiated 15 to 20 miles out from center, from around Riviera Beach to around Boynton Beach, and weaker winds, but still hurricane force, were present much farther out. By comparison, Andrew, which devastated an area south of Miami in 1992, would be a tight storm, with an eye only about 15 miles across and hurricane-force winds extending outward only about 30 miles.

Late in the afternoon, as the full force of the storm began to arrive in West Palm Beach, auto repairman Milburn A. Bishop left his home at 722 Sunset Road and sought refuge in a nearby house.

"The sky turned that peculiar color," he wrote later, "and then, Oh Boy!"

The wind was coming out of the northeast and "the rain just came down by the bucketfuls. The ladies then set the table and had plenty of hot coffee so we sat down at the table and were eating when it started in again, as we thought, 'full blast.' In about five minutes we felt the house quiver all over and heard a great crash to the rear. It was the roof off the [adjacent] apartment, which had come sailing into the house. Of course, that scared Mama half to death."

Five minutes later, a garage at a nearby home smashed into the other corner of the house. Each time, Bishop wrote, he expected the house to collapse. "Somehow, through the grace of God it held on, and the wind continued to blow for another two hours." Bishop watched, like a spectator in a gruesome flying parade of homes, as the structures on the street lost their roofs one by one.

At the county courthouse, skylights in the Criminal Court of Record broke and water poured in.

About a mile to the north, at 520 13th Street, Good Samaritan Hospital stood as salvation for Kate Maynardie West. Kate was pregnant—

and due. Some doctors and weather researchers theorize that a hurricane's low air pressure can induce labor in women who are close to delivering, although they say the stress of being in a storm may be just as responsible. For whatever reason, the time to deliver had come. Kate, from Waycross, Georgia, was just twenty-two. She had one child from a previous marriage and one with her husband, twenty-three-year-old electrician Eugene McCann Jr. He was the son of a man who had moved from Revere, Massachusetts, in the early 1920s and become a West Palm Beach cop.

West Palm Beach had gone decades without any formal medical center before local leaders had founded "the Emergency Hospital" in a modest five-room cottage in 1914. Three years later, it had moved into a larger building along the Intracoastal Waterway, at Flagler Drive and Palm Beach Lakes Boulevard, about a mile from the heart of downtown. At the time, leaders had complained about the hospital being "in the sticks." It had opened officially on May 19, 1920, with thirty-five beds, as Good Samaritan, the area's first permanent hospital. Now Kate looked to it for help.

The hospital had stayed open, its doctors and nurses bravely doing their best as the wind howled outside. Debris smashed out the windows, and eventually all patients were moved from their rooms into the hallway. Gene had somehow gotten Kate into a car, but he couldn't even drive the short distance to "Good Sam." The McCanns got out and began to crawl along the sidewalk amid the winds and flying missiles, even as Kate shook with labor contractions. Somehow they got in the front door of the building. Helping hands rushed to them. In minutes, right in the hallway, Kate had delivered a son, Eugene Joseph McCann, III. One birth certificate says 5:00 P.M., another 6:30. The doctor looked down at Kate, covered in scratches from the storm and exhausted from her ordeal. The baby was fine. He said to its bruised and exhausted mother, "Perhaps you should name him Windy."

Then came the eye.

Various reports give different times for the lull in West Palm Beach. Ruth Stewart, the dentist's wife, said it started at 5:40 P.M. Another West Palm Beach report, by Charles H. Ruggles, a consulting engineer who had his own barometer, puts it between 6:30 and 7:30 P.M.

Even then, savvy South Floridians knew that this was not the end of the storm, but rather the eye, and the storm would soon come back more furiously.

Tommie Rickards, fourteen, felt the lull. It was dead calm. A candle on a sill didn't flicker. His father Tom stepped outside the courthouse and saw a sky he would describe as "an inverted funnel, with stars shining through the opening overhead."

Ruth Stewart drank cold coffee while her husband and sons had some bread and milk. She knew the horrors of the last few hours were about to be repeated, perhaps even more viciously.

Milburn A. Bishop guessed he had thirty to forty minutes, so he raced back to his home "to nail up anything I could—provided there was anything left." Arriving home, he found one window off its hinges; two men helped him nail it back. He also nailed up other openings, added some braces, and raced back to the home where he'd waited out the storm's first half. He looked at a clock. He had been out about thirty minutes.

Then the wind returned even stronger—this time from the other direction. Bishop watched as part of another home smashed into the house he was in, and then its own chimney crashed in; finally a bedroom window blew in. Men huddled with nearly hysterical women in the center of the home as water poured in from the hole made when the chimney tore away. Bishop and the other men raced around the home, removing closet doors from their hinges and nailing them over windows; It took all four of them to hold a closet door over a window long enough to nail it.

As Bishop checked in the bathroom, he heard the wind screeching over his head. He climbed up and thrust a light into the attic and saw the sides of the house moving in and out like lungs expanding and contracting during a breath. "The hair still raises on my back every time I think of the tremendous, blood-curdling shrieks it would let out." He knew the roof could not last long and feared its inevitable separation would kill not only him and his companions but probably his neighbors as well. So he gathered with the other men and they agreed to try to get into the attic to brace its walls. Some passed shelves from closets up into the attic for two men to nail to the wall. Bishop thought to himself that if the roof gave way, he could ride one of the shelves down the street.

At Ruth Stewart's home, within fifteen minutes of the storm's return, the wind shredded the porch and rain poured in.

Just down the road in Lake Worth, J. Luther "Bo" Wright, the *Palm Beach Post*'s composing room superintendent, had worried that his home at Fifth Avenue and K Street would not survive the return of the hurricane winds. During the lull, he had grabbed his wife and small son and some blankets and food and raced down an alley to a nearby building. It was the two-story parsonage of the First Congregational Church at 10th Avenue and N Street. Wright quickly helped cover two blown-out windows and everyone waited out the second half. It came with such ferocity, "we all just thought it was the end of everything. I held the baby in my arms for hours and kept Vera close to me. There were nineteen people crowded into the dining room, and just a candle burning."

Parson Lillian B. Fulton took a Bible from a shelf. "All the women were on their knees, praying," Bishop would recall, "while the men snatched doors from the closets upstairs and nailed them to the windows. No lying. This was a horrible night."

Nearby, an Episcopal church was demolished and Lake Worth City Hall lost three of its walls.

Charles Ruggles, the West Palm Beach engineer, placed the height of the storm's second half at about 8:40 P.M. The walls of his home on Military Trail were vibrating and he could see them bowing out at the bottom. Fearing the roof was about to go, he grabbed his wife and the two threw open the door, which disintegrated almost immediately, as they crawled about 30 feet from their home, lying in the open in about five inches of water for the next two hours. About 11:00 P.M., the two developed the shakes from the chill. They decided they could get into their car and dashed the 75 feet to it in wind that bent them over. Ruggles found a pack of smokes and lit one with the car's cigarette lighter. The two spent the night in the car.

Post employees Beryl Lewis and Bill Matthews stood in the lobby of Matthews's apartment house, 325½ Gruber Place. They watched out a window, in amazement, as a service station across the street, built from strong concrete block, disintegrated piece by piece until all that remained were the pumps and the plumbing. A Buick coupe drove by at about 20 mph in the staggering winds and vanished down the street.

With the eye passing, Lewis, now separated from Matthews, sped in the lull to the offices of the *Post*. With no electric power, everything had stopped, except the wind. Outside the newspaper building, a man was clinging to a fence. As fearful as he was of the winds, he was just as worried that he wouldn't get to his post as a night watchman across the Intracoastal Waterway in Palm Beach. Lewis and another man dragged the watchman into the *Post* building.

Lewis and others then grabbed a barometer from the wall and began taking readings at fifteen-minute intervals. The dropping air pressure made their eardrums ache.

Nearby, workers at the American Telephone and Telegraph Company operated a barograph, a machine that measures barometric readings and prints them on a roll of paper the way a lie detector prints out. The lower the line, the lower the pressure and the more powerful the storm.

The line was going down, down, down.

The storm was probably about as big across as 1999's Hurricane Floyd would be. Floyd was about 500 miles wide and threatened the coast from South Florida to New England, sparking the largest peacetime evacuation in U.S. history, as some 3.5 million people fled coastal areas. And the 1928 storm may have been almost as strong as 1992's Hurricane Andrew, a storm so powerful that it flipped cars and knocked down parts of concrete buildings.

The barograph, the barometer printout at the AT&T office in West Palm Beach, showed a dip that might mean nothing to a layperson but is startling today to those who study such lines for a living. It showed air-pressure levels hanging steady through most of Saturday, September 15. Then, just after midnight, the line started a curve that turned to a free fall by noon. The line hit bottom at the mark indicating around midnight late Sunday. It showed 27.43 inches. With normal at 30 inches and a change of even a tenth of an inch a sign of a storm strengthening, that's nearly two-tenths of an inch lower than the 27.61-inch level reached by the furious hurricane, which had leveled boomtown Miami and inundated

Moore Haven in 1926. And it is the lowest pressure ever recorded in the United States to that time, lower even than the 27.49 for the killer Galveston hurricane of 1900.

Weather officials said at the time that, while the 1928 storm had a lower barometric pressure than its 1926 counterpart, they believed the 1926 storm had stronger winds. Their evidence: Trees in Palm Beach County had some leaves left, while those in the Miami area were completely stripped, even those in dense groves.

The low point measured at West Palm Beach in the 1928 storm was so low that most observers probably surmised it would never be matched again. But it was—and only nine years later—when it hit 26.35, more than one inch lower, on September 3, 1935. That "Labor Day Storm" tore through the Florida Keys with top sustained winds of at least 160 mph. The 1935 storm's barometric pressure set a low that still stands today. Because a hurricane's strength is measured primarily by barometric pressure, the 1935 storm is listed as the most powerful ever recorded in the United States; stronger even than Camille, which flattened Mississippi in 1969 with top winds at landfall of an unbelievable 190 mph but a barometric pressure low of 26.84 inches. The Labor Day Storm, Camille, and Andrew are the only storms ever to strike the U.S. mainland at Category Five on the Saffir-Simpson Hurricane Scale. Category Five storms have winds of at least 155 mph and barometric pressure of less than 27.17 inches. Weather bureaucrats, normally dry and scientific in their adjectives, describe this category as "catastrophic."

Official readings gave the 1928 storm a top sustained wind of 130 mph at its landfall at Palm Beach, about 25 mph short of Category Five. But considering the quality and quantity of instruments across the region, it's quite possible it rose to that wrath-of-God level. Estimates by observers at the two federal research stations along the Lake Okeechobee shore placed top sustained winds at 160 mph, and at the time of this writing, hurricane researchers were considering reclassifying the storm retroactively as a Category Five.

And, as have other great storms, it's quite likely the 1928 hurricane spawned numerous tornados, or rare straight-line wind streaks similar to those that did tremendous damage when hurricane Andrew struck South Florida on August 24, 1992.

• • •

In West Palm Beach's black section, at the Miller home, young Clothilda felt the winds grow stronger and the walls shake. Suddenly, the porch of the home across Henrietta Avenue came apart, flew through the air, and crashed through her bedroom window.

"We got out of the house and ran across the street," she recalled later. "You could see things flying. Afterward, I wasn't looking for anything flying. I was flying myself."

They ran to the home of their neighbor, Mr. Ewell, who had offered his place in an emergency. Clothilda would recall that for several minutes no one said anything. If they were praying, she said later, they were keeping it to themselves. Someone made coffee. Men tried to calm the women. Clothilda dozed in a chair. No one else slept.

The Palm Beach Yacht Club lost its pier. The Northwood warehouse district was heavily damaged. St. Ann's Church lost the roof of its school. Palm Beach High's brick clock tower came crashing down.

Two 75-foot Coast Guard cutters, from a base at Fernandina Beach in Florida's extreme northeast corner, had become caught in the worst of it just off the Palm Beach coast. The skippers, Morris Anderson on the "230" and Richard Abernathy on the "188," wrestled their ships through an inlet and into Lake Worth, the body of water between Palm Beach and the mainland that is part of the Intracoastal Waterway. The seas dragged their anchors, and ocean water poured into the engine rooms. The "230" lost its steering gear and the "188" its rudder, and both slammed into land. About 150 feet offshore, the eight men on each ship had thrown on life vests and dived into the rolling water. All sixteen climbed, exhausted onto land and slept where they landed. At first light, they found the "230" missing 40 feet of keel and the "188" punctured by holes at several places. They figured the ships were total losses. The crew members insisted on working street patrols and were still there at midnight late on Monday, September 17.

There was little concern about Palm Beach, the famed island of the rich. Most of its wealthy residents were part-timers and were up north, not to return until winter drove them to Florida's tropical climes. But Gus Jordahn stayed.

Jordahn, tough as nails, was a former officer in the Danish Army who had come to America in 1904, alternating seasonal lifeguard jobs at Coney Island and The Breakers, the famed Palm Beach resort. At Coney Island, he was once credited with twenty-eight rescues in one day off the Brooklyn shore. Once asked how many people he had saved over the years, he answered in a Scandinavian growl, "All I could get, keed."

In 1910, he founded Gus' Baths, a swimming complex with two pools and steam cabinets near Palm Beach's famous Worth Avenue. It was connected to the beach by a tunnel. Muscular and tanned, he was rarely seen in anything except swim trunks. His motto became the world-famous motto of Palm Beach: "Come to Our Ocean."

"Captain Gus" also would capture and ride loggerhead turtles, carving his name and the date on one animal's shell.

In 1924, Jordahn founded Cowboys of the Sea. The only requirement to join was having saved or helped save someone from drowning. The group, which came to boast some 500 members nationwide, was credited with rescuing hundreds of ocean swimmers. Gus once served as a U.S. National Guardsman on the Mexican border, and he was the first policeman ever in Palm Beach, hired a year after the town incorporated in 1911. He made the department's first arrest, of two men who were bathing nude. They each paid a $5 fine in time to get back to their jobs as pastry chefs at one of the resort hotels.

Gus had a flagpole outside his baths in 1908, and every day, he raised the American flag. As a ship passed, he would dip the Stars and Stripes in salute, and the ship would dip its colors or whistle in response.

While barrier islands, which would be the first victims of a land-falling storm, are now areas of mandatory evacuation, Gus and thirty-eight others—plus four pets—had decided to ride out the storm. The refugees were residents of apartments at Gus' Baths or nearby homes, along with a family of three from the mainland whose car had stalled on the beach Sunday afternoon. Young people kept up their spirits by singing and telling stories. Also inside: Cowboy, an Airedale terrier and a full-fledged member of the Cowboys of the Sea; Rainbow, another dog and mascot of the nearby pier; Ginger, a collie; and Sugar, official cat of the nearby Wertheimer Coffee Shop. Suddenly, Gus's wife realized with a start that her kitten, Cat's Pajamas, was still back at their apartment. Her husband stepped out into the winds and vanished. After what seemed like an eternity, he returned. He reached into the pocket of his bathrobe and pulled out a squirming cat.

About 3:00 P.M., as the thirty-nine huddled in a cellar behind one of the swimming pools, the ocean roared in on them, sweeping over the building and knocking down the walls of dressing rooms. About half the rooms were destroyed. Eight fishing-club trophy cups were washed away, but four were saved. The coffee shop was flattened. The only victim, missing and presumed drowned: Cowboy, the heroic Airedale.

At The Breakers, leveled by fire in 1925 and just reopened in December 1926, a chimney crashed through the roof and water damaged the interior. The island's other great resort, the Royal Poinciana, lost much of its roof and twisted on its foundation. Whitehall, the mansion built by Henry Flagler, lost several windows. Behind The Breakers stood the old pier, built in 1896 to jut out from the surf so ships could load cargo from railcars and guests could board steamers for trips to Key West, Havana, and Nassau. In storm after storm, waves had washed it away piece by piece. Now the surge knocked its remnants into the ocean. Palm trees were down everywhere. Underneath them on Palm Beach's Ocean Boulevard, sand a foot deep covered the asphalt. Yachts in safe harbor the morning before were now sitting atop the seawalls.

About 11:00 P.M., the wind finally died down. In West Palm Beach, Milburn A. Bishop returned to his home. "I would have had it two to one that I was going to find one big pile of tile, but no, there it stood." The outside was in good shape. But when he opened the door, he saw rain pouring down into his home from where the roof had been.

Meanwhile, somewhere else in West Palm Beach, Coot Simpson had survived the night.

But the monster wasn't spent. It was still moving, toward the Glades. That's where Clothilda Miller's parents were.

The Outer Bands

"A four-bottle blow."

The storm came straight over the West Palm Beach area, but its damage was not limited to that city. The pattern of destruction suggests it was a behemoth. It left damage along 130 miles of coastline from Vero Beach to Miami.

Bessie Wilson DuBois had come to the beautiful Jupiter Inlet, in 1914, when she was eleven. She would later recall hearing, on the day of her arrival, what sounded like people applauding politely. It was thousands of mullet boiling the water of the Loxahatchee River as it emptied into the Atlantic Ocean. It's a sound long since washed away by commercial fishing and development along the river and inlet. DuBois would later become the Jupiter area's unofficial historian, writing several small books about the region.

Back in 1928, her home stood right on the inlet, across from the historic Jupiter Lighthouse. Starting in 1854, the lighthouse had been built over six years, its progress slowed by Indian attacks. Its designer had been George Meade, later the hero of Gettysburg. It was first lit on July 10, 1860, and is the oldest structure in Palm Beach County. In 1928, it stood 90 feet above the water. The little town around it numbered no more than 300 souls. West Palm Beach was some 20 miles away but might as well have been 100. Bessie would later recall getting to school not by road but by water, using a lifeboat salvaged from the *Maine,* whose sinking in Havana Harbor had started the Spanish-American War.

DuBois was one of three sisters. On that day in 1928, she was also a young bride of some three years and the mother of Susie, 3, Doris, 2, and Louise, 7 months. The family had read the increasingly alarming newspaper reports about the approaching storm. Bessie's father, brothers Bob and Jack, and sister Grace gathered in the home Bessie shared with her husband John. "Papa wanted to take refuge in a reinforced concrete building," she wrote. But John refused. He had built the home and was confident it would hold up in the strongest winds. So they all stayed put.

Bessie spent the morning baking bread and a ham, boiling potatoes, and fixing pudding for the children. With no electric refrigerator, the food she had prepared was placed in an icebox. The family took up rugs and took down pictures. John DuBois tied up boats and pumped full a large water tank attached to a tower, hoping the weight would keep it from blowing over. Some of the men decided to drive to the nearby U.S. Navy station for the latest weather report. Just as their car passed under the water tower, the tank slid off its perch and crashed down onto the road, narrowly missing them.

Dairy farmer Noah Kellum Williams had driven south on Sunday morning to the plant in Kelsey City that bottled his milk. Owners of buildings in the town were boarding up windows. He returned to his farm in Jupiter, around where Florida's Turnpike now crosses Jupiter's main east-west road. Normally, Sunday morning would find him at church. Instead, he began boarding up his own home.

About 3:00 P.M., a neighbor came by. A large fruit company had built a high-powered radio station nearby to communicate with its farms in Central America. Someone at the station had sent the neighbor around to tell people they had to get out. The neighbor had no doubt embellished his story just a bit at each doorway; by the time he got to Williams, the storm had 200 mph winds and was accompanied by a 50-foot tidal wave. Williams knew the ridge on which his home sat was only

25 feet above sea level, but it was five miles inland. The house wasn't very strong, but the barn was new and sturdy. A tenant said the people who were calling for escape must have known what they were talking about. Williams stepped into his barn and gave his employees the bad news. The men had just milked and fed the first group of cows. He told them to fasten the big barn door open so it wouldn't blow shut and to unyoke the cattle.

Williams finally decided the safest place was the area's new $160,000 schoolhouse. He piled everyone into two trucks, along with bedding and pillows. At the schoolhouse, the winds reached their peak at 5:30 P.M., Williams recalled. He watched from a giant window as lumber and tree limbs flew and trees snapped. A dog sheltered from the wind against a building suddenly decided to make a dash to safety. When the animal got into the wind, it rolled him over; he crawled back to the wall and was still there when darkness hid him from Williams's view. Windows and doors were smashed in by flying debris. The group grabbed lumber left by workers on the newly finished building; two men would force a door shut while others hammered the lumber across the door and frame to brace it.

"Strong men prayed who had never prayed before," Williams would recall. "Strange to say, those who were in not in the habit of praying, prayed the loudest."

At the inlet, the U.S. Navy radio compass station wired a report that winds were at 90 mph and the tide was five feet above normal and its tower had blown over. The station was in the middle of advising that the wind was increasing when the dispatch stopped in mid-sentence.

"The winds galloped over us like a thousand freight trains, accompanied by that high-pitched whine that beggars description," Bessie DuBois wrote. "Huddled on the lee side of the back porch it was still light enough for us to see the great breakers coming straight across the ocean as if the beach no longer existed."

The water surged into the inlet and up the Loxahatchee River and into the DuBois front yard. "The tremendous surges were breaking among the palm trees in our yard. As every new crest swept in a few more cabbage palms went down."

The tide was higher than any of the family could remember. Foam from the waves crashed against windows.

The men gathered by the coffeepot while the women stayed in the bedroom with the children. The old house up on the hill, where John DuBois had been born, was vacant at the time, and Bessie had packed food and clothes in a basket for a hasty retreat should the water continue to rise. Susie saw her and asked her mother repeatedly, "When are we going up the hill?" As the winds howled, Susie danced on the porch, her eyes showing the excitement of innocence. Bessie had assigned one child to each man. But as she saw them watching the water swirling around the falling trees, she realized even a grown man alone could never get up the hill, let alone one carrying a child.

Her father and uncle decided to shave and dress—to make, they joked, "handsome corpses." But soon the strain had overcome even gallows humor. The tide had risen so high that seawater ran several inches deep over the home's floorboards. The wind pushed on the uncovered windows, turning the clear glass at their center white with pressure. They held. The family heard a crash and discovered the front porch had lost its roof and was separating from the rest of the house. They feared the home would come off its foundation and begin floating off. The children, oblivious to their danger, played happily with crayons and paper Bessie had bought for her Sunday-school class. "It seemed as if things were approaching a crisis," Bessie DuBois said.

Across the inlet, at the lighthouse, then emerged one of the most dramatic stories to come from the hurricane—and one of the more disputed. The lighthouse swayed as much as 17 inches at the top, its mortar squeezing from between its bricks like toothpaste from a tube. Somehow, the venerable tower held. It is a matter of pride for lighthouses that their beam never goes dark. During the Civil War, Confederate loyalists had temporarily removed the light to keep Union blockade ships in the dark while the local blockade-runners, familiar with the waters, slipped by. Except for then, the Jupiter Light had shone strong and true all these years. The lighthouse had only recently converted from old mineral burners. The light had earlier been turned by a series of weights that had to be pulled down, like winding a cuckoo clock.

Now a motor did the work. But just before dark, early in the storm, power went out. A backup diesel generator, recently delivered from Charleston, South Carolina, stubbornly refused to start; it turned out to be missing a critical part.

What happened next?

This is the version told to Bessie DuBois: Charles Seabrook, the keeper since 1919, had previously contracted blood poisoning in his hand. But he was bound to his duty. He found the old mineral lamps that had lit the tower before electricity, but he could not find the giant weights that wound to turn the light mechanism. The assistant keepers' first loyalty was to stay with their families. Seabrook would go to the tower and turn it by hand. His son Franklin, sixteen, saw red streaks running up Seabrook's arm from the infection and insisted on going in his stead. Four times, young Franklin tried to climb the stairs. Four times he was blown back by the wind as he tried to climb the steep steps. He finally reached the top. The mechanism made a fearful clang as Franklin Seabrook struggled to turn it. He heard the mortar ground out from between the bricks near the iron bolts holding the light's cage in place. One of the four giant lenses, each about $3\frac{1}{2}$ feet in diameter, shattered. The timing was off, but the light stayed on in the storm. For the next two nights, other people at the lighthouse, including Charles Seabrook's wife, alternated turning the light until a neighbor rigged a substitute.

But the son of an assistant keeper says that's not how it happened. "It was totally exaggerated," Ray Swanson said in 2001. "My dad, Ralph L. Swanson, turned the thing by hand."

At the schoolhouse, Noah Kellum Williams finally stretched out on the floor to try to sleep. Less than an hour later, he was awakened. An older couple lived in a second-story garage apartment nearby. It turned out they had stayed as long as they dared, then tried to make it to the schoolhouse, but the winds had knocked them down. They were huddling under a stairway on the side of the building away from the wind. But the second floor had blown off and the garage had tottered, trapping the couple. The man had been able to crawl to the school for help. It took several men to get the stairway off the woman, who was badly hurt. The wind was starting to die down but the rain was still coming down in torrents. A carload of men began to drive around, looking for people in distress. Often the road was blocked with debris. They finally went back to the schoolhouse.

In Boynton Beach, about 30 miles to the south, thirteen-year-old Eunice Lewerenz watched the plaster come down from the ceiling of the new high school. Boynton Beach was in a string of towns scattered between West Palm Beach and Fort Lauderdale that were then connected only by the railroad, but now constitute a suburban sprawl. The school had been built just a year earlier, and Eunice, an eighth-grader, spent her weekdays in it.

Her grandfather in Milwaukee had married three times. The last marriage had produced Eunice's father, Walter. Later, Walter labored in a sawmill until lungs weakened by tuberculosis made it too hard for him. His doctor told him he needed a change of climate, so he went to Florida. From 1912 to 1913, he was a surveyor in the wilderness of Military Trail, now a jumble of strip malls, before returning to Milwaukee to marry Hattie Petrella. Two years later, they came back to Florida, and Walter bought property west of town and started a farm. One day, a water moccasin bit Hattie on the ankle, and soon after, the couple moved their residence back into town. In the fall of 1928, there were five children: Eunice, Aileen, Harriett, Lorraine, and Walter, Jr.

When the storm arrived, Walter decided his home wasn't safe. The obvious alternative was the brand-new high school. They went first to the room used for manual training, now called shop class. It was on the west side, and they believed it would be safer than the home economics room on the east side. Other families had also come there. Soon, plaster started to fall. Suddenly the entire ceiling started to come down. The second-floor auditorium came with it. Eunice and her family were in a corner of the room and weren't hurt, but one boy was seriously injured.

They raced over to the home of ornamental-nursery owner Alfred C. Shepard, just across the street to the north of the school. Inside were Shepard, his wife, and three children. The home had French doors, and Shepard feared they would blow in. Someone placed a chair under the door handle and sat in it.

Then came the eye. Walter ran to his home. The yard was full of dead chickens. He gathered them up and returned to the Shepard home. He was gone less than a half hour. The wind picked up again. When it was finally gone, the problems of freshly dead chickens and hungry refugees solved each other quickly.

The high school survived and was repaired, but the storm had destroyed Town Hall, the Hotel Cassandra and the First Methodist Church. Florida East Coast Railway freight train "130" had gone into a ditch and railroad crews later furiously cleared tracks of debris for both regular and relief train traffic.

But the southern end of the eye wall was still farther south. In Delray Beach, the next town to the south, strong winds began at about 2:00 P.M. Sunday and the city's emergency alarm sounded at 3:00 P.M. Winds seemed to reach their height at 5:30; after a lull that some witnesses said lasted 30 minutes and others 90, the second act of the storm blew for about three hours. A boxcar on a siding in Lake Worth had broken loose and gone hurtling down the track, pushed by the winds to speeds approaching 75 mph. It finally derailed 11 miles downtrack in Delray Beach. Many buildings in Delray lost roofs or came down altogether. A lumber company, an ice plant, and a grocery were almost total losses. Houses of God were not spared. Two older churches were leveled, a third left irreparable. Two new churches suffered water damage and broken windows. Firefighters had set up a first-aid station at the Chamber of Commerce building. When it was smashed, they moved to City Hall. Delray Beach officials later reported 227 homes destroyed and 730 badly damaged, with a total of 1,268 buildings suffering some damage. Linda Simon and her husband returned to their Delray Beach home to find most of their roof gone. Their Boynton Beach furniture store was in ruins. Upholstery was soaked with water and the tops of wooden tables curled upward. Electrical wires and trees were down everywhere.

In Boca Raton, just south of Delray Beach, ten boxcars were overturned. Two cars had come right off their wheels, leaving the framework and wheels standing naked on the tracks. South of that, across the Palm Beach–Broward county line in Deerfield Beach, another freight train was blown off the track. In Fort Lauderdale, a 60-mph gale whipped down-town about 2:00 P.M. A large plate-glass window at the Florida Power & Light office shattered and was sucked into the street. The city would later report downed trees, broken windows, collapsed garages, roofs torn off homes. But damage was considered manageable, and officials suggested the town would be cleaned up in a week. Miami, which only two years earlier had been all but flattened, experienced top sustained winds of only 60 mph—not even hurricane strength—with gusts up to 75 mph on Miami Beach. The storm still managed to break plate-glass windows and knock out power and telegraph service, but the city was almost back to normal by Monday morning.

Jupiter pioneer Bessie DuBois would later call the hurricane a "four-bottle blow" for the amount of whiskey a sane man required for fortification. But as the long night had gone on, the DuBois family heard a dramatic sound. The ship's bell on the back porch, used to call the family to dinner, begin to ring. Jupiter was apparently north of the eye, and as the northern portion moved across the land, the wind had shifted direction. The surge was receding. The storm was passing the coast and heading inland.

The storm raged for three to four hours, all the time marching toward the interior at about 15 mph. Soon it was at Lake Okeechobee, some 40 miles inland. As it crossed, the wind shoved all the water toward the edge of the lake. The low dike along the lake's south shore was made of muck, marl (a crumbly earth containing lime), and sand. The storm's eye was moving toward a point on the shore near Canal Point. That brought the winds along the southeast shore first from the north, then from the northwest.

The winds drove the water toward Belle Glade and South Bay, the most populated area of the farming region around Lake Okee-chobee. They pounded that water against the flimsy dike that protected those people from the giant body that brought both life and death.

The dike broke.

The Glades

September 16–17, 1928

"Lord, Somebody Got Drowned."

On the sixteenth of September, in the year of nineteen twenty-eight, God started riding early, and He rode to very late.

He rode out on the ocean, chained the lightning to His wheel, stepped on the land at West Palm Beach, and the wicked hearts did yield.

In the storm, oh, in the storm, Lord, somebody got drowned. Got drowned, Lord, in the storm!

On Sunday morning, September 16, 1928, in Sebring Farms, fourteen-year-old Vernon Boots had decided to build a windmill to catch the climbing gusts. He found a boat propeller, speared it on a nail, and pointed it at the wind. By noon, the propeller was whirling so fast, it burned a groove into the peg. Boots and his brothers thought this was great fun. Lake Okeechobee stood just 300 feet away.

Hoffman Construction Company was helping build State Road 80 between Belle Glade and Clewiston. Earlier Sunday, the supervisor,

95

Captain Edwin E. Forbes, had contacted Ivan L. Van Horn, who skippered a tug for Hoffman, hauling supplies. Forbes told him to set up a pump on the company's giant quarterboat, a vessel where workers ate and slept.

On Saturday word had reached the Bootses and their four young sons about a coming storm. They had taken refuge on the quarterboat. But when the storm hadn't shown up right away, they heard a report it had changed course and would miss Florida. They had decided to go home.

Charles Ashton "Mutt" Thomas, then only thirteen, stood in his family's cottage. Mutt's father had borrowed $100 in 1921 to move from North Florida to Ritta Island, at Lake Okeechobee, to grow green beans and onions. In 1922, after heavy rains had left the island in standing water for weeks, they moved to Fort Lauderdale, where Mutt's father worked to build the homes going up by the minute in the real estate boom. By 1923 he'd earned enough to buy a Model T. The 1926 hurricane almost killed the Thomases and all but killed the real estate boom along the coast. Within a month the family had moved back to the Glades, to the Sebring spread. Their neighbors were the Bootses.

Mutt's father commuted to Ritta Island to farm; the family would often go out to help, wading back to the canal, then swimming home, a distance of about a mile and a half. The canal came right behind the Thomas home, serving as a swimming hole. A small schoolhouse practically in front of the Thomas home was run by Edna Denniston Hughes, forty-one. She lived with her husband John and four-year-old son Paul on a houseboat in the canal three miles away. Every morning she would row herself and the boy to the school. The day before, Mutt's parents had gone into West Palm Beach to buy clothes for the new school year, set to start Monday. They returned with word a hurricane was coming but was in no danger of turning to the Glades.

Jabo Tryon was only seventeen but was already working, at a Belle Glade icehouse, handling 400-pound blocks. When he'd started work about 4:00 A.M. Sunday, he had noticed it was starting to sprinkle. As he went about his deliveries, he saw the rain coming down harder. His father called the weather office. He told Jabo the storm was coming to the lake.

By afternoon, a strong gale had come up. Captain Forbes, the Hoffman construction supervisor, sent his two sons into the winds, already up to 60 mph, to warn South Bay's estimated 400 residents. Nearly 200 piled onto the quarterboat, preferring the solid vessel, secured to pilings by steel cable, to their flimsy homes. Its strong mooring didn't stop it from rolling in the waves. Van Horn kept to the boat's pump, smearing grease on the overworked parts to keep them operating, as those on board used buckets to try to bail out the rising water.

On Sunday afternoon, Mutt's family had spent the early afternoon boiling peanuts. The wind was beginning to blow, and Mutt could see the wave action over the little muck dike that protected the mainland. Around dark, having thoroughly enjoyed the peanuts, the Thomas family decided it might be a good idea to go inside. Mutt's father, Charles E. Thomas, tried to decide which action might mean salvation and which death. He opted to abandon the home and took his wife, three sons, and three daughters to the nearby home of V. F. Thirsk, caretaker of Thomas's farm. Charles Thomas thought it might be safer. They waded through waist-deep water in strong winds; as they entered the house through a back door, the water followed them over the jamb. The Boots family went there as well. In all, 60 people—about 20 whites and about 40 blacks—sought refuge there. Mutt's Uncle Minor stayed in the Thomas home.

Mutt looked down. Water was squirting up through cracks in the floorboards. In minutes it was up to his knees. Women pulled their children onto tabletops. At one end of the home, men began hacking holes in the ceiling. By the time people began crawling into the attic, the water was up to the windowsills.

Suddenly there was a surge. The house started to move. Mutt's father had gotten a hole in the ceiling big enough for another man to crawl into the attic and started ripping away the panels of corrugated sheet iron covering the roof. Suddenly the man vanished, tossed by the high winds through an opening in the roof and out into the black night. As the house broke apart, Mutt scrambled toward the hole in the roof, deciding his chances were better in the open wind than the collapsing structure. Suddenly a strong hand grabbed his wrist and lifted him through the hole. He said later he believed it to be Mr. Thirsk's. He grabbed onto the roof for a few moments before he was tossed into the water. He grabbed a piece of floating wreckage and held on. His father had vanished.

A pumping station near Pahokee, one of several installed along the lake to keep water from flooding the fields, had been operating around the clock since the August storm raised the lake level dramatically. Around noon, pump operator Edward Jensen's supervisor told him a storm was coming and he should shut the pump down and go home. But Jensen's father and neighbors had just planted fall crops, and he was determined to keep the pump going. Later, Jensen somehow dozed amid the winds, and he was awakened by a crash as pieces of sheet metal flew off the pump house. He finally decided that keeping the pump operating might be as worthless as draining the fields with a thimble, so he shut it down. Fearful of being cut to pieces by the flying metal, he dove into a subfloor well beneath the pump. But the water down there was rising. Jensen abandoned the collapsing building and raced to a fuel tank, where he met another man, a black farm worker. The two held on until the wind and rain stopped. They discovered six or eight other black farm workers who had crawled along the levee. The other workers wanted to walk the levee back to Pahokee. But Jensen knew they were just in the eye and the worst was still coming. Only the man who had waited out the storm with Jensen at the fuel pump opted to stay; the rest continued down the levee, now only a foot above the spreading water. Jensen watched their outlines grow smaller. Then the strong winds suddenly resumed; the second half of the storm was bearing down.

Jabo Tryon finished his rounds. The family car and truck were both in the shop, and Jabo asked his boss for permission to take the ice truck into town to get his father's car out of the repair bay so his family could flee north to Sebring. But the winds were getting strong. Jabo had brought some friends—for ballast, he would joke later—but after a gust lifted the truck about three feet off the road, he and the others fled to the porch of the Belle Glade Hotel. Five minutes later, they watched as winds slammed the big ice truck into a rubber tree.

Jabo had had nothing to eat all day, just a cup of coffee, so he went down to the hotel's restaurant for some pie and more java. The building was rocking so much the coffee sloshed out of his cup. Plaster fell from the ceiling. Jabo said to another diner, "This building ain't gonna stand much of this." Jabo tried to flee down an alley, but the wind pushed him bank. A giant rainwater-collecting tank crashed down to the street, just missing him. He ran back to the building. Water was rushing over the hotel floor.

"Well, the dike's broke," Jabo said. "Nobody expected that mud dike to hold anything anyhow." The other men worried about a panic. Jabo said, "You ain't gonna keep that a secret. It's coming."

State engineer F. C. Elliot later reported that trash and debris indicated water levels in Lake Okeechobee had reached 26.3 feet above sea level. This meant storm waters in the lake, already near the top, rose 10 feet above the lake level, 12 feet in South Bay. The rising water damaged the levee for a distance of 114,242 feet—more than 21½ miles—of the lake's southeast corner. In a few places, the dike was completely breached; in others, its top 2 to 3 feet washed away. The water could flow over and through the dike's remains unimpeded.

A weather observer at Moore Haven said the winds were greater than in the 1926 storm, but the portion of the dike from that city along the lake's southwest corner to the Palm Beach County line, did not fail. The storm surge was estimated at six inches at Moore Haven. At Canal Point and Port Mayaca, on the lake's northeast shore, the water level is believed to have risen only 1½ to 2½ feet. State engineer Elliot cited the storm's winds being nearly parallel to the east shoreline and noted that as close as 600 feet from shore, the lake fell to its deepest parts, and that depth diffused the water's energy.

The rise in lake level in the storm wasn't really the result of rain. Although gauges around the lake either didn't catch all the rain in the driving wind or were blown away, it was estimated at no more than about 9 inches. What did in the dike was the wind pushing the lake's water. A kitchen worker can't walk a cake pan full of water across the room without sloshing some. And water will rise and fall in a swimming pool in even moderate winds. Okeechobee is a giant, shallow lake, not really much deeper than that swimming pool. It is never more than 21 feet deep and usually 6 to 10 feet, and it's three-fourths the size of Rhode Island. On gusty days, there's considerable wave action. These were

150 mph winds. And with wind speed, the power is exponential. The 1928 storm was a Category Four on the Saffir-Simpson Hurricane Scale, and at 155 mph, would have moved into the realm of the most catastrophic storms, but even 150 mph winds produce up to 250 times the damage of a minimal Category One hurricane.

And the lake was already brimming. According to the Everglades Drainage District report, it stood at nearly 16½ feet above sea level during the week ending September 15. The day after the storm, it stood at nearly 17½ feet. The land around the lake ranges from 17 to 19 feet above sea level. Along the lakeshore, the elevations of the levee were 22 to 28 feet above sea level.

Maximum winds probably reached the lake's eastern shore an hour before the eye reached Canal Point. As the storm crossed, at a slight diagonal, it passed over the lake's southeast corner. A hurricane's winds blow counterclockwise. That means the eye wall—the most powerful part of the storm—struck the southeast corner not from the east, as the storm moved across the lake, but from the north, and eventually the northwest.

This was the worst of all scenarios. The wind bands passed from the northwest corner of the lake, driving a wall of water toward the southeast—the most vulnerable and heavily populated portion of the lake.

"While considerable water doubtless moved against the south shore of Lake Okeechobee during the first half of the storm," R. V. Allison, researcher at the Belle Glade agriculture station, would write later, "it was during the latter half that the southeast and eastern sections received the heaviest damage and consequently greatest loss of life occurred during this period."

Pretty soon the water was up to Jabo Tryon's knees. He could feel muck from plowed fields working its way up his pants leg in the water.

When the eye arrived, Jabo found himself enveloped in overwhelming heat. People ventured outside. Jabo borrowed a car and started helping look for people who might need help. He saw his mother's "washwoman." Jabo could do nothing for her. Her lifeless body drifted up onto the shore of the Old Pahokee Road. He walked to the railroad and carefully worked his way up the tracks. He heard a woman shouting "Yoo-hoo, yoo-hoo," but he could not see her. He found another woman who had tied herself to a telegraph pole with parts of her clothes. He and others got her to a building for shelter. Farther up, a large building had floated off its foundation and lodged on a bank. Jabo found two women, each holding a child. Pointing to himself, he said, "Grab the babies and load one in each arm. You get out yourself." He wrapped the two children in blankets and ran through pouring rain. His arms ached from the weight. He didn't know if the babies were faceup, water pouring into their nostrils, but he couldn't stop to check and had no place to lay them. Someone finally took the children from his arms; he never learned who it was.

Then the storm's second half began.

Jabo finally ran to another building and squeezed under a shelf in a back room. It was now close to midnight. He'd been up for almost than twenty-four hours. Although he was soaked he somehow got comfortable in a corner and went to sleep. Someone offered him a bed and he flopped onto it, but it sloshed with rainwater. He returned to the corner and went back to sleep.

At 6:00 P.M., Lawrence E. Will had finished filling the tank of Arthur Wells's Model A Ford and shut down his Pioneer Service Station in downtown Belle Glade. Will went to the nearby, unfinished Glades Hotel and had some dinner downstairs with two carpenters helping finish the building. They sat and listened to the growing wind. When electricity, furnished by the adjacent Belle Glade Hotel, failed, they lit a kerosene lamp. Water leaking through the ceiling doused it.

The winds died and Will and some others ventured out of the Glades Hotel. A new Ford repair shop across the street was flattened. Several homes, including Will's, had lost their roofs. Will says the lull lasted for only some fifteen minutes. Someone frantically grabbed him to help look for a lost child.

"Hardly had we started when the wind, as was to be expected, returned in full fury," Will recalled in his book.

Will and several others struggled to a nearby bridge they knew to be high ground. At most, Will reckoned, the water would get knee deep. The canal was jammed with wreckage: a barge, a houseboat hull, trees and the wreckage of houses. Will found some people in the wrecked barge, soaked but alive. The group walked back to the Belle Glade Hotel, across from the Glades Hotel, where Will had first waited out the storm. They found its entrance blocked by an overturned car. They returned to the bridge and made plans to crawl into the barge for shelter. But the vessel broke loose and began floating away. A cable caught it up midstream, just out of reach. Will and another man again tried to return to the Glades Hotel. The water had, in fact, reached their knees, but it was not finished with them. They got a quarter of the way to the hotel, gave up, and returned to the barge again. They found a large hole just above the waterline. They got a bilge pump from the houseboat and began pumping. Will noticed in the dark a clump of floating trash. On it were a kitten, a rabbit and a large water moccasin, a deadly snake. All three seemed to concerned more with survival than the normal rules of predation.

On Kreamer Island, W. C. Sutton and his wife, fearing the house would collapse, went onto the porch. As Mrs. Sutton watched, the water rose so fast it soon covered the island, and the trees vanished in the winds. She didn't realize the water had become so deep and, sensing a turning of the wind and perhaps the start of a lull, Mrs. Sutton stepped off the porch and disappeared under the waves. Sutton reached down, found her, and pulled her back up, gasping and sputtering. The house was floating. It floated a half mile, across a pear orchard and a five-acre tract; Mrs. Sutton later surmised that what she thought was the wind turning was actually the house pivoting into the wind as it floated. The Suttons climbed back from the porch through a window and stood on a table as the water rose inside. They would finally be rescued after the water subsided.

Helen Sherouse was thirteen. Her family had heard the storm would pass. But on Sunday morning, her uncle went to Belle Glade to deliver milk and came back with grim news: the hurricane would strike any minute. Sherouse's mother said she'd rather stay than fight the road in the family's car, roofless in the style of the times and open to the elements. Nineteen relatives gathered around the table that night. They would have dinner, and then prepare to wait out the storm. Water started coming through the door. Helen watched as someone cut a hole in the roof. The piano was now floating, and men pushed it across the room like a boat. People climbed onto the piano and onto the roof and huddled on one corner. Helen was holding on and calling to her mother. She'd shout, "Mama, are you there?" and her mother would answer. After a while, she didn't answer anymore.

Suddenly Helen found herself in the water. She surmised at the time that she had fallen off the house. She would learn later that the house had fallen away from her, turning over onto its roof like a capsizing boat. She could feel furniture falling around her. Her stepfather had instructed her that there was less chance of being struck by something if she were underwater, so she stayed under. She worked her way back to the house and inside. But the house was upside down, with part of it underwater.

She was freezing and exhausted. She heard someone stomping above and screamed. Believing all her relatives were still on what had been the bottom of the house, which was now the top, she continued to scream until her stepfather swung down and grabbed her. They huddled in a doorway until the morning.

Ruth Ellen Shive Carpenter had traveled in early August from the Midwest to Florida. Her parents, a minister and farmer, and her sister and her family had visited from Pahokee; Ruth, pregnant and due in December, and her husband and four-year-old daughter Dorothea, decided to return with them for "a much-needed vacation and the joy of a change." On the way home, they learned Ruth's brother Paul had been struck by a car and killed in North Florida as he changed a tire. Their leisurely, joyful adventure turned into a fast-paced, somber excursion. They arrived at their relatives' home along Lake Okeechobee and stayed there for five weeks, until September 16.

On Sunday morning, the wind had begun to blow briskly, but Carpenter and her sister did their housework leisurely and without worry. Her husband was playing checkers with her sister's brother, finishing six weeks of bed rest to recuperate from heart problems brought on by hookworm.

About 9:00 A.M., Ruth's father arrived suddenly and ordered everyone to pack. They were going to go to his home or into town. Ruth was surprised. Her father was known not to budge in the face of any danger, and her brother-in-law was so weak that moving him was a bad idea. But her father insisted. They moved first to her father's home, then to another relative's home across the street; it was also on the ridge, but farther back from the lake. As the wind grew, so did the number of people in the six-bedroom home. Occupancy had reached thirty by 2:00 P.M. Children and old people were placed in beds. Outside, the wind was so strong a person couldn't stand up. Inside, it was too loud for people to hear each other without shouting.

Ruth, the only person in the group who knew shorthand, pressed her ear to a radio and jotted down the storm's new location and track just before the broadcast faded. The paper was passed around, and everyone knew with sickening certainty the storm's center was now heading straight for them. "Nothing was left then but to wait and wait dumbly, like cattle for slaughter," Ruth wrote in her 1929 memoir. About 10:00 P.M., the wind ebbed, and the family thought hopefully that the storm was over. They opened the door and let in a few more neighbors. They had no sooner shut the door then a sudden blast of wind shook the house.

"It was as if all the devils in hell were shouting in our ears. The house shook like a leaf. A gable was taken off the upstairs room and, all at once, we noticed water coming up in the floor, just an inch or two at a time."

Ruth said everyone was silent, perhaps praying. Ruth began worrying about her unborn child, not due for another two months. She sensed it might come into the world amid this tumult.

Floyd Wilder was ten. His mother had died of blood poisoning when he was an infant and his father—grieving, in poor health himself and fed up with hard times in Arkansas—had followed the sun to Florida. Floyd had four sisters and two brothers, ranging in age to twenty-five; he was the baby. The family had moved around from Central Florida down to the lake and eventually to Bean City, a settlement south of South Bay.

The family had huddled through a July 1926 storm without injury, though their home was flooded. The September 1926 storm, which did so much damage in nearby Moore Haven, did almost none to the Wilder home. Wilder's father built a new home in South Bay, just south of the railroad tracks and a quarter of a mile from the lake. To take advantage of the breezes in pre-air-conditioned Florida, the elder

Wilder put a projecting room, with a door and window, on each of the house's four sides for cross ventilation.

On Sunday morning the boys were skipping rocks along the North New River Canal. The wind was up, and soon they and their families and some neighbors were settled in the Wilder home with a hearty meal of fried chicken.

"Just before dark, we noticed the water coming up, and my father, Clarence, and all of us boys ran out and began gathering up chickens, putting them in the corn crib," Wilder recalled in a memoir. They were chasing about 200 chickens, and the task appeared futile because the water was rising fast and the sky was growing dark. So the boys gave up on the chickens and ran inside. The water kept rising and Wilder's father got everyone into the ceiling loft. There were fourteen of them. Something slammed into the house. Wilder later suspected it was the grandstand from the baseball park north of the home. The house was knocked right off its pilings. It shifted and leaned amid the swirling water. Wilder's father shouted for everyone to hold on to the roof. But the roof went "zing" as it was torn from the home, and then it was gone. There was no sound except the sound of the wind and the rain. The house disintegrated and the fourteen people in it were tossed into the water.

Floyd Wilder came up to the surface in complete darkness, with others kicking at him. Glass, tin, and wood flew all around them. He saw a blinking light that he later determined was a neighbor's flashlight. Young Floyd grabbed what he would later realize was a piece of sheeting from a shack. It was jammed in a large tree and helped serve as a windbreak. Wet, cold and exhausted, he climbed onto the sheeting and dozed off and on.

To the south, at the Boots place in Sebring Farms, the dike and the high land of U.S. 27 formed a basin, with the home in the low-lying middle. Inside the house, water rose through the floorboards. Everyone moved to the attic. Neighbor Charles Thomas, Mutt's father, brought an ax and started chopping at the roof to make an opening to the outside. Many had flashlights. The water followed, and by the time they got into the attic, they could hang their feet down and touch water. Boots noticed the whites sitting quietly and the blacks praying loudly and crying. They waited.

Then the house actually lifted off its foundations. It was now floating. The home moved 75 to 100 yards at a speed a building had no business traveling. Then it struck the raised roadbed of the unfinished U.S. 27. It slammed into it three times. The third time, the building came apart like a cardboard house crushed by a giant's foot. Everybody tumbled into and under the water.

Boots grabbed a piece of ceiling and floated. He was on its smooth side and had to keep struggling for a handhold. The wind formed waves, some cresting as high as four feet. Boots had to turn his head into the wind constantly or it would have thrown him from the board. He held tight to rafter boards still nailed to the chunk of ceiling. The wind screeched without cease. The darkness was all enveloping, split only by bolts of lightning. Vernie Boots saw none of his three brothers as they floated all night, but he did hear Willie and Ray. They had been floating nearby, and they were able to call to him in the dark until he finally lost contact with them. He never saw Virgil, and Virgil never called out.

Frede Aunapu was a dragline operator in Belle Glade. He and twenty-one others, including his girlfriend, Elizabeth Beader, had gone to a packinghouse made of corrugated tin. Wind and waves battered the place and floating trees banged against it. Strong men broke into tears and prayed for rescue. A ceiling joist broke and snaked its way down Aunapu's back and through his pants leg. He was carried underwater as his belt wrapped around the wood. Aunapu struggled desperately underwater for what might have been as long as five minutes. He ran out of air and began breathing water and began to sense what it was like to drown.

But somehow he got free and shot to the surface, his throat burning as he spit up water from his lungs. He grabbed his girlfriend and the two crawled through a hole in the roof. They worked their way to a floating tree. A wave knocked Elizabeth off. She stayed under and Aunapu dove for her. He searched through black water 10 feet below, felt a body, brought it up and placed it in a tree. He ran his hand through the person's hair. It was kinky. Aunapu had pulled up a black man. Elizabeth was still down there.

He searched again, and this time he found her. He pulled her up and pounded her back to get the water out of her. The two climbed aboard a floating clump of trees. Aunapu left Elizabeth on the edge and moved to the middle, figuring it was safest. But as his girlfriend watched, the cluster of trees rolled inward, squeezing Anaupu like a wringer.

At 8:18 P.M., the anemometer at the University of Florida's Agricultural Experiment Station, near Belle Glade, was destroyed; its last wind speed reading was 92 mph. At almost that exact moment, a similar instrument was destroyed at the U.S. Agriculture Department's Cane Breeding Station in Canal Point, about 15 miles north along the lakeshore. Its last reading was 75 mph. As had happened at the telephone company at West Palm Beach, the Everglades Experimental Station showed a dramatic drop in air pressure.

About 9:15 P.M., the winds died down at the Everglades Experimental Station. Researcher R. V. Allison timed the lull—apparently the passage of the eye—at 25 minutes, with the winds returning at 9:40. The Canal Point station timed it at 9:30 to 10:05. Right in the middle of the eerie calm, Allison saw a remarkable sight. A Ford automobile emerged from the darkness. Inside it were four adults and eight children. They had somehow kept the car on the road at the height of the storm.

Allison said later the station's rain gauge measured 11.35 inches, but he wondered about giving that number any reliability. He said later the top of the rain gauge blew off, and the rain was coming at strange angles. And, he said, as water rose around the building, it was picked up by the winds and whirled into the air. During the storm, the dike surrounding the station's small property suffered a small breach. But there was so much water around it that the station's small pump was of little effect. The winds destroyed a five-room bungalow, two labor cabins, a garage, and the west side of the greenhouse. Except for two bungalows and the greenhouse's service house, every building suffered roof damage, and the two-story boardinghouse was so damaged that it had to be torn down later.

"During the height of the storm in this section there is little doubt that the wind reached velocities as high as 140 to 150 miles per hour," Allison would write later from Belle Glade. If those were sustained winds, then after having crossed 40 miles of land, the storm was still a strong Category Four, and perhaps as little as 5 miles per hour below the threshold for Category Five.

Storms usually lose punch as they pass over land and are denied their rich supply of energy in the form of warm ocean water. So the next question is, how was the 1928 storm as powerful when it crossed Lake Okeechobee as when it first tore through Porto Rico and the other small islands of the Atlantic Ocean?

The answer, once again, is in the eye, the quiet center around which the storm rotates like a massive wheel on an axle. The eye is where the storm sucks up warm ocean water to feed its wind. Send the eye over land, and it weakens. But that center had to cross only 40 miles, much of it swamp, from Palm Beach to Lake Okeechobee. The eye was 25 miles in diameter. As the western eye wall was almost upon Belle Glade, the eastern eye wall had just crossed the coast, The eye had been continuing to draw warm water—and energy—from the ocean. It hadn't had much time to weaken.

"It is important to note that if this hurricane had made landfall any-where else but South Florida or Southern Louisiana the hurricane would have weakened much faster," National Hurricane Center forecaster Brian Jarvinen said. He said friction with the ground kills hurricanes, espe-cially when they pass over trees, buildings, hills, and other obstructions. But this hurricane, once it got through the thin strip of development along the coast, was crossing flat fields and swampland. And, of course, it could then feed on the waters of the lake itself.

Jarvinen said the storm probably did weaken between the coast and Lake Okeechobee, but only by about 10 mph. He estimates a top wind speed of about 145 mph at West Palm Beach—just 10 mph below Cate-gory Five. He then calculates it took the storm two hours and 45 minutes to get to Canal Point, where he believes the center of the eye crossed. By then, Jarvinen estimated, top wind speeds were about 135 mph.

Jarvinen's calculations would also show that the storm was moving not directly east to west, but at an angle, toward the west-northwest, since Belle Glade is due west of Lake Worth and Canal Point is about 13 miles north of Belle Glade. Had it stayed on a directly western line, its eye might have traveled south of the lake, and damage would have been less.

Carmen Salvatore had no idea what a hurricane could do. So he had stayed at his home in Pahokee and taken his chances. After all, his home sat on a ridge, protecting it from Lake Okeechobee, just feet away. He felt the wind shaking and heaving the walls. Inside, his children huddled. There were Carmen Jr., 9, Mary, 7, Iris, almost 5, and Lucille, 3.

"Oh Lord, don't let the house blow away," Mary prayed.

Carmen, Jr. piped up, "The Lord's asleep."

Carmen decided that if he and his family stayed, they would die. He said flatly, "We've gotta get out of here." He gathered up Iris and Mary. Ella grabbed Carmen, Jr. and Lucille. They opened the door and headed for the landmark cypress tree in front of his home. They tried hiding behind it or along the ridge, but eventually aimed toward their friend Oscar B. McClure's two-story house, about 300 yards away. It took them nearly 90 minutes to go the 900 feet. At one point, Carmen fell into a flooded canal. Mary was only seven, but she would remember all her life how good the warm lake water felt as it surrounded her in the cold, driving rain. Her father popped to the surface, sputtering, still holding the girls. Ella and Carmen, Jr. dragged him through the standing water from the canal to the ground, where his feet again caught land.

The wind was so strong and the rain so thick that Carmen had to wipe the water from his nose and mouth to breathe. He couldn't see his hand in front of his face. Wind drowned out his shouts. When Carmen finally felt a vacuum, he knew he'd reached McClure's home. He found McClure outside, holding on to a tree root. The home had come off its foundation blocks. McClure had been trying to get to Pahokee for help. "Mac, there's nowhere to go," Salvatore said. "The wind's so strong you can't stand up." The Salvatores went inside, where twenty or forty people were taking shelter in a living room, singing and praying. Carmen looked down. His daughter Iris was almost unconscious from having inhaled wind-driven water as she lay in Carmen's arms. Another twenty minutes, Carmen figured, and she would have drowned in his arms.

The eye was upon them. Carmen went to check on an older couple, the Hunters, two houses to the south, as he had promised he would. The Hunters were gone. Carmen and others walked the ridge, shouting their names. By the time they got back to the Hunter place, the wind had started in the other direction. They stayed until dawn.

Outside, a small burial plot lay close to the Salvatore home. The water washed out one of the graves, exposing the coffin of a World War I veteran who had died in the worldwide flu epidemic of 1918. Old death was meeting new death.

But the storm's wall of water was not done. The surge moved up the east shore of the lake, toward its north end, at the town of Okeechobee.

"If it had been daylight the people on the north shore would have seen the water receding away from the shoreline and the bottom exposed with fish flopping around or trapped in small pockets of water," hurricane forecaster Jarvinen said in 2002. As the storm pushed all the water to the southeast, it was as if the giant lake had been tipped, and the north end drew down to the lakebed. As the storm continued its northwest track, over a two-hour period, winds shifted until they were coming from the south. The rest was elementary physics. The water soon came rushing back, then kept moving to the north end of the lake. Up there, there was no dike—not even a little one. Why would there be? The water normally flowed *toward* the lake, not the other way around. So the water poured north into the town of Okeechobee.

Charles Sears, Jr., and Effie Sears Ransom had been born into a home in South Bay with a big tree in the yard. It was less than a mile from the dike. Their parents had come, like so many, from the Bahamas. They'd come from Exuma. Charles Rufus Sears, Sr., one of seventeen children, had come from Forbes Hill around 1917, and Lucinda from Mosstown around 1920; they were married in Miami in 1921. They found no jobs in Miami and heard there was work in the farm fields around the lake, picking tomatoes and beans. Lucinda had had two boys and a daughter and was ready to deliver her fourth child when the storm came. An aunt and her two sons decided to leave. They went down the road and were never seen again, alive or dead.

As the wind grew, the roof came off and rising water approached the porch. Lucinda grabbed little Effie, not yet 2, and Charles reached Cleo, 5, and Charles Jr., 3. They looked for a high spot, but saw only an old tree in their front yard. They ran to it and climbed high into the branches. The mother went first and the father passed the boys up. As the wind howled, Charles was losing hope. He kept saying, "We're going to die." His wife didn't want to hear it. She began to sing:

> *Jesus, lover of my soul, let me to Thy bosom fly.*
> *While the nearer waters roll, while the tempest still is high.*
> *Hide me, O my Savior, hide, till the storm of life is past.*

Lucinda saw three bolts of lightning and took that as a sign from God. But some time in the long night, three-year-old Charles, Jr., slid from his father's arms. He was gone.

In the Morning

September 17, 1928

"The suffering throughout is beyond words."

At dawn, Tom Rickards and his family stepped out of the Palm Beach County Courthouse in downtown West Palm Beach. It was the only building standing for blocks, stark against the rolling hills of scattered lumber. Debris on the street came almost to the shoulder of his young son, Tommie. A piece of a tall flagpole was hurled several feet into the ground. Buildings were splintered across the horizon. Three weeks later, on October 3, he would write: "The suffering throughout is beyond words. Individual tales of horror, suffering and loss are numberless."

Clothilda Miller and her siblings looked out of Mr. Ewell's home, back to their own. All that remained was a pile of wreckage and a few clothes the family would salvage.

Clothilda sat down on a piece of lumber that had come off of the house. She said sadly to herself, "What must we do?"

In Jupiter, a bleary-eyed and disheveled Bessie DuBois and her family surveyed the damage to her home, the lighthouse, and the area around the inlet. Everyone and everything was wet and stayed wet. The house hung from the chimney and porch. The dock was standing out of the water and was covered with debris. Boats were scattered or smashed. The DuBois men had to chop away trees just to get out of the house. They learned later that John DuBois's sister's home had been destroyed and the woman's infant, less than a year old, had been killed when the winds pulled her from her father's arms and slammed her into a building. The baby was never found. Her empty casket had no flowers; after the storm, there were none to be found.

Nearby, a cement-block home belonging to a black family had collapsed and several people were dead; another report placed the deaths at six. Six people were killed west of Jupiter when a school building where they had sought refuge collapsed. The only survivors had found sanctuary huddled under oak and metal desks.

Bessie DuBois's father and siblings returned to their home, about two miles away, and found it twisted around the central chimney; stairs were at angles, dishes were broken and the house was off the blocks. The U.S. Weather Bureau Building south of the lighthouse along the inlet was destroyed.

Around daybreak, Jupiter dairy farmer Noah Kellum Williams, who had driven around as the storm was subsiding, looking for people who needed help, returned to his refuge in the schoolhouse. Williams took his son, Kenneth, and two dairy hands and tried to get to the farm. Here, the storm surge had not been 50 feet, as some had feared, or even 25 feet, and it had not topped the ridge. But it had pushed water up the Jupiter Inlet, and bridges were washed out.

Why wasn't there more of a storm surge along the coast?

Miami, farther south, has been the victim of large storm surges because Biscayne Bay and the Atlantic Ocean east of Miami Beach are relatively shallow. As with the lake, wind-driven energy needs somewhere to go. But of all the Atlantic seaboard, the three-county, 75-mile stretch of coast from Boca Raton to West Palm Beach to Fort Pierce is the least vulnerable to storm surge.

That area has some of the deepest water close to shore anywhere from Key West to Cape Cod. Storm-driven water carries tremendous energy. But off Palm Beach, where the ocean drops to thousands of feet just 17 miles offshore, the deep water dissipates most of the energy before it comes ashore.

Another factor is the slope of the land. Along southwest Florida, the land slopes gradually, averaging a rise of less than a foot for every mile away from the coast. On the southeast side, for much of the 75-mile coastline from Boca Raton to Fort Pierce, there's a ridge—a cliff of sorts—that rises up to 25 feet above sea level close to or along the coast of the mainland.

"Least vulnerable to storm surge" is a relative term; even a minimal hurricane would put barrier islands and the immediate coastline underwater. Studies show that in a Category Five storm, the strongest, the ocean would rise 11 feet above normal in West Palm Beach and Jupiter, nearly 12 feet in Boca Raton, as high as 14 feet in Martin County, and 15 feet in St. Lucie County. The barrier islands of Palm Beach, Martin and St. Lucie counties, separated from the coastline only by the Intracoastal Waterway, would be washed over by a rising tide. It would severely damage oceanfront condominiums, hotels, homes bridges and roads, and cut channels, carving new islands, sometimes permanently. The surge would roll right up inland forks of the St. Lucie and Loxahatchee rivers to and over property far inland.

Noah Williams and his party finished surveying the damage to their farm, turned around, and headed back to the schoolhouse where they had waited out the storm. There, 125 people were exhausted and hungry. Williams, who was a county commissioner, took charge. He led a group to downtown Jupiter. They entered a store. Most of the food was ruined, but some was in cans. Williams kept track of what they took so the owner could be reimbursed later.

After breakfast, Williams and a group again tried for his home, taking a longer route. On the way, they passed the two-story home of a neighbor. It had been made of concrete, and many had gone there, figuring it would stand the storm. It had not. As Williams passed, he saw men laying out bodies in the yard. Four were dead; another would die later.

Williams finally got to his farm and home. The two buildings were in shambles. The barn had been pulled apart almost to its concrete foundation. The house had been blown 10 feet off its foundation, the upper story broken off. Upstairs furniture and tiny pieces that had been part of the roof were strewn around the area. The north wall had vanished as if by explosion and the second floor hung crazily in midair on its north edge. One tenant's house had also flown 10 feet, but amazingly stayed mostly intact, its furniture barely moved. The group would later decide it was easier to move foundation blocks than the house, so they jacked it up and put blocks back under it. Eleven of Williams's cows were dead, probably from flying debris. Several were later found alive, some as late as Wednesday, three days after the storm. They'd been wandering, their udders swollen from lack of milking.

Williams retrieved his wife, Birdie, at the schoolhouse and brought her to her homestead. When she saw the destruction, she sat down and cried. Their farm was heavily mortgaged, and now they had lost everything.

"For twenty-three years, we have worked and slaved to get something ahead," she sobbed. "We got it and now it's gone in a night." That was true. Williams had mortgaged the cows to build the barn and, with the economy already sour even before the storm, he later had to sell his property and could get only enough to pay off back taxes. But on that wet morning, Williams told his wife he didn't feel like crying at all. They had survived without a scratch. All around them, people were dead.

On Monday morning, a woman was brought to Fort Lauderdale's Memorial Hospital from Deerfield Beach, just south of Boca Raton. She'd rode out the storm alone with two small children and had tried to flee when the storm was at its worst. Her five-year-old son was blown into a ditch and drowned; her one-year-old was lost. Flying timber broke both her hips. Later, in the same hospital, another woman gave birth to triplets.

In Pahokee, Carmen Salvatore surveyed the material possessions of his world. His home was gone. His crops were washed away. His seed had vanished in the wind or was soggy, rotten, and worthless. He had nothing in the bank. But he and his family were alive.

Lake Okeechobee was brown with mud, torn vegetation, and

debris. Dead snakes and turtles and rabbits rocked in the wake, along with swarms of fish that had suffocated in the stagnant water. All Carmen found of his home was a single ice chest, bought from Sears, Roebuck. Later, Carmen and others found his neighbor, Mrs. Hunter, in her eighties and less than 100 pounds dripping wet, hanging to a tree root, too weak to speak. They found her husband in a field, alive, clinging to a dead cow.

Carmen also took a clandestine side trip, to the home of Horace Redding, the moonshiner whose drum full of booze Salvatore had once dumped, earning him a death threat from old Horace. Salvatore had heard Redding had died in the storm. He needed to see for himself. Only then did he finally tell his wife what had happened so many years earlier.

Charles Sears, Sr., still in the tree with his wife and daughter, wept for his three-year-old son, Charles Jr., torn from his arms in the night. Suddenly he heard moaning. It was the boy. He had not been washed away, but had lodged in some lower branches and eventually fallen asleep. Charles reached down and grabbed his baby. Three of the Sears nephews showed up. Their clothes had all been torn from their bodies. Charles, Sr. would stay in the Glades to help bury the dead. Many were people he knew. Later, he would not talk about it to his family.

Frede Aunapu, crushed inside a pile of swirling trees, somehow survived. When he pulled off his clothes later, his body was a crazy quilt of bruises. Half of the twenty-two people who had been with him in the packinghouse didn't survive. Frede and Elizabeth were married the next May and eventually had three sons.

Ruth Shive, praying for her unborn baby in the house where she had sought refuge, had seen one side of the home suddenly cave inward, then stop. The water stopped rising. The wind had begun to slow. People snatched minutes of sleep. It was dawn. Her father's house was off its foundation and leaned drunkenly; the back end, along the lake, was gone. Had they stayed there, Ruth wrote later, they probably all would have died. They found friends and relatives and heard the horror stories. A neighbor had clung to something for hours in the water and realized later it was the back of a dead cow. Another had stood on a rooftop with her three small children and fought off snakes, rats, and other animals fleeing the rising water. Outside the Pahokee schoolhouse, where hundreds had waited out the storm, more than a dozen building rafters had neatly impaled a royal palm tree, almost in a perfect vertical line. Ruth's father's car, parked nearby, was unscratched.

The family had originally been on the list of missing, and Ruth's uncle in West Palm Beach had fought his way to the Glades to see if they might be alive and safe. The Red Cross offered passage to refugees. Ruth's husband wanted to send her and their daughter home to Tulsa, but she wouldn't leave. Finally she agreed to go to West Palm Beach. For the first time in their lives, the Shive and Carpenter families accepted charity, taking sacks of coffee, bacon, canned vegetables, meat and milk, baking materials and, most importantly, spray for the mosquitoes that had descended like a biblical plague.

Helen Sherouse had huddled in the doorway of her shattered home until morning. She and her stepfather were the only survivors out of twenty people who had sought shelter there. Helen had lost her two brothers and sister, her mother, her aunt, and several other relatives. As they walked to the Pahokee road, she saw railroad tracks twisted like copper wire. Some black men walked up with babies in their arms. They were dead. Helen's stepfather could not look at them.

Floyd Wilder found his siblings, alive, and later, his father, dead. The man's skull had been crushed. Floyd also lost his youngest sister, Laura. An older sister lost her three children. A woman neighbor who had gone to the Wilder home also died, along with her three children, one of them a pal of Floyd's named Philip. In all, eight of the fourteen in the house had died.

Out in the giant freshwater inland ocean that had been farmland twenty-four hours earlier, little Vernie Boots called for his brothers, Willie, Ray, and Virgil. Six decades later, as he stood before students in a Belle Glade classroom, recalling his experience, he got to the part where he reunited with Willie and Ray, and suddenly stopped, unable to continue. In the loud silence, there was squeaking as students shifted in their seats. Boots tried to gather his composure.

"That's all right, take your time," the teacher said. "It's a hard thing to relive."

Vernie finally said in a cracking voice, "I heard somebody groan. Of course, it was joyful. It was my youngest brother [Willie]. Funny thing. He'd never learned to swim. We heard another groan. . . ." Vernie had to stop again. Then he went on: "That was my brother, Ray."

The three Boots boys had decided to leave their wooden floats and soon found themselves in chest-deep water. They had floated $2\frac{1}{2}$ miles to the southeast when they heard another boy hollering and approached him, desperately hoping it was their brother Virgil. But it was their neighbor Mutt Thomas. Mutt had also floated in the darkness until the water receded, then sat on a large piece of floating wood until daylight. He had waded three miles before finding the Bootses. The group began wading back to their home. With the land covered in water, they had to use palm trees, the Bolles Hotel, and draglines as landmarks. Mutt heard someone shout his name. He looked across the canal. It was his father. The boy leaped into the canal and swam to his dad for an emotional reunion. Charles Thomas had held on to the cross-arm of a telephone pole all night.

The exhausted Thomases slept on the floor of the Bolles Hotel. At first the caretaker refused to let them in, but he eventually relented. The Bootses later hooked up with their half-brother Bill Rawle, who was in a small boat. They made their way back to Sebring Farms. Later, Boots's father and brother Virgil would be found dead. They were buried in the Ortona cemetery along the Caloosahatchee. Vernie's mother was never found.

Mutt and his father returned to Sebring Farms. There, they saw Mutt's Uncle Minor, his father's brother, who had stayed with the family home. Minor said he'd clung flat to the roof when it came off the house. On Tuesday, the Thomases found the bodies of Mutt's mother and all five of his siblings, along with Charles's brother Richard and his wife. Richard's two children, aged seven and five, were never found. The bodies of the Thomas family were taken to the Bolles Hotel, wrapped in sheets, and placed in pine boxes. They were taken on Wednesday to high ground, and then trucked to the Ortona cemetery, where thirteen-year-old Mutt helped his family bury the dead at midnight. Later, he learned his teacher, Edna Denniston, had clung to her husband, John, and son, Paul, in a cypress tree in the rising water. Edna and little Paul had drowned in John's arms.

For years after the storm, Mutt's father, who would die in 1942, worked the farm furiously. Sometimes, some of his workers came up to him for instructions, but he wouldn't answer. It was as if he were somewhere else.

The experimental station near Belle Glade was surrounded by three feet of water. It later subsided to two feet, but would stay there for nearly two months and destroy all the crops surrounding the station that the agents used for their research. "The condition of the country," soil specialist R. V. Allison wrote a supervisor on September 24, "is entirely beyond description. There is about two feet of water over the property station still. Many of the buildings are ruined. The greenhouse is badly wrecked." Allison reported that the little cottage, in which forty white people huddled, and the greenhouse service building, where blacks had gone for refuge, had held up.

On Monday, September 17, lighthouse superintendent W. W. Demerritt telegraphed H. E. Randall in Moore Haven. Randall was the superintendent in charge of the navigational lights along Lake Okeechobee. Demerritt, 160 miles away in Key West, asked Randall to "promptly report extent of all damages to your lights."

In New York, Harry Kelsey opened the Monday-morning paper. It said: "Palm Beach destroyed by storm." He tried to call his wife in South Florida. Lines were down. His employee, Charles Branch, who had waited out the storm in Geneva, near Orlando, had also heard the grim reports. He and a colleague loaded a car with an ax and other tools, food, and about five gallons of water, and headed south.

A reporter for the *Orlando Reporter-Star* made for the coast at Vero Beach and began working his way down. First he found a few roofs blown off and windows broken. At Fort Pierce, he found more substantial damage and wires in the streets. Fort Pierce officials later reported the winds and high water tore up the town's riverfront, wiping out piers and a bridge as well as a fish packinghouse and warehouse. By the time the reporter had reached Stuart, he found himself in a world of destruction. He thought to himself that it just couldn't get worse. But it did get worse, and exponentially, as he made his way down the coast to West Palm Beach.

Around midnight Monday morning, even before the full depth of the catastrophe was known, Alexander J. Mitchell, head of The U.S. Weather Bureau's Jacksonville station for more than three decades, observed grimly, "This is really one of the great hurricanes."

The U.S. Weather Bureau advisory for the morning of Sunday, September 16, had posted hurricane warnings from Miami to Daytona Beach and, on Florida's Gulf Coast, from Punta Gorda, about halfway between Fort Myers and Tampa, and the Cedar Keys, a small chain of islands about halfway between Tallahassee and Tampa near the inside curve of the Florida peninsula. Now, on Monday afternoon, in Miami, U.S. Weather Bureau chief meteorologist Richard W. Gray reported the storm was 600 miles across and that Sunday had marked the first time warnings had gone up on both sides of Florida's peninsula. "The storm was of remarkable strength," Gray said. Neither Mitchell nor Gray said anything of the U.S. Weather Bureau's flawed forecast.

In fact, at no point are forecasters found ever conceding that the information they were distributing was, up until the eleventh hour, absolutely wrong.

Alexander J. Mitchell, the U.S. Weather Bureau man in Jacksonville, would write later that the morning reports of Sunday, September 16, "showed the unmistakably rapid approach of the hurricane." Switching from the antiseptic to the melodramatic, he added that the observations of 8:00 P.M. that day "were convincing—the hurricane had reached the coast; and like a thing of life, the great atmospheric panorama was moving inland, the center eventually passing over Lake Okeechobee, where its fury converted peaceful communities into shambles, and contented firesides into morgues."

It wasn't much of a leap for Gray to describe the storm's fury at 8:00 P.M. Sunday, when it had already pounded the coast for some four hours. But how could Mitchell and Gray and all the other forecasters have confidently insisted as late as Saturday evening that the storm would miss the Florida coast? They don't say.

Mitchell rejected complaints about lack of warning, saying that the weather service issued two advisories a day for every day of the storm's march across the Atlantic, providing the storm's intensity and its direction and speed of advance. He said the advisories were distributed via radio, telephone, and telegraph.

In an October 12 letter to his supervisors in Washington, Gray said he advised Miami newspapers, which operated as many as six telephone lines passing on advisories, and his staff answered some 200 calls an hour from September 14 until almost midnight on September 16, when the storm was inland, and topped 250 an hour on the day of September 16, with many of those calls being long distance.

"On the 15th and September 16, The U.S. Weather Bureau office and the two newspaper offices answered 1,000 telephone calls per hour," Gray wrote. "The strain upon the operators of the telephones was such that they had to be relieved at frequent intervals."

Of course, as often happens, most of the attention was focused on Miami. It was the largest city in southeast Florida, it had already been struck two years earlier, and that's where the weather office was. Mitchell doesn't say how much conversation he had with authorities up the road in West Palm Beach.

But on October 24, Mitchell wrote his bosses in Washington: "Warnings of the storm were widely disseminated to the profit of all; and many who lost their lives on Lake Okeechobee was [sic] due to the ignoring of the information in possession of all."

But Mitchell must have known that such information was of value only to the few people in 1928 who would have the means to receive it, through radios, newspapers, and telephone.

And, of course, for most of that time, while he was giving plenty of advice, it was the wrong advice.

Clearly, forecasters' technology in 1928 was downright primitive compared to that of their twenty-first-century counterparts. But today's forecasters have a certain humility and pragmatism. Even with their best computer models, given the same track today, the best they can offer twenty-four hours before landfall would be a "cone of probability" stretching from the Space Coast to the Keys.

And, the Hurricane Center's Brian Jarvinen said in 2002, even as the storm left the coast of Porto Rico on September 14, it wouldn't have taken much to jar the arc. "A small 5 degree change [at] Porto Rico means [it] could totally miss our coastline," he said.

The difference is that, while the forecasters of today admit they can't be sure, the forecasters of 1928 believed—were even convinced—that they knew where the storm was, and was not, headed. They were wrong.

Weather officials continued to track the hurricane on Monday morning, September 17. The 10:20 A.M. advisory placed the storm east of Tampa in central Florida and moving northwest. Forecasters weren't sure if it would move into the Gulf. Warnings extended from Savannah to Jacksonville and to just south of Titusville and along Florida's Gulf Coast from the Cedar Keys to Apalachicola in the eastern Panhandle.

The *Times* of London reported that, at 4:15 A.M. on Monday, a radio station at Gordon City, on New York's Long Island, picked up a ham radio broadcast from Tampa: "A raging gale is blowing my house until it is shaking like a leaf. Wires are down all over the streets and telephone connexions went out several hours ago. I do not know how long my power will last, for I am in the centre of Tampa. No one has been reported killed or injured, but the storm seems to be still mounting. I cannot get in touch with any other radio station in Florida. I am badly scared."

In the Orlando suburb of Winter Park, Professor Lewis Elhuff, of the science department at Winter Park High School, later sent the U.S. Weather Service a list of hourly readings that showed the storm topping out at 70 mph at about 7:00 A.M. Monday. A report from Bartow, east of Tampa, showed the storm was at its strongest about 11:00 A.M. The writer said he had no record of wind velocity "but it was the worst storm in many years." E. H. D. Brown of Eustis, north of Orlando, reported later that, although the storm passed 35 miles away, he experienced a dramatic gust hours later. "I have been keeping tabs on our different storms here for the past 35 years, and cannot understand such a terrible blow."

At 4:30 P.M. Monday, the U.S. Weather Bureau placed the storm's 2:00 P.M. position at about 75 miles north of Tampa, moving northwest. Warnings stretched northeast to Georgetown, South Carolina, near Charleston, and west to Mobile, Alabama. That afternoon, the outer fringes of the storm caused a factory smokestack to collapse in Apalachicola in the Florida Panhandle. At 8:00 P.M., the storm was placed in extreme North Florida, between Jacksonville and Tallahassee, and was arcing toward the northeast, having begun that turn east and northeast at Tampa.

The storm had finally begun the "recurve" forecasters had so confidently said would occur long before it reached the Florida coast. It had come a little late, and that delay had brought far different consequences than those the forecasters had predicted so boldly.

At 9:30 P.M., warnings were extended to Virginia's eastern shore. But, the advisory said, the storm's intensity was "considerably less."

The storm passed west of Jacksonville about 2:00 A.M. on Tuesday, September 18, and then angled northeast across land toward the Georgia coast. Jacksonville reported top winds of less than 40 mph. By 9:30 A.M., the storm was near Savannah. C. M. Strong, assistant meteorologist in the Savannah office, said winds had begun picking up as early as 5:00 P.M. on Monday and were at gale force from 10:50 P.M. until about 3:45 A.M. Tuesday. It decreased rapidly at 7:00 A.M., then picked up again, apparently as what was left of the eye passed over Tybee Island, on the Atlantic coast and east of the historic city. The top sustained wind was only 52 mph, with a gust of 60—well below hurricane strength. But by then, despite having traveled hundreds of miles across land, the storm still packed some power.

"The noise of rain and wind were terrifying but there was very little damage done by the storm in this city and vicinity, mostly being confined to the drenching of houses, hundreds in number, by the rain, breakage of telephone and light wires by falling limbs, and the temporary interruption of railway, postal and telegraph service." Strong reported.

The storm was northwest of Charleston, South Carolina at about 2:00 P.M. Tuesday, and that city also reported top winds of about 50 mph, a fraction of the storm's greatest power but enough to damage piers, beach small boats, down trees and knock out telegraph service both there and back in Savannah.

On parts of the coast where lighthouses couldn't be built close enough to the coast to be effective, ships were outfitted with lights and moored offshore. At Cape Lookout, on North Carolina's Outer Banks, the master of such a "lightship" reported hurricane force winds about 4:00 P.M. Tuesday and vicious seas all night. About twenty-four hours later, at 4:00 P.M. Wednesday, it lost its 2½-ton anchor and chain and tore loose from its moorings. It tried to return to shore but, despite having both boilers at full steam, it couldn't negotiate the high winds and heavy seas. Finally, about 9:30 P.M., the ship was able to secure itself 11½ miles off the coast. At 9:00 A.M. on Thursday it got under way again, getting back to its pier around midday. Miraculously, except for the lost anchor and chain, it was undamaged.

The master of the Diamond Shoal lightship, also in North Carolina, later reported in the *Lighthouse Service Bulletin* that at 8:00 A.M. on Tuesday the ship rode out winds that reached 70 mph. He said the ship suffered no damage and the anchor dragged no more than 100 yards.

The storm had taken a turn to almost due north in southeastern North Carolina and was now passing through central Virginia, headed toward Pennsylvania. But as it did, the portion north and east of the eye was over the coast, and pounding it. Hundreds of families were moved out of coastal North Carolina as rivers rose. By the weekend, as many as 600,000 acres of farmland would be inundated, with losses approaching $5 million—about forty-five million in today's dollars—and Charleston, South Carolina, to the south, would be isolated by washed-out roads.

Soon the storm had lost its hurricane characteristics. But storm warnings had been posted as far north as New England.

On Tuesday, officials aboard the train carrying presidential candidate Herbert Hoover from Trenton, New Jersey, back to Washington, had been warned they might have to roll through some of the storm's winds. On Wednesday, an edge of the storm passed over Baltimore, where a fifty-year-old man was crushed to death by a falling tree. Winds gusted to 45 mph over the city and 60 mph on Chesapeake Bay, sinking or wrecking pleasure boats and oyster schooners in Annapolis.

On Wednesday night, the master of the lightship off Fenwick Island, near the Delaware-Maryland state line, reported 90 mph winds and 120 mph squalls and high seas that rocked the ship, sending water rushing over the aft rail.

Arthur Graham of Fort Lauderdale, who had been attending a plumber's convention at a boardwalk auditorium in Atlantic City, New Jersey, reported later that the storm blew out windows, stopping the meeting and prompting conventioneers to lay sandbags and sawdust on the rain-soaked floor. A local paper reported winds there at 72 mph on the coast and 46 mph inland at Philadelphia, where seven were reported dead.

Three were reported dead on the New Jersey coast. Heavy seas pitched a man off his boat near Atlantic City. A butcher in Seadrift was killed, apparently when power lines fell on his car and he tried to move them. And a seventy-six-year-old man in Cape May died of "nervous shock" after watching two century-old buttonwood trees crash down near his porch, the *New York Times* reported on Thursday. Hamilton Kean, candidate for U.S. Senator from New Jersey, was on his way to a speech in Union City with aides when a tree landed on the car's roof near Perth Amboy, pinning everyone in the car until passersby could rescue them. Kean went on to the gathering. The storm washed out railroad tracks in Ocean City, tore out 400 feet of track in Point Pleasant, and knocked down a 250-foot tree in Roselle.

On Wednesday, the storm, now nearly over Pittsburgh, brought twelve hours of driving wind, up to 60 mph, and heavy downpours to New York City, holding up traffic and knocking out four telephone exchanges. It tossed a man through a plate-glass window, leaving him with cuts, and threw a horse into a bay in Brooklyn. It downed trees across the city and out to Long Island and sank small boats in Westchester County, north of the city.

A critical baseball game between the New York Giants and Chicago Cubs was canceled, meaning the two would have to play a doubleheader at the very end of the season that could decide the National League pennant. Bad weather delayed departure of the relief ship *Bridge* for Porto Rico, the storm itself now blocking help to one of its earlier victims.

Later that day, Wednesday, September 19, 1928, what was left of the storm crossed the border from New York State's Finger Lakes and into its last country. It was last seen merging with a storm near Parry Sound, Ontario, about 150 miles north of Toronto. The barometric pressure was now up to a benign 30.30 inches.

It had been ten days since the S.S. *Commack* had recorded a gusty wind from the northeast. The storm had marched from Africa to the Caribbean to Canada, killing more than 7,000 people along its path.

In Brownsville, Texas, along the Mexican border, people noticed hundreds of pink flamingos. The storm had driven them from Florida clear across the Gulf of Mexico.

From New York, the correspondent from the *Times* of London, in his September 17 dispatch, described the storm as "the hurricane from the Bahamas," no doubt ever-mindful that his editors wanted everything to come from the angle of England and her possessions.

He dutifully reported the hurricane had swept across Florida, but said "the loss of life however, seems to have been small." He made two gross exaggerations, one low and one high, reporting only two dead in West Palm Beach but forty "buried in the collapse of a school building in Boynton."

He went on to say that "fragmentary dispatches . . . agree . . . that the storm, while severe, had nothing like the force of that which exactly two years ago to-day took 600 lives." Getting a date wrong wasn't as grave an error as misstating a growing death toll, but he had in fact been wrong again; the 1926 storm had been on September 18, not September 16. The reporter went on to say that no one had heard from Nassau for thirty-six hours and people were worried.

Two days later, the correspondent's lead was, "There were far more deaths in Florida from the hurricane than was first reported."

Frank Stallings's family had been the fourth to move to the southeast corner of Lake Okeechobee early in the twentieth century. His father, Festus, started farming and built Stallings Grocery on Avenue A in downtown Belle Glade. He spent nine months a year in Dawson, in southern Georgia, and twenty-year-old Frank was driving his father there in mid-September 1928. About daylight, they stopped at a store. There, Festus's glance fell on newspaper headlines. A monster storm had struck South Florida. Festus and Frank did not hesitate. They leaped back in the car and turned around.

On Tuesday, September 19, Alexander Mitchell's 10:00 A.M. telegram to Washington from Jacksonville was terse:

"Death list storm incomplete, probably several hundred confined chiefly southeast coast and Lake Okeechobee district STOP."

Help

"Urgent! Urgent! Urgent!"

About 6:30 A.M. Monday, a radio transmission crackled through the early morning air: "This is 4AFC at Palm Beach, Florida. Urgent! Urgent! Urgent!"

The report was brief and grim. Hundreds were dead, thousands of buildings demolished. Assistance was desperately needed.

Palm Beach firefighter Ralph Hollis and his friend, police officer Forrest Dana, had set up equipment and backup batteries on the second floor of the police station just after midnight Sunday. Ralph lived at the town's firehouse and kept his amateur radio equipment there. By Sunday night, the winds had downed his aerial and partially flooded the room. But in those early hours of Monday, Hollis and Dana were the first to tell the world of the storm's fury. By the time they finished at 3:00 A.M. Thursday, they had transmitted for 70 hours, sending out 10,000 words of news copy, 170 personal messages, 16 Red Cross messages to the agency's national headquarters, and 17 public messages, including an official appeal for troops. Palm Beach Mayor Barclay Warburton later offered the gratitude of his constituents for the men's work. The

Associated Press gave them engraved wristwatches. Thirteen years later, Hollis and another West Palm Beach man, Claude Rich, would be vaporized as they stood in the radio room of the battleship *Arizona,* docked at Pearl Harbor on the morning of December 7, 1941.

Other radios hummed as well. At the Hialeah station of the Tropical Radio and Telegraph Company, fifteen men, a woman, and a boy worked 55 hours straight, transmitting as many as 20,000 press reports and up to 75,000 personal messages during the storm.

John Wellborn Martin must have had his radio off.

On Monday, the head of the Florida National Guard had contacted Martin, the governor of Florida, for permission to activate troops. Martin said he'd think about it. "If necessary, of course, I will act on the request," he said, adding, "I do not think the storm has done much damage."

If Martin, a lawyer and former Jacksonville mayor, had at first been clueless to what was going on in South Florida, he may simply have been looking through rose-colored glasses. Born in 1884 near Ocala, he had seen the drainage of the Everglades, and it was during his tenure as governor that Florida's real estate boom reached its peak. Riding that prosperity, Martin pushed through several programs, including the building of highways statewide, the financing of public schools through state money, and the supplying of free textbooks to all students through the sixth grade. In 1925, when the Stuart area, north of West Palm Beach, had wanted to split off and become a new county, savvy organizers had assured its passage by saying they would name it "Martin."

But even as John W. Martin had taken office, in 1925, the boom was starting to lose momentum, and it was now in a rapid downward spiral accelerated by the 1926 hurricane in Miami. Undaunted, Martin had already filed to run for the U.S. Senate by the fall of 1928. The election was in November, so Martin was now a lame-duck governor.

On Tuesday, Martin and the state's comptroller and treasurer met as the Board of the Everglades Drainage District. They convened just long enough to approve previous minutes, then broke up, according to the secretary, F. C. Elliot, the state's chief engineer. The full board, now including the attorney general and agriculture commissioner, reconvened in special session at 11:00 A.M. Wednesday. The telegrams from the south were grim. Martin told Elliot to head down immediately. The governor said he would be leaving that afternoon to see the damage for himself.

The National Guard had not waited for Martin. On Sunday, the state's adjutant general had telegrammed George E. Grace, captain of a Tampa unit, to take a group and head for Okeechobee, the town at the north shore of the lake.

The president of the United States also had not waited. Calvin Coolidge's reputation as reticent and reserved had earned him the nickname "Silent Cal," but now he was anything but silent. As early as Sunday night, with hard reports of devastation already back from Porto Rico and the news from Florida growing worse by the hour, he had already been in touch with the Red Cross and told the War, Commerce, and Labor departments to make themselves available to relief agencies. On Monday afternoon, he issued a statement that "an overwhelming disaster has overtaken our fellow citizens." He was asking the Red Cross to lead the effort and urged people to give promptly and generously.

By Wednesday, the *New York Times* ran a full-page announcement titled: "An appeal to the Citizens of New York." It said the storm had "left a dark trail of disaster and death," adding, "the efforts of the entire country have been summoned." It bore two signatures. One was that of Jimmy Walker, the colorful mayor of New York. The other was President Coolidge.

Red Cross headquarters in New York soon was reporting a flood of donations. Millionaire J. P. Morgan gave $10,000. People of more modest means came in to give what they could. A timid man said he'd made a collection at the workplace; he handed over $750. A weeping young girl gave her jewelry. By Friday, September 21, the Red Cross was estimating that relief in the islands and Florida would require $5 million. Leaders called on each chapter, suggested a quota, and urged the chapter to exceed it.

Help came from benefactors large and small.

In West Palm Beach, a truck pulled up with a Georgia farmer at the wheel and potatoes in the back. He'd been on his way to market when he heard of the storm. He turned and drove for hours to South Florida.

He found the Red Cross headquarters, turned over his truckload of the precious spuds, and went home to Georgia. An unnamed relief organization inexplicably sent a shipment of red plush tasseled piano covers. Resourceful black relief laborers, many in threadbare clothes, used them as cloaks.

The black St. Patrick's Catholic Church in West Palm Beach had suffered $40,000 damage and the white Holy Trinity Catholic Church $17,000, with lesser damage reported at Catholic churches from Micco, in southern Brevard County, to Deerfield Beach, in far northern Broward County. Two months after the storm, on Sunday, November 18, every Catholic church in America would devote its offering to hurricane relief; $202,800 was collected, with $84,200 of it going to South Florida and the rest to Porto Rico.

William J. "Fingy" Conners, the Buffalo newspaper man who had built the for-profit Conners Highway from West Palm Beach to the Glades, wired *Palm Beach Post* publisher D. H. Conkling $5,000. Conkling himself threw in another $1,000. And Colonel E. R. Bradley, owner of the famed casino that operated in Palm Beach with impunity for a half century, sent a $10,000 check from his Kentucky horse farm. In San Francisco, where only two decades had passed since the great 1906 earthquake, grim city council members voted without discussion Tuesday to send $10,000 to their suffering neighbors across the continent. Also voting to donate: the Red Cross chapter in Issaquena County, Mississippi. The previous year, that region had been swamped in the great Mississippi River floods. The Red Cross had rushed in to help there as well. U.S. Masonic lodges sent more than $107,000. Florida's two U.S. senators also appealed to the federal government to rush in help.

Floridians had not waited.

Within an hour of hearing the grave reports from West Palm Beach, Miamians sprang to action. About 7:30 P.M. Sunday, Red Cross workers from Miami began working their way up the coast highway, pushing away debris that grew thicker by the mile, in winds still gusting almost to hurricane strength. Miami city officials later authorized donations of 20 barrels of disinfectant, 24 lanterns, 2 tanks of chlorine, and 5,000 paper cups.

"When Miami suffered its hurricane disaster in 1926, it was the recipient of much needed outside assistance," Monday afternoon's *Miami Daily News* said in a front-page editorial. "Sunday's hurricane found Miami prepared to meet such an emergency and it regarded it as a privilege to lend assistance to its suffering neighbors." An accompanying cartoon showed a nurse leading a procession of ambulances into the "stricken area" and carrying a box reading "Miami Relief." The headline read, "Miami Does Not Forget."

The next day's editorial was as forceful. In 1926, it said, "Miami, weak and helpless, following its saddest visitation, raised its hands in supplication. And quickly the cry was answered. Other cities and states answered that cry of distress from Miami. And in its saddest hour, the stricken area to the north and west of Miami may be sure that this community does not forget." Tuesday's *Miami Herald* printed an urgent plea from its neighbors to the north for sightseers to stay away. While relief help was welcome, rubberneckers were getting in the way and blocking help.

The Tuesday morning *Palm Beach Post* saluted Miami in a front-page box titled; "Light of Memory Burns Bright as Miami Rushes to Aid City." The building on Datura Street that housed the *Post* had caved in and much of its machinery was smashed and twisted. But the *Post* had gotten a paper out. *Post* composing-room manager Bo Wright wrote his mother in Union Springs, Alabama, to say he wasn't sure if he would stick around even if he still had a job when things settled down. "I'm pretty much disgusted with the whole thing and if the job does 'go' we may see you soon," he wrote. "I know I am 10 years older than I was at this time last week."

The *Palm Beach Times* had handset a small edition that came out Monday afternoon. The *Fort Lauderdale Daily News* also got out a paper, turning the printing press with a belt attached to a motorcycle.

The American Legion conference set for Sunday morning in Fort Pierce had drawn a small crowd, and with the storm threat hanging over them, everyone decided to skip out on the event and head for home. Dr. E. W. Ayers, post commander in Miami's Coconut Grove neighborhood, had driven up with his wife Sunday morning, and at 2:30 P.M. he began his return trip. Someone had told him the storm would strike around

Jupiter, but not until about 8:00 P.M. By the time he and his wife got to Jupiter, around 3:30, winds were blowing at about 70 mph. An hour later, they got to West Palm Beach and were in the heart of it. They found shelter in a hotel and left their car in a garage that later collapsed. Ayers began helping at 6:00 A.M. Monday at an emergency hospital set up at the Pennsylvania, a businessman's hotel in downtown West Palm Beach. Other Coconut Grove legionnaires, including Ayers's son Erling, the post's historian, had driven up Monday morning with a relief caravan. Everyone began to fan out Tuesday morning to Lake Worth and Delray Beach. Dr. Ayers found his car. Someone had found it pinned under debris, but people pulled it out Monday and found remarkably little damage. Ayers was able to drive it away.

Almost 10 inches of rain had fallen from 8:00 A.M. Saturday, the day before the storm, to 4:00 P.M. Monday, the day after. By the end of the week, another 9 inches would fall, piling soggy misery onto the disaster. Later in the week, rumors began flying that a second storm was aiming at South Florida, causing such uproar that the *Fort Lauderdale Daily News* felt obligated to run a front-page item debunking the scuttlebutt. It ran another one in later editions that day, discrediting a report in the *Miami News* that the stricken region was in danger of being struck by a wave of the bubonic plague, the rat-borne disease that had wiped out one-fourth of Europe in the 1300s.

Telephone officials reported 32,000 accounts out of service, 400 poles broken and another 2,500 poles leaning. Telephone linemen got the word out about the damage, and soon Southern Bell and AT&T workers were rushing south with equipment from centers in Atlanta and in Jacksonville, where employees worked in inches-deep water left by the hurricane as it left Florida. The phone company shipped down 150 tons of copper wire from inventory and another 75 tons from factories, as well as 20 railcars full of poles and a railcar full of switchboards. The phone company's office in Delray Beach was almost destroyed when the roof caved in. Workers set up service in a nearby building while a team, in a 48-hour turnaround, raced 150 miles to Titusville and commandeered equipment there to get Delray Beach's service up and running. In February 1929, the phone company would hang a bronze marker at its West

Palm Beach station, at 326 Fern Street, "in grateful appreciation and to hold in remembrance the men and women of the Bell system who so faithfully and courageously exemplified the spirit of services during the Florida hurricane, September 1928." The marker stayed on the wall of the building until Southern Bell's successor, BellSouth, moved out of the building in 1998. It sat in a closet for about three years until the company placed it outside its central switching center at 120 North K Street in downtown Lake Worth.

The Palm Beach County Commission met at 10:00 A.M. Wednesday. Only three of five commissioners were there, plus a clerk, and they met for only a half hour. Only one item was on the agenda: to wire the governor for help. "The county has exhausted its general welfare and poor farm fund, and there are thousands that need food and shelter," said the resolution, which noted that Red Cross help was a week away and said the county would need at least $100,000 in immediate relief. Vincent Oaksmith, mayor of the city of West Palm Beach, said in a front-page statement in Wednesday's paper: "A time like this tries the caliber of our citizenry."

Back in Palm Beach County, private engineer Karl Riddle surveyed the bridges from the mainland and reported three spanning the Intracoastal Waterway from West Palm Beach south to Delray Beach were damaged and unusable, including the drawbridge at Lantana, which had been pulled off its turntable and was lying in the water. The engineer concluded it could be repaired. He also said he had found the coast road impassable about halfway between Boynton Beach and the southern end of Palm Beach and had had to turn around.

Trains were still South Florida's most critical means of transportation, and with rail signal devices blown away and telegraph service down, they had to crawl through the stricken coastal areas, arriving at Miami hours late. Stations were damaged from Kelsey City south. Stations in Boca Raton, Deerfield Beach and Pompano Beach were reported destroyed. But by Monday morning, trains were getting through, and full service was back by 9:00 A.M. The trains would play a critical role in the days to come.

On Monday morning, a relief train had headed north with 10 tank cars of drinking water and three baggage cars loaded with food and medicine, including 1,500 gallons of milk. Twenty doctors and as many nurses, all volunteers, were aboard as well. Arkansas U.S. Senator Joe T. Robinson, running mate of Democratic presidential candidate Alfred E. Smith, had arrived in Miami on Sunday. That night he called off his campaign appearances and had his private railroad car and one used by his press entourage hooked up to the relief train. The entourage stayed in the West Palm Beach area until Tuesday night.

"Conditions are indescribable," Robinson said when he arrived in Jacksonville. "It is inspiring to witness the courage displayed by relief workers. They are laboring, however, under a serious handicap."

And a note was dropped off the *Palm Beach Post* office, unsigned and without elaboration.

"God, please never let me be a refugee again. . . . I went home yesterday to see if I could find just a few little things—so full of memories; his watch, the little orphan boy's pictures of his parents; the little motherless girl's new shoes. . . . Our experience that night when we held our little ones close and were ready for Thy will not ours, to be done brought us so close to Thee that we will always walk a little nearer to Thee."

In Lake Worth, federal lawman Clarence H. Parks wrote to J.R. Merritt, the sheriff of St. Lucie County, 50 miles north at Fort Pierce. Parks was a Prohibition agent. And he was asking for booze, of all things.

"We have several hundred people who are in very bad need of stimulants and if you happen to have any that you could turn over to Mr. Harwell who in turn will turn it over to physicians to be prescribed for patients that are in need of same," Parks wrote. "We have no whiskey at this office as we destroyed everything except just a small sample to be used as evidence." The sheriff fulfilled several requests for the good stuff, sending down bottles he'd seized from smugglers running contraband into Florida from the nearby Bahamas. One receipt showed that on September 24, eight days after the storm, Merritt sent down "15 Sacks Whiskey in Quarts, 228 loose quarts whiskey, 40 quarts Bacardi rum, 184 loose pints whiskey." Merritt himself struggled down the coast with a mule and wagon, carrying clothing. Roads were too torn up to handle motorized vehicles. Rattlesnakes driven by the high water spooked the mules, but Merritt got through.

Help

Some had been smart before the fact. At the Southern Dairies Creamery in West Palm Beach, managers had decided not to trust the rosy forecasts that the storm would miss. They had worked the pasteurizing machines nonstop Saturday and Sunday until the power went out. As a result, as residents staggered out of their homes Monday morning, the creamery had 1,400 gallons of milk to provide a hungry populace.

Looting became a problem almost immediately. Resident Helen Buchanan called to say her garage had been blown down and people were "carting off everything," a West Palm Beach police clerk wrote in the blotter. "Watch out." But few incidents were reported. That didn't stop Police Chief F. H. Matthews from ordering a sundown-to-dawn curfew, saying everyone must be off the streets "unless an EXTREME EMERGENCY demands it, and then must have a pass or permit signed by the chief of police or his assistant." Officials also worked quickly to squelch rumors that bodies had been found in the lakes that served as the city's water supply. Palm Beach County Sheriff Robert C. Baker ordered checkpoints on the main highway at Jupiter, to the north, and Lake Worth, to the south, and allow in only those with legitimate business. On Friday, September 21, relief worker R. T. Eubanks, who had driven from Miami to West Palm Beach with a load of furniture, reported that two gunmen had robbed him on his way back as he passed through Fort Lauderdale. They took $13 and his pants.

At the island town of Palm Beach, mansions had been reported open and being looted. One wealthy family reported priceless paintings had been torn from their frames by the winds and were lost. Officials declared martial law for the island on Wednesday but rescinded it the next day. One by one, the wealthy denizens of the island called from their primary residences up north to approve repairs. Mayor Barclay Warburton, like almost everyone in the town a part-time resident, finally arrived from Philadelphia September 23 and right away began directing cleanup. His home, on the west side of the island, had itself been among the most damaged in Palm Beach. Warburton found a shrine to the Virgin Mary surrounded by floating debris. But the lady was undamaged. Warburton predicted the catastrophe would be no setback to the coming winter season.

By Saturday, September 22, Joe Youngblood, superintendent of Palm Beach County schools, called on children in adjacent Broward County to donate clothing, "especially underwear, sizes 2 to 14." The vice mayor of Lake Worth wired Fort Lauderdale's mayor, saying, "several gangs of negro laborers were badly needed." The Delray Beach city council ordered all able-bodied men pressed into service and said anyone seen walking the street without a job will be given one, and that everyone would be fed "and properly cared for."

Help had come by water as well. In a flotilla of flat-bottomed skiffs and fishing boats, a team of volunteers, many of them members of the city's swimming team, left from Fort Lauderdale and worked up the North New River canal toward Lake Okeechobee. Still, the coast—and the world—had only a small idea of what had happened in the interior.

But slowly, slowly, slowly, everyone was beginning to realize they were looking at more than a bunch of damaged buildings.

The *Miami Daily News* on Tuesday placed the unofficial total death toll at 225. The next night, that estimate had nearly doubled, to 400.

In Pahokee, Carmen Salvatore's brain could not absorb what he was seeing. He walked almost like a zombie. He found himself in town, where survivors gathered to share experiences, each more horrible than the last one. But they also knew it was time for action. They organized a group and gathered 400 volunteers. The time to grieve and swap war stories was over, at least for now. They had to start cleaning up.

The Interior

September 16–25, 1928

"Ugly death was simply everywhere."

Why did so many die?

The myth is that a hurricane will kill you by hitting you on the head with flying timber or a flying car or bring your house down around you or throw it, and you, across the street. But the deadliest storms on record have not killed that way. It was the water, the water, the water.

"Storm surge" is an ominous term for what forecasters say is the deadliest aspect of hurricanes: a rising tide of water, aided by the hammering effect of breaking waves and driving wind, that can arrive as much as five hours before a storm. It can cover tall buildings and drown people many miles inland.

In Galveston in 1900, storm surge raised the Gulf of Mexico on one side and Galveston Bay on the other, and the barrier-island city was essentially underwater. The surge knocked down houses and created a giant line of debris that smashed everything in its path.

The two most powerful storms on record did most of their killing that way as well. The "Labor Day" storm in 1935 washed a rescue train and the track into the sea and inundated the low-lying Florida Keys.

During Hurricane Camille, in 1969, the surge was 23 feet at Pass Christian. It washed away a Gulf-front apartment house where about two dozen people had decided to stay and have a "hurricane party." A famous "before and after" photo set first shows a three-story concrete building—and then just its concrete slab.

In fact, Andrew, the storm by which the great monsters of the early twenty-first century will all be measured, was, for the most part, not a killer. Probably more than a half million people experienced hurricane force winds on August 24, 1992, and someone looking at photographs of entire neighborhoods that were flattened might presume a death toll of hundreds, perhaps thousands. In fact, only fifteen died. Not surprisingly, that apparent contradiction has spurred conspiracy groupies to allege authorities hid hundreds of bodies in refrigerator trucks or burned them hurriedly. They theorize leaders didn't want public panic, and since the victims were migrants anyway, no one would come looking for them—an ironic twist on the 1928 storm, when so many migrants were never identified.

Why did Andrew kill so few? Because their homes protected them, even as the buildings came down around them. Andrew made Biscayne Bay rise nearly 17 feet, but the actual stretch of coast south of Miami where it struck is not nearly as densely populated as areas just a few miles to the north. There is no protection from a flood. That's why meteorologists and emergency managers use the elementary mantra "hide from wind, run from water."

And so, in 1928, the second deadliest hurricane in history had killed so many not from strong winds that smashed buildings, not from buckets of rain that turned streets into waterways and creeks into raging rivers, not from the ocean surging onto land like a bulldozer. It had killed thousands in a way unlike any storm before it and, probably none since: Its wind had pushed water from an inland lake and spread it across the land in a moving engine of death. And it had been aided by the flimsy dike built in a foolish bid to stop it. Had the water poured out of the lake gradually, it would have killed many. But by building up behind that five-foot dike, then bursting out, the water washed people and houses away and killed thousands.

How many would die today? Probably very few. Today, people would be warned and evacuations would be ordered. The lake now has a towering, presumably trustworthy dike. Like a twenty-car pileup, the recipe for catastrophe at Lake Okeechobee, Florida, in 1928 required a series of unrelated conditions to all collide in one place at one time; a shallow lake, an inadequate dike, lack of communication, few evacuation routes, a flawed forecast. And a storm coming at such an angle that the surge came not from the coast, the most populated area, but onto the land from the great lake.

On Monday morning, Glades resident Chester Young began helping with the bodies.

"Ugly death was simply everywhere," he would recall.

Arriving at one site, Young was handed an ax and told to start chopping at debris while another man dug.

"Within minutes, I caught sight of what he was after. A human hand appeared above the mud beneath the treetop. I felt a little sick at the gruesome sight, but I knew that would not work. I steeled myself and tried not to look." The hand was that of a woman of about twenty. The crew found four more bodies, of an older man and woman and a young man holding a small child. All of them were washed off in a water hole—perhaps for dignity's sake, perhaps just to help with identification—and placed beside the road where they lay mute, until another crew in a truck came to take them away.

Just who ended up in a coffin and who in a funeral pyre depended on the availability of a coffin, a passable road, and a vehicle. And coffins were not wasted on black victims.

About noon, Young's crew found an older woman who was alive but had a foot caught in the branches of a downed tree. She said her name was Aunt Hattie and she was waiting for her son and grandson to come and free her. Young's crew cut the limb that trapped her foot and set out to find her family. First they found the bodies of a young woman still holding a two-year-old in her arms. Aunt Hattie identified them as the wife and child of her grandson. The next body was that of Aunt Hattie's daughter-in-law. Then two boys, of about six and nine, and two girls, of about twelve and fourteen, were uncovered. Soon Aunt Hattie's son and grandson were found, also dead. The crew loaded a stupefied Aunt Hattie on a truck with the bodies of her family.

Young's team worked until it was too dark to see, then gathered around a fire; Young didn't learn who had been able to find dry wood. There, they had some hot food, coffee, and water brought in by truck. There was little conversation around the fire, and even that was hushed and muted. As dawn broke, the teams started out again. Within a half hour, workers found two bodies 50 feet from where they had slept. Young made the observation that bodies were always found north of their homes.

Later in the week, C. L. Reddick, an old settler, was found dead, his dog still standing by him and barking at rescuers. The animal had stood faithfully by his master's body amid the carnage for five days.

Dr. William J. Buck, Belle Glade's pioneer doctor and civic leader, worked for eighty-two hours straight both before, during and after the storm. His first acts called on his skills not in medicine but in leadership. He assigned American Legionnaires as foremen and had them recruit volunteers who used any tools they could to start clearing roads. The roads were choked with junk; some even had houses on them. By Tuesday afternoon, Dr. Buck's road brigade had made passable the three miles from Belle Glade to the agricultural station, the four-mile road to South Bay, and the mile-long road to Chosen. Most of the other roads were still flooded. Buck sent men to break open a nearby icehouse to provide fresh water. Some men broke the latch with an ax. A man, nearly frozen but alive, popped out. He'd gotten inside from the storm, but the latch had jammed, trapping him.

Buck then issued an edict: all women and children were to be evacuated to the coast. And there was only one way to do it: walk. More than one hundred women gathered their children and some belongings and, grumbling, began the grueling 40-plus-mile walk to West Palm Beach. They were hot and bone-tired and bruised. But they went. They got to the bridge 6 miles east of Belle Glade, where cars sent by the Red Cross began to ferry them to the coast. On September 25, Buck had a reunion, of sorts, with Glades residents in West Palm Beach, in refugee camps at the county courthouse and the Methodist church. They crowded around the man who had gotten them out of the flooding and into the shelters and camps, where they could get good food, clean water, medical attention and a roof on their heads. They said he had saved their lives by steering them down that road.

By Tuesday, people were already coming in to West Palm Beach from the Glades, dead and alive. The living arrived for help covered in scratches and cuts; the storm had torn their clothes away, leaving them helpless against the razor-sharp sawgrass that stands waist-high or higher in much of the Glades and had slashed victims as they struggled through floodwaters. Three Seminoles, who apparently had not seen the blooming sawgrass, were rescued in high water Monday night. They said they'd been separated from others in the storm and feared many were lost.

Frank B. Willits and Noel McAlister, who had been camping at Yellowstone National Park and followed Noel's hunch back to Florida, had driven almost straight through for three days and two nights to West Palm Beach. They found Noel's mother in a hospital. She said Noel's father and brother were dead. The three had piled into the family car and tried to flee the storm for the Hoffman company's construction barge, tied to the dock in South Bay, but the car had been blown off a bridge and the father and brother had drowned. She had grabbed wood and floated to a canal bank, where she lay stranded for two days.

On Monday, West Palm Beach blacks, eager for information and solace, had begun to gather at their unofficial town hall, Industrial High School. There, people were starting to come in from the Glades. The first to come in had been survivors, many of them hurt. All had stories to tell. Later, the dead began to arrive. They, too, told a tale, at least by their numbers. There were shouts of joy as families separated in the storm were reunited and shouts of despair as people learned their loved ones were among the dead. One man who had walked 12 miles from the Glades with his wife and several children was looking for his twelve-year-old daughter, who had become separated from the family during their exodus. Suddenly, the girl was brought in, alive. Rescuers in a car had found her on the road. By Tuesday night, survivors at the black school numbered more than 1,200.

For the first time, Clothilda Miller learned the storm had been even worse in the interior. That's where her parents had been. Clothilda and her siblings went to the school. Perhaps her mother would be there. "After all, a mother will try to get to her children," she would recall decades later.

On Tuesday, after two excruciating days with no news of her parents and brother, Clothilda was finally reunited with a relative from the Glades. But it wasn't her mother. It was Ernest Rolle, the brother-in-law, roommate and business partner of her father, Isaac Miller. Ernest had found the children at the wreckage of their home. He had to tell them what they did not want to hear. He said he and Isaac had sat down in their shack and watched as the water came up until they were floating out the door. They got separated. Isaac was a good swimmer. The two kept calling out to each other, trying to determine each other's location. Soon Isaac did not answer.

By the end of the week, Clothilda and the other children had made up their minds that their relatives would not be coming back from the Glades, at least not on their own power. They might already be here, among the dead. The kids would not look for them.

By that first weekend after the storm, relief workers had a new problem. To the north, rain-swollen waterways from the swollen Kissimmee River valley were emptying into the big lake. And the canals that spread like a spiderweb south of the lake, draining water to the coast, were jammed with debris or broken locks. As a result, instead of finally receding, the level was rising and the swollen lake lapped over what was left of the dike that had failed so spectacularly on September 16. Areas of standing water stretched to the western neighborhoods of West Palm Beach. Many of the few passable roads were flooding again. Officials issued an urgent call for motorboats.

The Coast Guard's Fort Lauderdale base, normally active at sea, found itself in the less-common practice of working inland. Boatswain C. C. Baum and four men, on a cutter and four dinghies, worked their way toward the Glades. Along the way, it picked up, on Thursday, 18 more men and four boats. They met up with 27 men from the West Palm Beach station and 56 men and seven boats from the Palm Beach station and a mobile reserve based at Fort Lauderdale. Over the next several days, the Coast Guard found 14 survivors and recovered 475 bodies.

Six bodies were brought in Monday morning to a hotel in Belle

Carmen Salvatore lived his entire adult life in Pahokee, dying at 98 in 1994. (1993 photo by E.A. Kennedy III, *Palm Beach Post*)

[INSET] Young Carmen Salvatore in his doughboy's uniform. He survived the horrors of World War I only to nearly lose his family in the great storm. (Salvatore family)

Clothilda Miller Orange lost her parents, brother, aunt and two cousins in the 1928 hurricane. In this December, 2000, photo, Clothilda, then 90, holds her parents' marriage certificate, the only family document to survive the storm. (James. W. Prichard, *Palm Beach Post*)

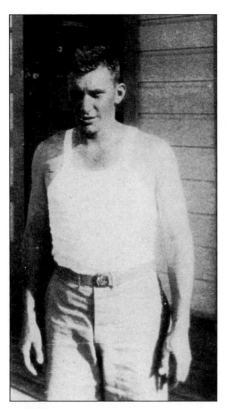

[LEFT] White National Guardsman Knolton Crosby shot and killed black laborer Coot Simpson on a West Palm Beach street. Simpson had been conscripted into the recovery effort. The shooting was ruled justified. (Cassie Mae Brooks) [BELOW] No photo of Coot survives. Simpson's son, Sanford, died in 1997. (Michele Julian)

The drainage of the Everglades early in the 20th century created a farming region along the shores of Lake Okeechobee that today is one of the largest sugar and vegetable growing areas in the United States. (South Florida Water Management District)

The Cathcart building in downtown Delray Beach, as it stood before the storm. (Delray Beach Historical Society)

The Cathcart building, smashed to rubble, after the storm. (Delray Beach Historical Society)

The yacht *Marchionese* is left smashed atop a seawall in Palm Beach. (*Palm Beach Post* archives)

Palm Beach County Courthouse (far right, with columns) is one of the few buildings left standing in downtown West Palm Beach. (*Palm Beach Post* archives)

[BELOW] The smashed Palm Beach Times building. (*Palm Beach Post* archives)

[ABOVE] A boy walks through the wreckage of his West Palm Beach home. (*Palm Beach Post* archives)

Downtown Belle Glade after the storm; roofs are torn off and a car overturned. (University of Florida archives)

An American Legion relief unit toils on body-burning detail at South Bay. (University of Florida archives)

[LEFT] One of the many bodies found floating in standing water in the interior. Rescue workers pulled them out and cremated them in giant pyres. (University of Florida archives) [BELOW] Seventeen bodies being burned with oil. Heavy rains hampered the burning. This fire started at 11 A.M. on Sept. 25; the photo was taken at 3:45 P.M. (University of Florida archives)

Bodies are loaded onto trucks at Belle Glade for transportation to the coast and burial. (University of Florida archives)

More than 5,000 people attend a funeral on Sept. 30, 1928, for the 69 white victims buried in the mass grave at Woodlawn Cemetery in West Palm Beach. (Florida Photographic Collection)

A 1999 map shows the site of the mass grave for 674 black victims of the 1928 hurricane, on Tamarind Avenue in West Palm Beach. Over the years, the tract that held the 1½ acre grave in its northeast corner hosted a slaughterhouse, a dump, an incinerator and a sewage plant. Map shows rerouting of 25th Street in 1964, which sent some of the road over the grave and neighboring graves from a pauper's cemetery. (City of West Palm Beach)

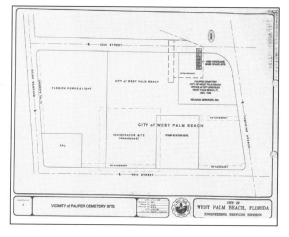

Robert Hazard, president of the Storm of '28 Memorial Garden Coalition, says a prayer Jan. 29, 2002, during the dedication of a historical marker at the mass grave. (Richard Graulich, *Palm Beach Post*)

[ABOVE] Artist's rendition of proposed memorial at site of mass grave of black victims of the 1928 hurricane. (Storm of '28 Garden Memorial Coalition) [BELOW, LEFT] Florida author Zora Neale Hurston immortalized the 1928 hurricane in her classic novel *Their Eyes Were Watching God*. (Florida Photographic Collection) [BELOW, RIGHT] Sculpture memorializing the 1928 hurricane stands in front of the Palm Beach County library branch in Belle Glade. (Belle Glade Chamber of Commerce)

Glade and laid out on pool tables. At the lake's north end, in the town of Okeechobee, twenty-five were reported dead. In Clewiston, west of Belle Glade along the lake's south shore, five people were reported dead and twelve homes destroyed, but there had been no flooding. At the Southern Sugar Company in Clewiston, later to become the industry giant U.S. Sugar, damage was minimal to both crops and buildings, including a new sugar factory not even finished. At the county cemetery in Ortona, 25 miles west of Clewiston, burials were under way. By Thursday afternoon, twenty-eight people, presumably identified, had been interred. To the north, Moore Haven—swamped almost exactly two years earlier the first time a hurricane toppled the Lake Okeechobee dike—reported no deaths or damage.

Lawrence Will had made his way from shattered Belle Glade to the experimental station Monday afternoon and hitched a ride in the trunk of a Ford to Fort Lauderdale, where he reunited with his family. His grim and frantic description to locals of the carnage inland helped spark relief. A flotilla of private and Coast Guard boats made their way up the Hillsboro Canal. Will helped navigate. The 50-mile trip took sixteen hours. A doctor on the boat warned his fellow rescuers his oath was to the treat the sick and injured and he wouldn't be stopping for the dead. Soon the rotting dead would themselves pose a threat to the living.

When the Coast Guard had arrived in West Palm Beach, the National Guard had not yet arrived. At Belle Glade, the Coast Guardsmen found people in private boats haphazardly trying to round up survivors and the dead and took charge, with the OK of Governor Martin. Later, the Coast Guardsmen commandeered a group of labors and, over three days, cleared the 13-mile road between Belle Glade and Pahokee, thick with tree trunks, muck, and "debris of all kinds of depth of from two to five feet," reported R. L. Jack, commander of the Florida East Coast Patrol Area. In fact, Jack reported, Coast Guardsmen found themselves playing "police, courier, mechanic, road building, burying the dead, butchering live animals, milking cattle." Along with its other supplies, the Coast Guard had brought 25 gallons of a special supply of Prohibition contraband. It was grain alcohol and strictly for the volunteers, to give them strength for their awful work.

Jack later suggested, perhaps optimistically, that "the loss of life would have been reduced by one thousand souls" had there been a house of refuge, 14 feet above the water on pilings. How he planned to get 1,000 people into one shelter, and keep out those who still wanted in once the place was full, Jack did not say. He did suggest Congress find the money or pay the price later once farming and population returned. "We can no longer stick our heads in the sand and say hurricanes do not strike the Middle Florida east coast," Jack wrote.

On Monday night, a relief worker and *Palm Beach Post* employee, R. N. Jones, had joined a caravan out to the Glades. He came back with a truck bearing the bodies of thirteen black people—and a grim pronouncement hinting at the carnage in the interior: he said this was "a small percentage of the corpses found floating in the hyacinth choked and muck filled canals," and added, "the loss of life was terrifying."

Relief workers fed survivors and took aside the able-bodied blacks, putting them to work collecting bodies.

About 11:00 A.M. on Monday, a team from the Florida Board of Health, based in Jacksonville, grew frustrated at the lack of news from the south and decided to head out. The group finally got some information from the *Orlando Sentinel,* but not much. Eventually, a messenger arrived with a note from West Palm Beach Mayor Vincent Oaksmith saying the area needed tetanus antitoxin and vaccines.

The following morning, the group made its way down the interior between Tampa and Orlando, arriving in Okeechobee in the afternoon. That night, the various agencies met and talked strategy. The next day, a survey team traveled by boat along the lakeshore.

In Clewiston on Saturday, September 22, American Legion officials asked for airplanes to survey the destruction by the air. The same day, at South Bay, some forty-one bodies still lay in a field within 200 yards of the main part of town. There weren't enough people to handle them, and relief coordinator V. C. Denton said they would stay there, covered with lime, "until we can get enough men to pile them up and burn them."

As individual corpses were discovered, they would be sprinkled with lime by searchers and a pole with a white flag set up beside them, to guide the gatherers. Hundreds of remains, so bloated they could not fit in caskets, were stacked like cordwood on flatbed trucks.

Considering the general sanitary conditions present in the 1920s, the fear that the storm's death and destruction and standing water would open the door for disease was a valid one. Health officials reported some cases of typhoid, tetanus, and influenza. But a report of a flu epidemic in Clewiston was later debunked. The Board of Health workers treated drinking water wherever they could with sodium hypochlorite and started administering typhoid shots at once; more than 8,000 people started the series of shots and the Board reported 6,490 completed the treatments. The group reported no great outbreaks, crediting its extensive vaccination program over previous years. By September 28, the state Board of Health declared area health conditions as "excellent," saying the anticipated outbreaks hadn't happened. Crews began putting screens on the barracks for blacks, to keep out mosquitoes, and building privies on the canal bank.

Ellsworth L. Filby, chief engineer for the state's bureau of sanitary engineering, kept a log of what he saw:

On September 20: rescue of a man who'd been clinging to a telephone pole since the storm. That day: intermittent rain. The wet stuff just added to the misery of those looking for survivors, collecting the dead, cleaning up debris, and trying to rebuild. Saturday, September 22: Began discussing plans for disposing of bodies. They agreed on cremation, using driftwood and oil. The gathering of bodies into piles was almost impossible, probably due to their state of decomposition. "Water $2\frac{1}{2}$ feet deep. Work very tiring and depressing," Filby wrote.

"Sanitary situation western part of Palm Beach County increasingly serious," disaster relief director A. L. Schafer wired Washington on September 20. "Bodies coming to surface. Necessary to bury bodies without identification." He also wrote that a new "negro cemetery" was being established at "Loxahatchie, sixteen miles west of Palm Beach."

In the town of Okeechobee, where twenty-five were reported dead, managers reported that bodies could not be buried there because the ground was too saturated, so they were being buried in Sebring. On the lake's northeast shore, a small informal cemetery stood on high ground in a settlement called Port Mayaca. Soon bodies were being sent there.

Eventually, a mass grave would be established at Port Mayaca. A marker atop it says it holds 1,600 bodies.

On Wednesday afternoon, in Belle Glade, people started constructing caskets. Palm Beach County Sheriff Robert C. Baker came in about 4:00 P.M. and said he was short of caskets. He told officials to load them on trucks. They would be driven to a collection area at the airfield in West Palm Beach to await burial.

In West Palm Beach, at the black cemetery along Tamarind Avenue, a large hole had been dug. By Wednesday night, 250 black corpses had already been laid into it. Orel J. Myers, the assistant medical director for the Red Cross, told the newspaper, "All white bodies will be held for 12 hours at Woodlawn," the official—that is, white—cemetery. "Colored bodies are being buried immediately."

It wasn't unusual for the newspaper to carry lists of name after name: "Marvin Lee and entire family. Three grandchildren of Oliver Wilder. Mrs. Raus and four children, newcomers to the community." Then: "Six negroes. Two negroes. There are from 100 to 150 negroes dead and missing in the South Bay section." The newspaper said 34 blacks had been buried in Pahokee and Belle Glade. No names. Brief announcements on the front page served as a bulletin board. James Felton of Lake Worth, feared dead, was safe. H. L. Douglas of Chosen, near Belle Glade, was looking for his wife and children and could be reached at the courthouse.

Thursday's newspaper carried a list of names of people for whom Western Union had undelivered telegrams. It ran across three columns.

Among the dead listed in the paper; five from the Schlecter family of Belle Glade. There was E. E. Schlecter, 50, and four children: 18, 11, 4, and 3. The four were Erma, Emma, Johnnie, and Kathleen, a neighbor wrote to a cousin in Indiana on September 20. Only Clara Schlecter had survived. She had floated on a log, holding little Johnnie, until a wave swept him away. Walter Schlecter had been out of town when the storm killed his parents, three sisters, a brother, and a niece. "I can't realize that the folks are gone and never to see them again on this earth," Schlecter wrote from the Glades October 25. "I feel like this is all a dream. I know it is so, but I can't realize it, but Mother and Father always taught me that if we lived our lives on this earth pleasing in His sight that we would meet again in Heaven; this sure helps to bear the burden we have to bear."

Charles Green had clung to the crossbar of a light pole outside the icehouse in Belle Glade. Separated from his wife and children, he held a memorial service for them, but he didn't stop working. Three and a half weeks later, he would enter a refugee camp in West Palm Beach and find his family, alive.

At mid-morning on Wednesday, 1,000 storm refugees in West Palm Beach, some of whom had been brought to the coast from the Glades, climbed aboard fourteen rail coaches—half white, half black—for relief centers farther south. The whites went down to Miami, the blacks to Pompano Beach. "As we walked through the destitute places," famed black educator Mary McLeod Bethune wrote in an article carried by several black newspapers, "our souls cried out to God for help, because He alone could sustain us under such conditions as these."

Frank Stallings and his father Festus had been driving straight through from Georgia since they first saw the grim headlines about the storm back home. Somewhere near West Palm Beach, a patrol stopped the car and told them it was impossible to go farther. Frank told the officer he didn't know if his family was alive or dead and he had to find out. The cop sighed and told him he'd have to bounce the car through piney woods just to get to West Palm Beach. There they somehow came across Stallings's sister, shaken and weeping at a church. But there was no time to console her. The Red Cross needed help out in the Glades, so Frank and Fred headed there.

Laborers had already been at work with axes and saws, chopping away at trees and buildings. The debris was piled along the road for some 20 miles. Frank and Festus had the grim job of helping pull bodies from canals. Workers would tie them behind boats and drag them to where they could be collected. Eventually, local health officials stepped in and said the crews would have to burn the bodies were they had piled them. Because the ground was wet, they used driftwood and crude oil as fuel.

A month earlier, the two-year-old daughter of neighbors Ray and

Grace Teague had proudly shown Festus the bracelet she had received for her birthday. Now Festus reached and grabbed the arm of a corpse. It was the little girl. His hand closed around her bracelet. Then he placed her in the pyre. Festus would say for years that it was the hardest thing he had had to do after the storm. For four years, Frank Stallings helped raise Butchy and Sissy, the Teagues' two older children, the only surviving Teagues, now orphans.

On September 26 alone, presumably following the directions of health officials, workers burned 267 bodies, 87 of them in a single pyre.

A National Guard unit from the Tampa area had been sent to the town of Okeechobee, and unit leaders left by car from Tampa late Monday night. September 17. They arrived in Okeechobee about 4:30 A.M. Tuesday. By midday Wednesday, the guard had helped recover nine bodies there. Eventually twenty-five people would be found dead or declared missing and presumed dead. A scan of the list reveals grim groupings of surnames that tell a story of families destroyed. Five Lees: one 78, one 39, one 22, one 3, one 4 months. Five Frasers; one 40, the others 7, 4, 3 and 14 months. Two adult Stevenses, plus two toddlers, one 5-month-old. Four Lightsey children. Three children of the Upthegrove family. The list also includes Old Man Hamlet and Old Man Yeats, hermits, both unaccounted for.

Around that time, Thomas Richard Brown, a National Guard colonel, arrived in the Glades from Arcadia, a small town about halfway between Okeechobee and Sarasota. "This is undoubtedly as bad a mess as I ever care to see," Brown wrote his father. "They are bringing in dead people all the time and they are swollen up about as big as cows and stink something awful."

Brown described scattered housing materials and dead livestock, adding, "I don't know what I will do when I smell fresh air again." He said the big lake reeked from the dead things in it and workers were forbidden to even bathe in it; fresh water for drinking and cooking came in on boats, which also brought antibiotics, perhaps penicillin, discovered only that year. Guardsmen were even forbidden to shave for fear of cutting themselves and becoming infected.

As Brown watched, a man who hadn't slept since Friday and was searching for his family came to a pile of bodies and found his father, mother, and wife, their clothes tattered, and "in awful shape." One man had just identified his fifth dead child. His wife was still missing. A man of about eighty identified his wife, "and when they brought her in with hardly a rag on her, that was awful to see the old fellow." Some bodies came in with skin and hair gone, their eyes swollen until they'd burst, their tongues protruding "longer than your hand." One man looked as if he weighed 250 pounds, Brown was told he'd been closer to 110. Brown said workers were placing the bodies in coffins and trucking them to high ground at Citrus Center—an apparent reference to the cemetery in Ortona.

"They appear dazed," one unidentified St. Petersburg Red Cross worker said of the survivors, "and some who have lost entire families do not realize it, but keep wandering around looking for someone they will never find."

Henry Martin had searched the Glades in vain for two days for his wife. Now, at 11:00 P.M. Tuesday, he found what was left of his family at Jackson Memorial Hospital in Miami. In the storm, the water had been rising in his home at Belle Glade. He had cut a hole in the ceiling and crawled into his attic with his wife and seven children. A falling timber knocked Lucy, 6, from her father's lap and killed her. The house fell to pieces and the family found themselves in the water. A gust flipped the board Henry and Henry, Jr., were riding out from under them and tossed it 15 feet into the air. As the wood came back down, it slammed Raymond, 13, killing him instantly. Then Henry Martin was separated from the others. Martin's wife, Thelma, grabbed Aaron, 2, and Ernestine, 7. She set the two up on the roots of an upturned tree, even as the tree snagged her. Though pinned by the branches, she managed to keep the baby's head above water. After the winds died down, rescue workers found the three and they were eventually taken to Miami. Henry, Jr., 9, and Annie, 16, had also been found and were at the hospital. That's where Martin found his five children. The pressure of the tree limbs had injured Thelma's arms and something had punctured her skin. She had an infection and a fever, but managed to tell Aaron and Ernestine, "Everything is all right."

On September 25, a weary woman struggled up the stairs to the newsroom of the *Palm Beach Post*. Her name was Thelma Anderson Dey. Her husband, Lewis Francis Dey, from New Jersey, had come to the lake area in the 1910s to work as a carpenter. He had married Thelma in 1920 and joined her family's commercial fishing enterprise at Moore Haven, on the lake's west side. The 1926 storm had destroyed the family's fishing fleet. Now they were finally getting back into the black. Frank and Thelma Dey had lived on a houseboat tied up to a barge near Moore Haven with their baby son, Vernon. Two other sons were visiting Thelma's mother in Kelsey City.

Worried that the boy might fall off the houseboat someday, Frank had tied it securely to a barge. They had heard no warning of the storm. When the water rose, the boat smashed against the barge. Frank tied Vernon to him with a sheet and the two adults clung to a door jamb as the houseboat came apart around them. After the eye, the storm came back more furiously. With Vernon still tied to him, Frank lost his grip. Wearing just a nightgown and kimono, Mrs. Dey struggled in the water for nine hours, once tearing the kimono to free herself from a nail. Nails, wire, and thorns had slashed her body. Her knee was crushed. Eventually her clothes were torn off her. Finally, Monday evening, her feet touched hard ground, on a sandbar built up by the storm. She lay on a bank, exhausted until she saw the forms of some men. She whipped off the remaining neckline of the kimono and waved it furiously. Determined not to fall onto the sand piled with dead fish and live, desperate critters, she stood long enough for the men to reach her, then passed out in their arms. She was 20 miles from where her home had been. When the man brought her by boat back to Moore Haven, relatives were waiting for her. Her body, torn and battered, was almost unrecognizable. As soon as the roads were passable, her family took her to Good Samaritan Hospital in West Palm Beach.

Little Vernon was later found dead in the flooded grasses north of the lake. Thelma told the *Post* reporter on September 25 that she held little hope her husband was alive but was checking with the paper anyway. The next afternoon, Lewis Dey's body was found. He was buried that night at the cemetery in Ortona, southwest of Moore Haven, next to his young son. In all, at least twenty-four people—seventeen white and five black—were buried at Ortona. The largest group—fourteen—were buried September 19 and 20, with a Baptist preacher and a Methodist minister officiating. "Let me thank the people of Moore Haven for the kindness and sympathy shown during the loss of my loving husband and baby," Thelma wrote from Kelsey City in the September 28 *Glades County Democrat*. "May God bless you all."

One of the most compelling first-person accounts came from a mysterious "Fred Harries," who left it on the desk of a Red Cross official in early October 1928. The official later begged without luck for help in identifying Mr. Harries. The man had come up from southern Broward County, apparently on the morning of Monday, September 17, and found the damage starting in earnest in the northern neighborhoods of Fort Lauderdale. As he moved north into the towns of Pompano Beach and Deerfield Beach, Harries found homes smashed, land underwater, bean crops that had been in bloom "swept as clean as a concrete pavement." He said farmers were already out hauling muck onto the denuded land to replant. Harries did not go into detail about what he saw in coastal Palm Beach county, opting to focus on what he saw as he and the others fought their way west into the Glades in wheel hub–deep water. In Belle Glade, "nothing was standing and everything that had been planted was simply drowned out and would never come up again," Harries wrote. Harries was surprised to see no buzzards. Locals told him they believed the birds were spooked by all the relief traffic and were happy to gorge themselves on carcasses, both animal and human, in the back country.

"When you think that 99 percent of the deaths were preventable, and at least 50 percent of the damage, because all this was done by water, it makes one think," Harries concluded in a fervent plea to somehow improve on the flimsy Lake Okeechobee dike, which had now failed twice in two years. "It is no use fooling with the question any longer. Real work must be done and done at once."

The story of Pelican Bay reflected the poor communications of the era—and the limit to which people on the coast knew or cared about the interior. Within days of the storm, stories were emerging that Pelican Bay, a tiny peninsula that stuck out from the lake's southeast shore, had been cut off and perhaps as many as 450 people on it were dead. Rescue workers couldn't get to it because of the flooded road and debris. That was the last mention by the papers. No more was learned because there was no village of Pelican Bay strewn with 450 bodies. The name refers to an arm of the lake. A small sugar-company settlement called Pelican Lake was about six miles to the north, near Canal Point. And there were enough real dead for anyone to have to write about imaginary ones.

On Thursday, September 20, gubernatorial candidate Doyle Carlton showed up in West Palm Beach with $10,000 in relief money in his pocket. Carlton had driven to Okeechobee on Tuesday to survey the damage, then returned to his hometown of Tampa to gather donations. On Friday morning, he took a boat ride into the Glades. "If the people of the United States could see what I did today, they would contribute generously," Carlton said.

Carlton had especially wanted to look at the dike.

On Friday, Governor John Martin finally toured the area after having driven down from Tallahassee. Blaming the technology of the time, he said he would have come sooner had he realized the damage was so serious. He called it "appalling." A total of 537 had already been confirmed dead.

"The people of Florida know nothing of the extent of the damage," Martin said. "They believe that the storm was nothing more than the usual Florida hurricane. I have seen enough, and heard enough, to assure myself that this is not time to let our pride stand in the way of our physical needs. The world must be told, for the world will respond."

The next morning, he dashed off a telegram to all Florida mayors, urging their cities to donate what they could. "Without exaggeration the situation in storm area beggars description," he said.

About midnight on Friday night, Martin, clad in white overalls, returned worn and heartsick to the coast after yet another trip to the Glades. Sitting on a bed at his room in the Monterey, one of West Palm Beach's least-damaged downtown hotels, Martin spent an hour with a gaggle of newspapermen, recounting his grim tour. He described keeping count of the bodies floating, or in piles, or on the side of the road beneath circling buzzards, or still lying on their porches.

Martin had spent a half hour talking to Levi Brown, a black farmer in the region since 1921. Brown had brought his wife, four daughters, and three sons to the roof to escape the rising flood, but his home had been smashed and everyone thrown into the water. He heard cries in the darkness and recognized one as that of his twelve-year-old daughter. A water moccasin that had climbed aboard the same log showed its gratitude by biting Brown; the man's right hand swelled enormously, but Brown said he had found the pain passable if he slipped it underwater. Brown worked his way to his skiff and set out for survivors. The first three he found were two white men and his twelve-year-old daughter. Brown later got a dose of antivenin for his hand and spent the next several hours helping rescue dozens people and identifying the dead. On Thursday, September 20, he found the body of his eight-year-old daughter. He later found another child, his oldest, dead on a heap of twenty-five corpses. His wife and six of his seven children, all except his twelve-year-old, had died in the storm.

When Brown finished his story, the governor did something unusual for 1928. He extended his hand to a black man.

"Brown, I am glad to shake your hand, and I wish Florida had many more citizens of your caliber, for you are a credit to your country," Martin said. He gave the devastated man $25. Another official gave him $5.

Brown would soon be a celebrity again, but not for his heroism.

From Pensacola, as far away from Palm Beach County as you can get and still be in Florida, a legislator wired Martin to call for a special session of the legislature, so that money could be moved from the state treasury for relief. Martin, who had also rejected a special session after Miami's 1926 storm, would later deny one for this storm as well.

Martin was back in Belle Glade on Monday, September 24. It had now been eight days since the hurricane struck. He toured the Glades by car and boat and issued a statement that "the destruction of property is enormous." He said that, while driving the six miles from Belle Glade to Pahokee, he counted six corpses floating in the water or lying in the road. Martin called on all cities in Florida to send whatever cash they could.

Thursday morning's *Palm Beach Post* carried new estimates that were moving into the level of the unthinkable. They said the death toll could pass 1,000. On Saturday, September 22, the Associated Press reporter in the Glades was quoting National Guard Captain G. G. South's estimate that the toll would triple to 1,500; "That is minimum, I think."

The day before, Coral Gables health chief Dr. A. F. Allen had said from the Pennsylvania Hotel in West Palm Beach, " "We have gone over the death toll situation pretty closely. When the final report is written, the general agreement among our doctors is that the total dead will not be far from 2,500."

On Wednesday, September 19, Martin had had finally activated the Florida National Guard, including two regiments in the West Palm Beach area. But as early as the day after the storm, a local lieutenant, J. A. McIntosh, had already taken it on himself to activate Company C, 124th Infantry. By Thursday, four days after the storm, the number of militia patrolling the streets was up to 161 guardsmen and 11 officers. One of those called to service: nineteen-year-old carpenter Knolton Theodore Crosby.

Cleaning Up and Rebuilding

September 1928

"What a joy it is to hear the birds again."

On Wednesday afternoon, September 19, three days after Florida had suffered the greatest single assault of death and damage in its recorded history, Gus Jordahn, owner of the famed baths on Palm Beach, followed a tradition that has been repeated every time Americans struggle to recover from disaster. He walked out to the ocean side of his property, unfolded a new American flag and hoisted it up his pole. A passing freighter, one of many heading south—perhaps part of the critical commerce now resuming, perhaps a relief ship—blew its whistle in salute.

South Florida was coming back.

By Tuesday morning, water service was already back on in central West Palm Beach, It was expected to expand as the day went on. The post office said it would try to restart mail delivery in West Palm Beach that morning as well. Garbage collection resumed and workers toiled furiously to move debris, spoiled meat, and rotting refuse before they became a health hazard.

At 5:00 P.M. on Tuesday, September 18, Howard Danner and Elizabeth Decker were married in the storm-damaged home of Dr. C. K. Vliet.

They were to have been married that evening at the home of Elizabeth's sister, but it was wrecked. A night wedding was out; power was not yet back. Invited guests were too busy cleaning up. So Vliet married them. The couple went to their nearby home, to the kitchen—the only dry room—where they had a candlelight dinner.

The Seaboard Air Line Railway, which operated just west of the Florida East Coast tracks, was back in full operation by Wednesday night. West Palm Beach Police Chief F. H. Matthews decreed no one except authorities could carry a gun. All Girl Scouts and Boy Scouts were expected to report to Red Cross headquarters Saturday morning.

On Wednesday, Mayor Vincent Oaksmith issued a "no work, no food" order, saying all able and unemployed men must offer themselves for work within twenty-four hours or face being drafted.

"Every able-bodied person in West Palm Beach is ordered to work," the *Palm Beach Post* said in an editorial on Thursday, September 20. Praising the quick restoration of utilities, the paper added, "let us all take our lesson from these examples. They have started rebuilding, they have taken care of the emergency, and they are planning for the future. Face the situation soberly, for it is grave, but remember that while we have people of courage, we have hope."

While every able-bodied person in the region was being ordered to work, the bulk of the labor fell on the usual group. Official reports, correspondence and news accounts all refer not to the armies of workers but to "negro workers," "negro laborers, "moving negroes to the scene." Some were paid. Some were not. Some went voluntarily. Some did not. By Wednesday night, only a few blacks had showed up to volunteer for the cleanup. About sixty were rounded up and drafted to dig graves.

Coroner Tom Rickards and his family, including his young son Tommie, had a lot of work to do, and they got help as well.

"Well, a nigger here is tearing away the debris so we can move our piano out," Tom's wife, Helen, wrote matter-of-factly to her sister-in-law, Kate Rickards, in North Carolina on September 23. "We've had to cover it with roofing paper. The roof is mostly off and the rain comes in like a sieve. Rain, rain, rain—almost constantly on all the rugs, mattresses, and clothes hung all over town. It's been a great catastrophe. But we're all right."

On September 27, Sheriff Robert C. Baker wrote Kate Rickards to say he was "pleased to inform you" that both his family and Tom Rickards' had survived the storm but that their homes were damaged "and the city was completely wrecked." But, he added, "We are getting the town and different places in the county cleaned up the best we can and I think we are making wonderful progress." He added that "the spirit of the people in general is marvelous and we are going to come back again in spite of all."

Willie Rawls, fourteen, of West Palm Beach, went over the bridge to Palm Beach and spent four to five days shoveling a foot of sand off Ocean Boulevard, the road that parallels the beach. After a grader was brought over, Rawls and another fifty men, presumably all of them black, went to work in teams of two with crosscut saws, cutting down damaged palm trees. He would say later he worked from 7:00 A.M. to 6:30 P.M. Back in Georgia, that was called "can't to can't." Can't see to can't see. The workers returned at night to a house Rawls shared with five other families. Rawls's family had fled their home in time to see it blow apart and had dodged boards as they raced for shelter. Rawls spent his first paycheck on clothes and worked for the city of West Palm Beach for fifty years.

The *Palm Beach Independent* was a rag that tendered opinion as reporting, peppered its columns with the N-word and spent far more time on the status of blacks than the news called for. It reported on September 28 the good news that a relief headquarters had been established by the Ku Klux Klan at—no surprise!—the offices of the *Independent*.

And in the kind of condescending, self-righteous, pseudo-benevolent racism prevalent at the time, a pageful of commentaries in the paper that day included a call that only proper authorities, not just private businessmen, had the right to conscript area blacks for cleanup work. It added, of course, that the blacks deserved to be properly paid for their forced labor.

The paper raised this issue because its very own janitor, a likable fellow named A. O. Arnold, had been commandeered by two men, at least one of them armed. The villains ignored the pass West Palm Beach officials had given Mr. Arnold, identifying him as an employee of the newspaper and exempting him from conscription. They took him and another black man to their private property on the south side of town, where they worked the two all day without feeding them or paying them a cent. The column said the two men were later afraid to identify their kidnappers and that Arnold returned to work too sunburned and worn out to be any good and had to be sent home.

"This damnable outrage was the act of a two legged skunk, pirate, and enemy of the public welfare and a coward," the columnist gnashed. "If such things are permitted, they will demoralize negro labor."

The next column down defended lynching as efficient justice; still another column on the issue added that "if any man in Palm Beach County commits a crime that deserves lynching, we will not only pay our share of the expenses, we will help pull the rope."

On Sunday night, September 23, Jews gathered at a community house to hold joint services of two congregations for Kol Nidre, the solemn service that marks the beginning of Yom Kippur, the Day of Atonement. The local worshipers reflected on the previous year and asked forgiveness for their transgressions from a God some may have thought had abandoned them. Others believed that, in the brunt of a tempest, God had stood with them.

The newspapers began offering free ads for those seeking work or workers. It also warned of outsiders coming in to profit heavily from rebuilding storm-damaged buildings. Stores ran advertisements saying, "moved temporarily," "temporary quarters," "our merchandise is not damaged," "ready for you: a clean, fresh stock of groceries." By September 28th, newspapers were full of ads assuring residents things were returning to normal. Everyone's gas service should be back. The water was uncontaminated and safe to drink. As soon as Frost's Hardware's insurance adjuster released the stock, the place would reopen "with some very attractive sacrifices."

Even the *Atlanta Journal* opined, "The devastated sections will come back, stronger and finer than ever. It is the invincible Florida spirit that misfortune does not break."

The town of Palm Beach had been left out of relief efforts. The mayor, in a letter to the Red Cross, said the wealthy island had relief money for the few of its residents who needed help.

On Friday morning, September 21, after two days of rain and a week of hell, the sun came out.

Cleaning Up and Rebuilding

"What a joy it is to hear the birds again after thirty-six hours of the howling wind," The *Delray Beach News* said in an editorial that day. "The little bird breaks into song and rebuilds its nest after a calamity as great to him as it is to us. It may be difficult just now to smile and sing but that is the spirit that will win."

In the same edition, Delray Beach Mayor Lysle W. Johnson, himself hobbled by a bad ankle injured in the storm, said in a front-page message to citizens: "An all-wise Providence has seen fit to visit us with this disaster but we are taught that all things happen for the best and we certainly have plenty to be thankful for." He concluded, "Let us all go forward shoulder to shoulder. Carry on!" A week later, the newspaper sought to comfort readers by pointing out that separate floods had killed 100,000 and 900,000 in the past in China. "In China the people are killed like flies whenever a disaster comes," the paper opined. "The deathlist would have been a hundred thousand had Palm Beach County been a Chinese province." Apparently this was meant to make everyone feel better.

On Sunday morning, September 23, perhaps the most telling symbol that the famed resort region was returning to normal: the *Palm Beach Post* resumed its society column. Four days later, on September 25, in New York, the Giants split with the Chicago Cubs in a doubleheader. They had to make up the September 19 game that was rained out when the hurricane passed through the Northeast after slamming Florida. The Giants would eventually drop three of four to the Cubbies and lose the National League pennant to the St. Louis Cardinals.

On Thursday, September 20, the West Palm Beach city commission, in special session, approved an anti-gouging ordinance. Anyone selling something for more than its pre–September 16 price could pay a $500 fine and go to jail for up to 30 days. Within hours, a merchant who had doubled the price of hamburger meat, and a gas-station operator who had hiked kerosene from 20 cents to 25 cents a gallon, were each summarily charged and convicted in a special municipal court and sentenced to 30 days in jail. The shopkeeper was also fined $250 and the kerosene gouger $100. The jail sentences were later suspended, but the merchants still paid the fines. The town also required all local merchants to submit price lists. By Saturday, West Palm Beach police reported crime was down by 75 percent, with only ten arrests made for the week, most for drunkenness or reckless driving.

Arthur Stokes, a black worker arrested for murder before the hurricane, had to be released. All the witnesses had died in the storm. Deputy State Hotel Commissioner Pat Houston was believed to have fled with a large amount of state money. His name was cleared when his body was found near Pahokee.

The school year set to begin on Monday, September 17, obviously had not. But Palm Beach County leaders said damage to schools was less than $500,000 and was covered by insurance. Officials hoped to open for classes two weeks late, on October 1.

By the second weekend, September 29, the police had passed down the word to drifters: you have twenty-four hours to get out of town or risk being arrested for vagrancy.

As would happen six decades later, after Hurricane Andrew leveled southern Dade County, the 1928 storm brought up the issue of how well buildings were constructed.

"I have been on the east coast of Florida for more than 40 years," said Alexander J. Mitchell, the meteorologist in charge of the Jacksonville weather station. "I have seen many storms. The one which blew here a few weeks ago was no more intense than many which have blown in the past. The difference lies in the fact that today there are more buildings to face the brunt of the wind. And as so many of them are poorly constructed, naturally the damage is great."

In West Palm Beach, Nat Pierson, the city's building inspector, noticed something common in all the homes that had come off their foundations: those foundations were just blocks of concrete on which the homes had sat, secured by nothing more than gravity. When the wind slid buildings off their foundations in the wind, they usually collapsed. After the Red Cross arrived to make repairs, its building adviser, A. D. Rieger, prescribed bolts and poured concrete foundation anchors. Pierson said that would eliminate 80 percent of the potential for destruction. The Red Cross had become an early champion of a concept that hurricane researchers, engineers and government officials would preach with a vengeance in coming decades: mitigation. Build right in the first place, they said even in 1928, and you limit damage in a disaster.

The hurricane did do a favor for the Port of Palm Beach. It washed away a sandbar that had blocked the inlet to the ocean, deepening the channel from 14 feet to 17 feet and saving the inlet commission as much as $40,000 it had planned to spend to clear the inlet before the storm did it for them.

South Florida found itself in a "spin" quandary. If it downplayed the disaster, donations would drop. But extensive reporting of the catastrophe would also discourage tourism, the state's lifeblood, and the infusion of new businesses, so critical to pulling Florida out of the economic woes that had settled on the state even before the storm.

On September 27, Palm Beach County Red Cross Chairman Howard W. Selby traveled to Washington, Philadelphia, and New York with former Palm Beach Mayor Cooper Lightbown and *Palm Beach Post* business manager W. A. Payne. They wanted to counteract the newspaper reports that had understated the devastation. But Florida also declared October 1–6 "Post Card Week" and urged people to send as many as a dozen notes each to family and acquaintances up north to dispel rumors about damage and encourage Northerners to visit the Sunshine State.

Tampa banker L. A. Bize wrote state newspapers just days after the storm to say that grim news reports were hurting the state and that storm damage was "greatly exaggerated." Actually, Bize was correct in suggesting the damage, although staggering, had been mostly limited to coastal Palm Beach County and Lake Okeechobee. In fact, he said, with Porto Rico's crops so devastated, Florida had a chance to exploit the tragedy. "There is no occasion for any pessimism in Florida as a result of this little blow," Bize wrote, apparently still oblivious to the piles of bodies in the farm fields to his southeast.

Also in Tampa, Peter O. Knight, a lawyer and civic activist who would later have a municipal airport named for him, telegraphed national columnist Arthur Brisbane on Monday, September 17. "Dispatches sent out from Florida concerning so-called hurricane positively malicious and criminal," Knight wrote. "The velocity of wind in Tampa has not exceeded 30 miles per hour. No damage here and damage to entire state negligible."

Knight's arrogance, coupled with his obvious ignorance of the

situation, left overwhelmed relief workers on the other side of the peninsula astounded and furious. "We are face to face with dire necessity and are
in severe straits," Palm Beach County Red Cross Chairman Howard W. Selby
retorted. "Yet, Colonel Knight, from a comfortable office building in Tampa,
has the presumption to ask Brisbane to use his column for telling the people
of the United States that the storm did only 'trivial damage' to Florida."
Selby added in a telegram directly to Knight: "If you are to serve as
spokesman for entire state, won't you kindly make personal visit here? We
are distressed and need the help of the nation." And the *Okeechobee News*
called Knight "a jackass" who "stayed in his office and send [sic] out a message minimizing the worst catastrophe in the history of the United States."

Florida got support in strange places.

For years, northern newspapers had trashed Florida—partly from
envy and partly from panic as Northerners and their money fled en masse
to the new paradise. The *Wall Street Journal* wrote a series of editorials
pointing out that damage from previous storms had often been greatly
exaggerated and wondered if this was now the case in Florida. The *Journal*
insisted the $5 million Florida had initially requested for relief would prob-
ably cover everything. (The final estimate was $75 million). In any event,
the newspaper claimed erroneously, Florida was rolling in money anyhow.

The *Grand Rapids Herald* responded with an editorial on September 28 railing against its national counterpart. The Michigan newspaper was astounded that the *Journal* had charged the Red Cross's
dramatic cry for assistance was actually an attempt to "give Florida a
black eye" by exaggerating the disaster. The *Herald* opined, "If you have
difficulty following this logic, don't blame us." The editorial concluded,
"The *Wall Street Journal* may be content to serve up stones when the
suffering ask for bread. It is nothing short of ghoulish."

The *Fort Lauderdale Daily News,* all but untouched by the storm,
had a different complaint. It wrote on Friday, September 21, that a
Chicago newspaper had used damage pictures of the city from the 1926
storm and was saying Fort Lauderdale had been smashed by this new
hurricane. "These pictures . . . are published by the *Chicago Tribune*
which admits of itself and for itself that it is 'The World's Greatest Newspaper,' " the Fort Lauderdale paper fumed.

Shortly after the storm, a writer named Don Morris published and sold a booklet filled with details and pictures. He claimed to be the first reporter on the scene, even though the region had several newspapers whose staffers had lived through the storm, including those from the *Palm Beach Post*. And he said of the dead, "nearly two-thirds were negroes, and the death panic among the simple and superstitious black folk must have been terrible to witness."

By Friday morning, September 21, most people had been moved out of the Glades. Buzzards had returned and their lazy circling was helping crews find bodies. On Saturday, a group of blacks arrived with a new baby, born on a barge in the floodwaters on Tuesday. Also that day, a haggard man walked into the Salvation Army headquarters at the West Palm Beach Chamber of Commerce building. He had a pile of baby clothes to donate.

"You don't need these?" the attendant asked.

"No. She was blown out of my arms Sunday night."

The Florida Children's Home Society, in Jacksonville, arranged for the placement of orphans—white ones. Placement of black orphans was left to the Richmond, Virginia–based Commission of Interracial Cooperation. On Friday, the number of blacks housed at a Pompano Beach horse track had swelled to 1,000. Thirteen white survivors were taken to the Broward County Courthouse in Fort Lauderdale.

On Monday, September 24, a state agriculture inspector in central Florida blocked shipment of any fruit knocked off trees by the storm and now on the ground for more than a week. The same day, twenty-five Glades farmers met at the county courthouse in West Palm Beach with a federal agriculture agent. If they could get some money, the men said, they wanted to return to their farms and start to replant crops.

On September 25, the city of West Palm Beach had announced that 2,881 homes were damaged beyond repair and 700 were destroyed. Some 8,200 whites and 4,000 blacks were homeless. The Red Cross would eventually pay $471,770 to victims or vendors and help 12,707 families in the storm area. The agency set up twenty-two feeding centers where workers distributed prepared food packages. Shipping and railroad lines shipped used clothing to the region for free. Salvation Army volunteers labored to unload, sort, clean, and eventually divvy up the garments. Fort McPherson, Georgia, near Atlanta, shipped 2,000 cots and 1,000 blankets. The military sent more bedding as the demand grew.

Shelter became a dramatic concern. Homes still standing had lost roofs or at least windows, and the days of rain following the storm kept everything miserably wet. From 8:00 A.M. Sept. 15 to 4:00 P.M. on September 22, 18.42 inches of rain had fallen on the West Palm Beach area. Work crews started on homes, nailing down temporary paper roofing. Shelters were set up in schools, churches, government buildings and warehouses. The peak in West Palm Beach was Tuesday, September 20, with 11,000 people in shelters. Winter residents still up north sent word to have their empty homes opened for shelters.

At the height of its mobilization, the Red Cross had 93 cars of volunteers averaging more than 500 trips a day and some 50 trucks making about 200 trips from supply centers to the needy, plus 38 boats and 4 airplanes in operation.

But by November, the agency had to deal with politics as well as recovery.

On November 20, the Red Cross came under fire from George O. Butler, a West Palm Beach commissioner, over "alleged inefficiency" in the running of the refugee camps in the city. Butler called for the agency to open its books and said he'd received many complaints in the two months since the Red Cross first arrived, just after the storm.

"What I have been able to learn is not at all creditable to the Red Cross," he said. "It's a shame the way they've been doing business here."

Butler said people who asked for help were turned away and sometimes insulted. He said he worried that about $1 million raised to help Florida victims would go back to the general coffers in Washington. A similar complaint would dog the Red Cross and cause controversy after the September 11, 2001 terrorist attacks in New York and Washington.

Ruth Mettenger, the supervisor of nursing services for the Red Cross, said she had asked Ettenne Baker, one of the complainers, for a list of people not receiving proper care so she could look into it. Baker said she had a list, all right, but was taking it to the West Palm Beach City Commission.

"She made insulting personal remarks about the nurses and said that it was impossible for patients to get admission into the hospital tents," Mettenger wrote in a statement to supervisors. She said Baker listed one woman she said had received no help for a broken shoulder; "When I told her this was an untruth, she stated that I was a crook the same as all the other Red Cross workers, that we were keeping the money in order that we may dine at the finest hotels and receive exorbitant salaries, that the poor patients that were lying in bed were deprived of the cream off their milk in order that the nurses may use it. After more slander of the Red Cross, I felt there was nothing further to be gained by remaining, which was a fortunate decision on my part, as Mrs. Baker ordered me out of her house."

At its November 21 meeting, the West Palm Beach City Commission heard a letter from the Red Cross that both defended its action and expressed the wish that the commission would have brought its concerns directly to the agency instead of to the press.

In a November 30 letter to his bosses in Washington, A. L. Schafer, the Red Cross's West Palm Beach–based head of recovery, did acknowledge some problems with milk and clothes getting to the most needy but said they were being worked out. He also said that after the city commission meeting, other commissioners contacted the Red Cross to distance themselves from their colleague, George O. Butler. But Schafer reported that Butler's remarks had prompted an explosion of public criticism of the politicians and support of the agency. He said it was so overwhelming that everyone decided no meeting between the commissioners and the agency was needed.

"While we might have gone to the Commission and demanded retraction, I have thought it best to maintain a dignified silence and continue to saw wood," Schafer wrote to headquarters in Washington. He suggested the best strategy was to let the matter collapse of its own weight. Headquarters wrote back in agreement on December 7.

Even the *Palm Beach Independent,* more a racist and reactionary rag than a legitimate agent of local influence, stood up to support the Red Cross, saying "mistakes are going to be made" but that the agency was doing the best job possible under the circumstances.

167

In the 1920s, race infused every aspect of life, and while plenty of the usual discrimination followed the storm, complaints or exaggerated or nonexistent slights complicated matters.

"Our people are experiencing the worst treatment in refugee camps set up by the Red Cross," J. Winston Harrington, correspondent for the black newspaper *Chicago Defender,* wrote on September 21. He said National Guardsmen had arrested hundreds of the homeless men, women, and children on "flimsy charges" that they had stolen food and clothes. And the *Defender,* noting the state's history of lynching and brutal convict labor practices, said in an October 6 editorial, "Florida, despite its beautiful climate and tropical splendor, is one of the most unhealthy states in the Union as far as we are concerned." The paper wondered if the twin disasters, the hurricanes of 1926 and 1928, were a divine sign, adding, "justice has been known to come from such a chaotic condition of this."

While the correspondent was heavy on vitriol and short on facts, the National Association for the Advancement of Colored People was more pensive. The NAACP organization walked a fine line, standing strong for black rights but struggling to work within the system and refrain from the kind of exaggeration or inflammatory shouting that could only hurt the cause. After all, there were enough real outrages against blacks without people such as the *Chicago Defender*'s J. Winston Harrington making them up, or at least reporting rumors and exaggerations as fact.

On September 27, NAACP officials wrote their West Palm Beach contact, Alonzo Holly, about the various allegations. "We naturally would want to get the facts, but, our funds being limited, we are reluctant to spend several hundred dollars that an investigation would cost, unless we are reasonably sure that there is sufficient cause," NAACP assistant secretary Walter White wrote.

Harrington's diatribe would soon be eclipsed by a campaign that also mixed both real and imagined slights against blacks. In targeting the Red Cross, this new campaign picked on just about the only agency that was color-blind, or at least as much as any group could be in the Deep South in 1928.

Enter the Negro Workers Relief Committee.

Black and White

"Hurricane Devastation—Then Jim Crow Discrimination"

On October 30, 1928, Colin Herrle, the Red Cross's recovery coordinator for the Glades, wrote A. L. Schafer, the agency's West Palm Beach–based head of overall storm recovery. He reported on a meeting held that morning with A. L. Isbell, "field organizer" for the obscure Negro Workers Relief Committee, headquartered in New York.

"We had a very agreeable meeting and I believe he left satisfied with the idea that we were doing everything possible to eliminate any discrimination in the handling of the white and the colored cases."

Herrle said Isbell mentioned a black woman who was sick; Herrle got a nurse on it immediately. He said Isbell complained that white victims got to pick through donated clothing, but blacks were handed clothes. Herrle said this might have been the case early on, but not now. Still, he promised to look into it.

Herrle admitted most of the rationing was going to white families, but said that was because blacks were able to find work, presumably in cleanup or collection of bodies.

"Personally, I rather feel that the whites are getting a little bit better

169

of the argument on this point, but very little," Herrle conceded. He said he hoped to iron out the discrepancy.

Herrle continued that Isbell was in the area gathering information and that he'd asked Isbell to alert him to any complaints or special cases so Herrle could get right on it. "On the whole, I think he [Isbell] was pretty well satisfied when he left," Herrle concluded. "Should you ever see his report, I wish you would send me a copy."

Isbell reported, all right.

The workers committee distributed a blistering attack on the Red Cross in a circular titled "Hurricane Devastation—Then Jim Crow Discrimination," with photographs, dramatic headlines, and excerpts of letters it said it had on file. The testimonials, reportedly written the first week of November by black South Florida storm victims visited by Isbell, "tell their own pathetic story," the committee raged. The committee said most black victims had received no aid from relief groups, including the Red Cross, and blacks had had to depend on their own ranks "and with the white class-conscious workers who have from time to time co-operated with us."

The committee's circular then ran a list of incidents. Some of its reporting may have actually been true or partially true, but the organization provided no full names of alleged victims and offered no source or documentation for its claims. Among the claims: A Fort Lauderdale woman who lost everything was given $4 for food for a family of five. When she returned a third time, "They drove her away from the station." A family of nine got only $3, another only $5. The circular then described more serious charges, again without any documentation. A Fort Lauderdale man with a family to support said the Red Cross "has done nothing for them at all, but has tried to intimidate them." And one more, this one probably true: the "state militia"—the National Guard—had picked up a Fort Lauderdale man on his way to Belle Glade to collect his children and forced him instead to work collecting bodies for two days without pay.

The committee called on "all organizations, Negro and white, upon the fraternal orders, upon the churches, upon every individual who has a heart and enough imagination to visualize the sufferings of these thousands of Negro victims of the storm and of white discrimination in the administration of relief" to rush aid—to the committee.

For the most part, the circular and a longer list of complaints distributed by the committee—anonymously, "to prevent retaliation on the part of white State and Red Cross officials against these Negro sufferers"—allowed as how the Red Cross had, in most cases, delivered help, just not enough for their liking. They gave no consideration to the sheer volume of the demand for help that was overwhelming the agency in both the islands and Florida.

In fact, the letters began repeating certain phrases word for word, an indication they were form letters of sorts or that the writers were been coached.

A Delray Beach woman said her home was destroyed and all the Red Cross could mete out was "a few old pieces of clothes and a few cans of tomatoes and potted meat and a small can of milk for myself and kids." And tar paper. And 100 pounds of fertilizer. And tomato seed. Another testimonial said the agency provided money for building materials, plus clothes and food. A Boynton Beach resident said the Red Cross "promised us some lumber if their money lasts but we haven't heard from them yet." From Deerfield Beach: "The Red Cross promised help but have done nothing so far, not even to give us money for food."

The *Chicago Defender,* in a story published November 3, quoted Grace Campbell, chair of the workers committee, as claiming the relief was running 80 percent for whites and 20 percent for blacks.

A November 16 statement by Campbell was even more breathless: "Too long have we left our helpless brothers and sisters and their children to the tender mercies of the Red Cross with its notorious record for deviltry and the vilest sort of discrimination in the Mississippi flood." Campbell went on to charge that, after floods devastated Mississippi in 1927, the Red Cross had set up slave pens to house farm workers, used most of the relief money for rich farmers, and used guardsmen to whip and kill black refugees.

Campbell recounted some of the earlier anecdotes from South Florida and added some: Black families with four and five children got relief cards for $2 in groceries while white families, some childless, got vouchers for $6 and $7. A pregnant woman who had been ordered hospitalized was still waiting for a bed. The Red Cross had hired no black staffers and sent white staffers into black homes to strong-arm families into requesting only the most minimum of aid. Campbell said the workers' agent—presumably Isbell—actually joined a body-fishing crew, and he and others had to eat at the rear of a kitchen "among the garbage and flies."

The workers committee's rants got into all the black newspapers, as far away as California, and the Red Cross was staggered. The last thing the group needed as it tried to distribute money and raise more was allegations such as this.

The local Red Cross would later refute most of the alleged cases of mishandling, except for those that carried no name and thus could not be investigated. Schafer wrote his Washington bosses that his agency was employing blacks, although he admitted he had no black caseworkers but said his staff was "entirely sympathetic" to blacks. He said any delays in rebuilding black homes were attributed to labor agreements between white and black carpenters' unions that barred white carpenters from working in black neighborhoods.

Schafer said the state health department—not the Red Cross—was handling the collection of bodies, and so he couldn't respond to any of Isbell's allegations about that. And he said most of the difficult conditions under which blacks lived were the same ones with which whites were contending.

The Salvation Army also stepped in to back the Red Cross's refutations and vouch for the relief agency's work. Mary McLeod Bethune telegraphed the NAACP's national office to say that she'd found no evidence men were being forced to work without pay and that in general she found no dramatic injustices: "I reached the scene the day after the storm for the purpose of interceding for justice and helping direct activities pertaining to the relief of my people. No power could intimidate or prevent me from protesting any injustice measured out to them. Will you believe me when I say that as far as I have been able to determine, this game in this disaster has been played absolutely fair?"

To make sure no one was neglected, the Red Cross had early on set up a Negro Advisory Committee. It rushed to defend the Red Cross, sending a statement November 8 "to state with great emphasis that it has met with whole-hearted cooperation on the part of Red Cross executives. Investigations made by the committee prove conclusively that negro storm sufferers are receiving adequate aid."

The committee said that, with six weeks having passed since the storm, immediate emergency help had given way to the more laborious process of identifying the most needy for long-term recovery money. It argued that blacks were getting their fair share of relief and said that, as a group, it "cannot but be embarrassed when ungrounded complaints are aired by chronic kickers. In this era of discrimination, it is a positive stimulant to come in contact with a group of white people so free from the prejudice complex. Red Cross workers are not inquiring as to color, but as to need, and with reference to actual storm losses."

Around the same time, the Red Cross debunked one damning anecdote. It was about a black man named Levi Brown—the same Levi Brown whose heartbreaking story had moved Governor John Martin himself.

The Negro Workers Committee had said that Brown, after an exhausting day helping collect bodies, had gone into a Red Cross mess tent, and was eating a piece of ham given him by a relief worker, when the director of relief work in the Glades "grabbed an 18-inch ax and made a ferocious assault on Brown, uttering the vilest oaths and telling him that 'ham was not for niggers.' " The report said Brown was struck in the head and shoulder.

On November 29, Herrle, the Glades-area director, telegrammed Schafer in West Palm Beach to say he'd met with Brown. The man said he had been struck with a meat cleaver, but not by the director, for whom Levi reportedly said he has "never had anything but kind words" all his life, or any other Red Cross representative.

Herrle followed that with a longer note that same day, with the story he says Brown told him: Brown had gone to a restaurant and requested a meal ticket for himself and his daughter. Three white people, miffed at the celebrity Brown was getting as a result of his harrowing tale of rescue and tragedy, began to give him a hard time and, when he tried to leave, one of them grabbed him and struck him in the face and back of his head with the flat side of the meat cleaver. The three finally let Brown go. Brown had said the director hadn't even been there during the attack, and he would sign a statement about the whole affair as long as the Red Cross checked out his story with the others involved.

Herrle went on to say that Fleming Ruttledge, the man who apparently assaulted Brown, would be glad to himself sign a statement. Ruttledge later did, on November 28, saying he struck Brown "following an argument in which he became impudent and called me a liar." Ruttledge also said the director wasn't even there.

"Brown, I imagine, would like to prosecute Ruttledge, but I doubt whether he would have any chance before a white jury and I should imagine that the best thing for Brown would be to have the matter quieted down as much as possible," Herrle wrote.

While the Red Cross had managed to clear itself of complicity in the attack on Levi Brown, the workers' committee's A. L. Isbell continued to go after the agency. On November 28, Schafer, the West Palm Beach-based director of the Red Cross' relief efforts, wrote his Washington bosses to say every complaint being circulated by newspapers around the country seemed to originate with the same person. Schafer wrote that the local Negro Advisory Committee identified Isbell as the only one stirring things up and that the committee was trying to shut Isbell down. Schafer said he had cooperated with Isbell when the man first showed up a month earlier, and that Isbell had promised copies of all his reports. But Schafer said he got nothing from Isbell and learned of his allegations only in the newspapers and the agency's circulars. In fact, Schafer wrote, he'd been told Isbell had run out of money and had tried, without success, to borrow from advisory committee members.

On December 13, Schafer wrote his bosses to say that Isbell's reports had made their way into still more newspapers and so far he had no evidence that a penny collected by Isbell for relief was actually reaching victims. He noted that West Palm Beach City Commissioner George O. Butler had backed off his initial criticism and "commissioners themselves now feel quite humiliated." But he said Isbell and his shadowy group continued to fluster the Red Cross.

Schafer told his bosses they needed to check out this Negro Workers Relief Committee.

Black and White

On December 3, A. E. White, New York representative for the Associated Negro Press, a cooperative of black newspapers, sent a telegram telling all member publications to kill a story on the committee and wait for a new one by airmail. The telegram said the committee had been linked to communists. The new story sent to the newspapers took the angle that groups were fighting "what they say are unwarranted attacks that have been made upon the Red Cross by irresponsible agencies." The dispatch was mostly a repeating of the entire statement by the Negro Advisory Committee defending the Red Cross.

The Chicago-based Associated Negro Press wrote the Red Cross on December 6 that the *Newark Herald,* which had printed a particularly blistering report, wasn't a member of the ANP and that other black papers which had written stories about the alleged mistreatment of black storm victims actually knew little about the relief committee but presumed it to be legitimate because its executive committee contained some of the most important black leaders of the time.

Claude Barnett, director of the Associated Negro Press, said Isbell had visited the previous day, armed with details about problems as well as a November 20 *Palm Beach Times* article criticizing the Red Cross and demanding an accounting. But, he concluded, "To wantonly attack the Red Cross for the purpose of raising funds for their own organization to distribute is manifestly unfair."

Now the Red Cross decided to do its own investigating. In December, it contacted a group called "The National Information Bureau." which described itself as "a cooperative effort for the standardization of national social, civic and philanthropic work and the protection of the contributing public"—in other words, a charity watchdog.

The bureau reported that, after two days of searching, it couldn't find any offices for the Negro Workers Relief Committee. It had sent people to the Lenox Avenue address on the Committee's letterhead; they found it had moved. The bureau went to three Harlem addresses linked to the group but found all in "ramshackle houses" over cafés or nightclubs and people there had never heard of the committee. Nor had anyone from any of the "reliable Negro groups" in New York. At one

Harlem address, the bureau learned that a man identified as the president of something called the Turf Club—usually a term for an organization tied to a horse racing track—had been collecting money for relief. But no one knew much about the man, and the investigators couldn't find any Turf Club.

The workers' committee sent another missive on January 3, 1929, now identifying itself as "formerly Negro Committee for Miners' Relief" and listing a new address at 169 West 133rd Street in Harlem. In this circular, the committee said it sent an investigator—Isbell—into South Florida and that "he found the Negroes doubly victimized; on top of the terrible storm devastation they are obliged to suffer discrimination and terror at the hands of prejudiced officials." The committee went on to say that, although millions of dollars had poured into the region, white families were recovering while blacks were still struggling.

"Only through the Negro Workers Relief Committee can these victimized workers and tenant farmers hope to receive unprejudiced aid," the letter said, adding that Isbell himself was distributing money to the needy. This was, of course, the same Isbell that the Red Cross in West Palm Beach had reported was out of cash and seeking handouts for himself.

In January 1929, the National Information Bureau, the charity watchdog group, wrote the Red Cross to say it had tracked the workers' committee to the offices of the Crusader News Service. Its editor, Cyril Briggs, was apparently the director of what the information bureau called a "very loose-jointed" group formed after complaints of Red Cross discrimination or inattention during the 1927 Mississippi floods. The watchdogs said all the group had done so far was to send Isbell from Chicago to check out the situation in Florida and had hired a woman named Susannah Paxton, "an organizer and a known radical" for two weeks to run the money-raising campaign.

The information bureau then went through the "executive committee" the workers' committee listed on its letterhead. The bureau said the legendary activist W. E. B. DuBois, editor of *The Crisis* and an NAACP officer, had not allied himself with the workers' committee, but had donated $50. A National Urban League official said he'd never heard of the group. William Pickens of the NAACP said he'd allowed his name to be listed but knew nothing about the group and had never attended a board meeting. Another person listed on the committee denied she was on it. Also, the bureau reported, the rector of a Presbyterian church said there was distrust of the committee because many serving on it were communists.

On December 21, John D. Cremer, associate director for disaster relief at the Red Cross's Washington headquarters, had contacted DuBois, who was in Washington for an interracial conference. Cremer asked him to stop by for a meeting. The Red Cross was not happy with its public trashing at the hands of the Negro Workers' Relief Committee. According to a Red Cross memorandum, DuBois told Cremer the group was young and impulsive and had there been legitimate criticism, he would have heard about it. But he did say the Negro Advisory Committee set up to help the Red Cross in South Florida was too conservative and should include perhaps even people from these radical groups.

DuBois was familiar with the heavy criticism the Red Cross had taken for the way it dealt with victims in the Mississippi River Valley, most of them black, after the disastrous floods of 1927. Red Cross Vice Chairman James L. Fieser told DuBois the Red Cross handled southern disasters with southern chapters populated by southern members. And, while the national agency believed in impartiality, "we, of course, were not able to change the economic and social conditions that had existed in the South for many years," Cremer wrote.

Eventually, even the Negro Workers' Committee affair calmed down. Meanwhile, on October 6, the last shelters were abandoned and the families still in need were concentrated in two tent colonies. The region began to move on.

The Red Cross had spent more than $1 million, a staggering amount in 1928, for building materials and labor to help rebuild 3,624 homes. It was four times what the agency had spent in any other category. In 81 cases, houses were shoved back onto their foundations. Another 704 were anchored to concrete foundation piers. The already-collapsing real estate market had left many people "property poor:" their homes were destroyed, while the owner still held mortgages now on the brink of foreclosure. The Red Cross's policy was to help the homeowner, not the creditor.

The farm losses had also been staggering.

C. W. Warburton, director of extension for the U.S. Department of Agriculture, which at the time also oversaw the U.S. Weather Bureau, was asked by the Red Cross to go to Florida. He arrived in the Glades on September 30. He reported back that the storm had destroyed virtually all the crops. But Warburton also reported farmers were in excellent spirits and anxious to resume farming.

The planting season had just started when the storm struck, and the land stood in water for weeks. The Red Cross rushed in seed, fertilizer, feed for beasts of labor, and fuel and oil for tractors. The Ford Motor Company sent two truckloads of parts and two mechanics to fix up more than 150 damaged and soaked tractors. The Palm Beach County Loan Farm Fund spent $100,000 giving out loans of up to $300 at 5-percent interest. Congress approved $15 million in crop aid to southeast farmers, much of it in loans to buy seed and fertilizer. Most of the attention was focused on the Glades. "Those people are very energetic and enterprising and are trying to return to their little farms," Florida U.S. Senator Park Trammell told the Senate Committee on Agriculture and Forestry on December 19. "It is all they possess: the land."

Statewide, the storm ruined what would have been the best citrus crop in the history of the industry, the Florida Citrus Exchange reported on September 26. So much for the self-important protestations of Tampa activist Peter O. Knight that "damage to entire state [was] negligible." The exchange said the storm's winds scratched much of the fruit, reducing the quality. It also reported 6 percent of the oranges and 18 percent of the grapefruits were lost. Especially hard hit was Polk County, east of Tampa, which lost 12 percent of its oranges and more than 33 percent of the grapefruit. In the Indian River region, between Palm Beach County and what is now the Space Coast, 20 percent of the oranges and 40 percent of the grapefruits were lost. Managers said harvesting would be delayed until mid-October because groves were flooded.

The storm would have been devastating enough had the area been at the height of financial health. But it came at the time when the great 1920s real estate boom had collapsed and South Florida was already heading into the Great Depression. For Florida, the one-two punch of the storm and its 1926 Miami predecessor had hastened what had already been a steep slide. In Palm Beach County alone, fourteen banks had failed in the year preceding the storm and banks that two years before had $50 million in deposits now reported totals of $10 million to $12 million. B. D. Cole, founder of the West Palm Beach–based insurance company of the same name, founded in 1919, said later that, at least for West Palm Beach, the storm was a blessing in disguise. Cole, noting that the collapse had started in 1926 or even before, argued the flush of insurance money into the area helped start its recovery or at least soften its slide.

Nearly a month after the storm, on October 12, Richard W. Gray, assistant meteorologist for the U.S. Weather Bureau's Miami office, made the difficult journey into the still-ravaged interior to make a first-person account for his bosses in Washington. It was like a descent into hell. Miami, the town Gray had watched the 1926 storm tear to pieces, was about 70 miles from downtown West Palm Beach, but even it had provided hints of this storm's power, in the form of some torn awnings and broken windows. Next stop: Hollywood and Fort Lauderdale, up the road in Broward County. Gray saw only slight structural damage, along with some broken windows and leaking roofs. Most of the losses were from water damage, and Gray figured a few thousand dollars would cover everything in those two towns. North of Fort Lauderdale was Pompano Beach, and it was there that Gray first started to see what the storm had done. He estimated losses were in the millions of dollars.

Then he moved inland. At the settlements along the lake's southeast shore, "The small houses in these localities were washed away or inundated," he wrote on October 23. "Practically the entire Everglades region south of Lake Okeechobee has been flooded, making it impossible for growers to prepare the land for the usual early winter crops." Gray reported crops in the Glades were still flooded a month after the hurricane. He wanted to emphasize the lack of major damage to major buildings, something he noted in the 1926 storm as well. He said that proved that well-constructed buildings can withstand the most powerful of storms.

On October 23, Florida National Guard Major B. M. Atkinson reported roads were dry and in good condition from Belle Glade east to

West Palm Beach, north to Okeechobee and west to South Bay. On the side of the roads, two feet of water still stood. Most of downtown Belle Glade still was under standing water; Atkinson said it probably would be for at least another week. Only 150 people were in the town. No one was doing repairs; it was impractical until the land was dry. Atkinson reported some minor scuffles, blaming them on idle and discontented residents of the smashed city.

Atkinson reported spotting one industrious man. It was Levi Brown, who had lost nearly his entire family, whose story had touched the heart of the governor of Florida, and whose assault had been wrongly blamed on a Red Cross official. Atkinson said he watched as Brown waded through flooded fields, laboriously but steadily planting peas.

Christmas brought few prospects of joy to those still recovering. From Junior Red Cross chapters around the country, children sent thousands of dollars. The agency assembled Christmas packages, with books, candy, and handmade cards done by art classes in schools around the country. The Salvation Army provided toys. The Red Cross also spent about $5,000 on new playground equipment, books, and other supplies for schools ravaged by the storm.

The Red Cross finally pulled its recovery team out of South Florida at the end of 1928, with the Palm Beach County chapter set up to receive national money for another two years to finish the job of rehabilitation.

"What a change has been wrought since they first came to us in those hectic days following the disastrous storm!" the *Palm Beach Post* said of the Red Cross in a January 6, 1929 editorial. "What a difference their efforts have made!"

In its recovery efforts after the 1928 hurricane, the Red Cross would spend nearly $6 million, $50,000 directly from its coffers and another $5.88 million in contributions. State-by-state totals for donations from people and institutions ranged from $1,038 from South Dakota to $1.12 million from New York. The agency spent $3.23 million in Porto Rico and the Virgin Islands, and $2.7 million in Florida. The Red Cross pointed out two key differences between the relief efforts in South Florida and Porto Rico: the island was mostly rural and Florida more urban, and relief in Porto Rico was on a "mass" basis, while in Florida "the wide divergence in economic status made imperative a case-by-case determination of need." Again, these totals would be tenfold in current dollars.

Monday, September 24, eight days after the storm, had been the first day that no bodies came in from the Glades. Workers were still finding bodies, but they were too decomposed to transport. They would still be finding bodies in late October—ten in one day on October 19. In 1930, two years after the storm, workers clearing a large pile of debris and parts of the failed dike from a railroad embankment at the state prison farm would find the remains of Glades resident Dave Burnett. He was the last storm victim to be positively identified.

Also on September 24, 1928, the National Guard began releasing guardsmen to return to their homes across the state and in West Palm Beach. That would presumably include guardsman and carpenter Knolton Crosby.

Railroads offered free passage for bodies, and for refugees who wanted to leave South Florida. By the first weekend after the storm, some 800 survivors had accepted the offer of a free ride. The total reached 1,427 through 6:00 P.M. September 28. The railroads finally stopped the practice amid complaints that the not-so-needy were exploiting their generosity. After that, the Red Cross ponied up fares, either full or half. The organization also guaranteed the return fare of refugees likely to find themselves welfare cases at the other end.

The train was how Coot Simpson had left town.

Coot Simpson

". . . in the lawful discharge of his duty."

When the Negro Workers Relief Committee had issued its blistering dia-tribe complaining of the treatment of blacks after the storm, it listed as case number one, that of Coot Simpson.

Who was Coot Simpson?

He could have been Coot, Coote, Coute, Cootie, or Cooter; various documents contain those spellings. His descendants say his real name was probably Hezekiah Christophe, or something close to that. In the Deep South, that sort of French name usually meant an origin in Louisiana or Haiti. But no one can now say for sure. Coot was a black man born in the late nineteenth century, and relatives or researchers in that arena can usu-ally forget about finding such luxuries as birth certificates or other doc-uments, home addresses, work histories, or photographs.

His relatives describe him as very dark-skinned, about 6' 2" or 6' 3", of slender build. Relatives say he had small almond-shaped eyes.

His death certificate says he was born August 25, 1893, somewhere in Alabama. Parents' names and birthplaces: unknown. His family says that, when he was a young man in Alabama, he had come across a white man harassing a black woman. He tried to come to her rescue, a fight resulted, and he killed the man. Before he could be arrested, he fled to Georgia on a freight train. It stopped in Surrency, a tiny town about 70 miles west of Savannah. Hezekiah asked if there was work there. There was, in the lucrative industry of tapping turpentine from trees. Hezekiah changed his name to Coot Simpson. With today's technology, the law would have almost assuredly tracked him down. But not then.

Longtime Surrency resident Wayman Wilcox, who was eighty-seven in 2002, remembered Coot as "an all right person" but didn't recall much about him. At some point, Coot married Juanita Bryant, a local woman. His relatives say it may not have been an official wedding, rather part of an old southern black custom called "jumping the broom." It's a tradition believed to date back to the 1800s, when slaves were not permitted to marry in church. The Simpsons had a son, Stanford.

The 1920 census for Appling County says that "Coote Simpson" was the head of his household in the "settlement roads" section of Surrency. He was 29. He rented the place with his wife, "Warnida." She was 20. Also: their son, "Stanfort," $4\frac{1}{2}$. Somehow the enterprising enumerator had managed a trifecta; he'd misspelled the names of all three. On top of that, Stanford's death certificate, in 1997, says he was born in January 1919, meaning he would have been younger than two years old when counted in the 1920 census, not $4\frac{1}{2}$.

The listing shows Coot as a native of Alabama and Juanita and Stanford of Georgia. All could speak English. None had attended school in the previous year. The adults could read and write. The baby could do neither. Coot was a farm worker.

Relatives say that, when the turpentine business dried up, Coot— like so many before him—looked south to the land of opportunity. He took Juanita and their son and Juanita's young sister, Sular Bryant, and moved to West Palm Beach. Coot got work draining swamps. And he did some gambling on the side and even ran a gambling house. One longtime resident said he was a landscaper on Palm Beach.

He was a world apart from K. T. Crosby.

Knolton Theodore Crosby, son of Floyd G. Crosby of Georgia and Hattie Hannong of South Carolina, was born on November 1, 1907 in

West Palm Beach. In April 1927, Crosby signed up for a three-year stint in the Florida National Guard, Company C, 124th Infantry. He was nineteen. His paperwork says he was 5' 7½" and weighed only 137 pounds. He had brown hair and blue eyes. His eyesight and hearing were normal. He was missing four teeth: two upper, two lower. He'd never had venereal disease. He'd never been convicted of a felony. He'd had eight years of education and four years as a carpenter. He was unmarried and had no children.

The 1928 city directory for West Palm Beach says Knolton Crosby was living at 505 35th Street. Coot lived "across the tracks," at 524 22nd Avenue. On the morning of September 23, 1928, documents later showed, Coot was living one door down from that, at 522 22nd Ave. He was twenty-nine days past his thirty-fifth birthday.

Everyone agrees on how the day ended for Coot Simpson. Everyone diverges on the details.

This is what the Negro Workers Committee said in its November 16, 1928 circular:

At the corner of Eighth and Division streets, Simpson was on his way to work when guardsmen ordered him, "Get on that truck, nigger." Coot called back that he needed to ask his boss if he could go, and started across the street. He did not run.

And this is what Coot's relatives have said over the years:

As guardsmen went through the city, rounding up blacks to help clean up and bury the dead, Coot was drafted. He worked for a few days. Juanita did not know where he had gone. He said, "Now, I'm going to go home," and started to find the foreman to let him know.

The guardsman said, "You can't leave."

There's no dispute about what happened next.

Crosby lifted his rifle and fired.

Coot's family says the shot struck him in the lower back and blew out his abdomen. He was killed instantly.

Crosby's nephew, Fred Scurlock of Okeechobee, says this is the story he had heard: Crosby and other guardsmen were rounding up people to help bury bodies. Crosby went into a bar and told Coot to come with him. Coot refused, then came at Crosby with a bottle, and Crosby shot him. Scurlock, born two years later in 1930, admits that, like all the others', his information is secondhand.

Cassie Mae Brooks, whose mother was Knolton Crosby's sister, says the version she heard is that Crosby went to someone's home, the person refused to go and got belligerent, and Crosby shot him.

"The other family is right in feeling they were wronged," Cassie said in 2002. "My father, particularly, was pretty prejudiced. They just didn't talk about it. Of course, I wasn't even born then. When we were children, adults didn't talk about things in front of children. I think it was after he died and some of the parents were talking about it. My mother did tell us one time that her brothers were, back then, they were kind of uneducated and real old Florida crackers and the guy didn't do what he told him to do and it wound up him being shot. I got the feeling that it was justified in the way that the man wasn't obeying what Uncle Knolton had been sent out to do. He tried to force him to go and he wouldn't go and they had a confrontation and he shot him. That's all I heard."

Coot's relatives said they believe the guard just panicked. But clearly Knolton Crosby would have known, even in that split-second of decision, that he had no fear of penalty. He was a guardsman keeping the peace in a disaster area. More importantly, he was a white man shooting a black man in the South in an era when such an incident usually prompted no questions. And, Coot's descendants say, his relatives were in no position to make a stink.

The Negro Workers Relief Committee said Crosby opened fire almost immediately.

An Associated Press brief that ran in the *Miami Herald* September 24 says the soldier shot the negro—both not identified—"who was alleged to have attacked him in the negro section of the city." The story says the soldier fired in self-defense but was arrested pending an inquest. Even that is a surprise for the era.

The September 24 *Post* carried a one-sentence brief saying that an inquest would be held at 2:00 P.M. "over the killing of Coote Simpson, negro, Twenty-second street, who was killed by the rifle of a National Guardsman on special detail duty at noon yesterday." That was the only reference to the shooting.

Relatives say Crosby's lawyer was Eugene Baynes, who had just turned forty-four and had moved within the previous few years from Monticello, Georgia, about 140 miles from Coot Simpson's former home town of Surrency. Baynes would be a noted criminal lawyer for two decades. He died in 1965, at the age of eighty.

The hearing lasted no more than a day. It may have lasted a few hours, or even less. The September 25 *Post*'s two-paragraph brief said the jury investigating the death of Coots—another spelling—heard from witnesses, including a police officer. Its official ruling: ". . . do say upon our oaths aforesaid that the said Cootie Simpson came to his death in the following manner, to wit: By a rifle wound inflicted by Knowlton [sic] Crosby, a member of Company 'C' 124th Infantry Florida National Guard, while in the lawful discharge of his duty." The coroner's jury, "good and lawful men of said County District," had declared the incident a justifiable homicide. The portion of Coot's death certificate for "cause of death" said, "jury verdict: gun shot wound inflicted by soldier in discharge of his duty." It was signed by the county's coroner, Tom Rickards, who had survived the storm in the very courthouse where he now presided over the acquittal of Knolton Crosby.

"Negroes ordered to load bodies at Pahokee and other Everglade towns were forced to do so at the point of a gun," Rickards' son, fourteen-year-old Tommie Rickards, wrote his aunt Kate in North Carolina on October 3. "One negro in town was shot for disobeying. They were better then."

The Negro Workers Relief Committee's circular said: "Simpson leaves a wife, too sick to work, and two little children, one a girl of nine and the other a boy of ten."

Palm Beach County Sheriff Robert C. Baker sent Juanita Simpson to George Carr, the Red Cross disaster chairman, with a note that said, "The bearer is the wife of Coot Simpson killed today by one of the Nt'l Guards. She has two children no money and wants to ship his body to Surreacy, Ga [sic]. Is there any way you can assist her, she will explain."

Carr took her to Zoe Goodrich, a Red Cross caseworker. She contacted the Florida East Coast Railway about its standing offer to ship bodies of storm victims for free. "But when they learned the circumstances surrounding the death of the man they advised me they believed it the responsibility of the National Guards rather than the Railroad's," Goodrich wrote.

So the caseworker went to Major Robert Ward, in command of the guard. Ward responded that the National Guard apparently had no money in its budget to pay to ship bodies of people they had killed. Goodrich went to the Guard's brigadier general, Vivian Collins, who told him to send his office the bill and he'd take care of it.

On September 26, Juanita and two children, aged nine and ten, boarded a train for southern Georgia. They rode for free. Also loaded aboard: the body of Coot Simpson. The shipping charge: $15.81. Coot was buried in a plot at the rural Rachel Baptist Church in his former home town of Surrency, Georgia.

Goodrich wrote that she later learned Coot was a military veteran and that he'd been issued a service certificate. A 2002 inquiry to military records centers would find no listing for Coot, but such listings, especially for blacks, are not complete. Goodrich wrote that Coot's service certificate entitled his daughter, Mattie, to a death benefit. Goodrich urged Juanita to see her after she returned from burying Coot in Georgia so Goodrich could help the woman file a payment claim with the Veterans Bureau.

"Juanita has worked about half time since her return to West Palm Beach at $2.50 a day," Goodrich's December 12 note says. "She collected $265.00 insurance at the death of her husband and the payment on the adjusted service certificate will be about $182.00."

Goodrich also advised that Juanita Simpson had a son, about ten, from a former marriage. That may be a reference to Stanford, although Stanford's death certificate does list Coot as his father. And, Goodrich said, Mattie was Coot's daughter by a previous marriage. Coot's relatives today say "Mattie" may have been Sular Bryant, Juanita's baby sister, whom Juanita was raising as a daughter.

In April 1929, Crosby was one of dozens of Florida National Guardsmen who received a state service medal for service after the hurricane. A report by the state's adjutant general said guardsmen's duties were "confined chiefly to guarding property in exposed buildings and rendering such other assistance to the local authorities as they were called upon to perform." It does not say any of them killed anyone.

Six months later, on October 4, Crosby received an honorable discharge. A note says he was moving out of Florida. It said he was of good character and "sincere, honest and faithful." It had been one year and eleven days since he'd killed Coot Simpson.

Knolton Crosby's life went on. He presumably returned to carpentry, then went on to a lengthy but unremarkable stint in the military during World War II. He was a private, first class, in the U.S. Army, from March 11, 1941 to October 11, 1945. He served in the First Coastal Battery, Company D, 265th Coast Artillery Regiment. That unit, part of the Florida National Guard, was moved to Fort Crockett, Texas, then Fort Zachary Taylor in Key West, and to South Carolina, New Jersey and Washington state, and finally Alaska, where it disbanded in July 1944. Crosby received the World War II victory medal and a service lapel button, both standard issue for all veterans.

The 1928 city directory lists Knolton Crosby and a person named Dell. Relatives say that was his first wife, and he had a son nicknamed Buddy from that marriage. Relatives also say Dell later left him and married a man named Creech, who adopted Buddy. Court records show he married Irene Riopel, six years his senior, in April 1942. Court records show Crosby and his wife sold their home in Riviera Beach in 1946. Irene would die in the 1950s. Relatives say they don't know what happened to Buddy.

On Monday January 20, 1947, Crosby, then living at 712 Evernia Street, was found dead at 202 First Street. Crosby's obituary the next day says, incorrectly, that he died at his home. He left two brothers and two sisters. He was thirty-nine years, two months and nineteen days old. Cause of death was congestive heart failure due to alcoholism, according to his death certificate.

"He never talked about 'the incident,' " nephew Fred Scurlock said. "I know it affected him because he drank an awful lot."

At 4:00 P.M. Wednesday January 22, Crosby was buried at Lot 70, Block 1A, Woodlawn Cemetery, where so many white victims of the 1928 storm lay. His body received an American Legion escort and was placed in the veterans' plot.

And so Knolton Crosby had spent four years and fifty days on earth more than the man he had shot. The body of Coot Simpson, a veteran, had been the subject of an argument over who would pony up a little less than $16 to ship his body to a simple grave in a rural churchyard. But his killer, who drank himself to death, would be buried in his hometown's most prestigious cemetery—a white cemetery—with full military honors.

Coot Simpson died not of wind, or water, but instead of the sometimes-fatal condition of being black in the Deep South in the 1920s. His grave marker has long since fallen to the elements, as did the mass grave in West Palm Beach, so full of others who may not have died like Coot Simpson, but have been remembered as well.

The Dike

1929–present

"A panther by the tail"

Ten days after the hurricane, the Kelsey City laborer named Lonnie finally showed up for work. To supervisor Charles Branch, he looked like a zombie. His eyes were glassy. Branch asked if he had prayed during the storm. He didn't answer right away. Then he asked, "Where do the wind go when the wind done blowing?" Branch told him not to trouble himself with that because someday, the wind would surely come back.

And when it did, how would they stop the water?

The top of the front page of the *Okeechobee News* for September 28, twelve days after the storm, carried a grim cartoon. A woman was on her knees in front of her smashed home. A man lay still beside her. She held a baby up and shouted "Help!" in front of two specters, labeled "starvation" and "death Okeechobee."

Atop the cartoon, a headline read: "For years we have asked for flood control, and received canals that flow backward. Two thousand lives pay the price of politics, indifference and mismanagement."

The local American Legion post passed a resolution on September 28, urging that the state install a weather station there to supplement the stations at Moore Haven and Canal Point. The post's resolution came to the Everglades Drainage District board, quoting Alexander Mitchell at the weather service complaining that he'd raised the issue with F. C. Elliot, the state's chief engineer, but that Elliot had said a station there would be of no value because the lake was too shallow. Elliot told the district board, at its October 9 meeting, that he'd never said such a thing, producing a letter he'd wrote to Mitchell in July 1925 suggesting the bridge tender at Taylor Creek, where it entered the lake, could take measurements. The board said everyone seemed in agreement that it was a good idea. Within days Mitchell was in Okeechobee, making arrangements for the station. It would shoot rockets 200 feet high that could be seen as far out as 20 miles on dark nights to warn people on the lake of impending storms. And it would have a flagpole to hoist those now-archaic hurricane flags.

In an October 24, 1928 note to Washington, Mitchell, the official in charge in Jacksonville, passed on the suggestion that rocket signals be used at night. But E. B. Calvert, meteorologist in charge in Jacksonville, wrote back that the system was obsolete.

"We appreciate the fact that, at the present time, the people in the Lake Okeechobee region are in a state of unrest and distress and that it is proper for this office to take any reasonable action which may give them peace of mind as to future service," Calvert wrote. He continued that, while the agency doubted the effectiveness of rockets, it had no objection to Mitchell arranging for displays with whatever he had in stock but that if those didn't work, Mitchell was to do nothing until the agency looked into buying effective rockets.

Reporting was not the main issue. People wanted a dike. Not the little mud berm that had vanished in a wall of water. This time, they wanted a big one that would save their lives.

"We cannot and will not ask the people of the Everglades to take up their work under the shadow of death," West Palm Beach Chamber of Commerce President George F. Bensel said on September 28.

Just hours after the storm passed, the first cry had arisen to do something about the dike. Samuel L. Drake, president of the New River–Lake Okeechobee–Caloosahatchie Navigation Association, called for the state to turn over to its federal counterpart the task of making the big lake safe from future catastrophic floods.

"The time has come when the government of the United States can no longer shirk the duty of flood control of the great Lake Okeechobee area," he said.

F. C. Elliot couldn't agree more. The storm had provided the state's chief engineer an awful I-told-you-so.

"That there will be other storms is certain," Elliot wrote after the storm, in the 1927–1928 biennial report to the board of the Everglades Drainage District. "Levees must be built along the shore of Lake Okeechobee."

Elliot also said the flow into Lake Okeechobee in the three-month period before and after the 1928 storm was greater than for any other year on record, and had the outflow from the lake been greater, fewer might have died.

But, he told a Rotary Club luncheon in Clearwater in March 1929, "It would be feasible to lower Lake Okeechobee to an extent which would remove danger of flood to surrounding lands, even under hurricane conditions, but such lowering would result in the impairment, and possibly even in the complete destruction, of its navigable feature."

In November, the Everglades Drainage District board passed a resolution containing a scathing denunciation of the federal government.

"It is alleged that the maintenance of said lake and water level specified by the United States government presents a problem of hazard of life and property and citizens of the State of Florida who inhabit the territory adjacent to said lake," the resolution said. It said the 1928 storm showed the need for cooperation between Tallahassee and Washington about the setting of the lake level. And it urged Congress, in its next session, to get to the business of protecting the Glades from another catastrophic flood. On December 5, the board sent out a telegram to Florida U.S. Senator Duncan Fletcher that was even more specific: Build a big dike.

Word began to spread that people were afraid another storm would hit Florida during the snowbird season and Mitchell, at the Weather Bureau, had to explain that they don't form in the winter months. "A hurricane in Florida in the winter months is as unheard of relatively as a snowstorm in the central west in the summertime," he said. In fact, though, hurricanes have formed in every month except February, and four tropical storms have actually made landfall outside the historical hurricane season, which runs from June 1 to November 30. A tropical storm struck Florida in February 1952.

Not everyone wanted a bigger dike.

"They built us a wall of dirt to keep the water out and it traps us," Jess D. Lee of Torrey Island, his gnarled fist clenched, told the *New York Times* on September 19, 1928, at a refugee center in Miami. Lee had braced his home with a truck, a tractor, and other vehicles, and four times swam family members to safety; first his wife, then three children.

"The lake dumped over it and there's just enough left to hold the water from running off," Lee complained. "Nature used to take the water off to Shark River. Now these state engineers come along and trap us. That whole wall ought to be torn out."

On September 24, less than a week after the storm, E. G. Sewell, the mayor of Miami, suggested a giant canal, 14 feet deep and an amazing 250 feet wide, from the lake's eastern shore to the coast, as an emergency drain. Sewell suggested the canal would cost $5 million, the dike another $3 million. He said he didn't know where the state would get the money; perhaps from the road fund.

Within two weeks of the storm, Florida U.S. Senator Duncan Fletcher was calling control of the lake "an urgent government problem" and saying that as soon as state engineers finished studies they had started before the storm, he'd be pressing Congress for action. So in January 1929, the House Committee on Flood Control wrestled with what to do about a big lake that kept trying to drown everyone.

U.S. Representative Hamilton Fish, of New York State, even said a nice word for black people:

"We want to protect the lives of those people of African origin who sometimes have no [way to flee] and whose lives are just as dear to their families as those of the white man," Fish told the hearing. "Nobody knows how many colored people have been drowned by these floods."

At the hearings, some agreed with Jess Lee that the problem was insurmountable and that the best plan was to tear out the rest of the levee and let the lake return to its natural flow into the Everglades. Fred H. Davis, Florida's attorney general only since 1927, went so far as to tell the committee, "I've heard it advocated in certain districts of Florida that what the people ought to do is build a wall down there and keep the military there to keep the people from coming in there."

But that would have been a surrender to nature, and civilization had gone too far to let nature win now.

So the answer was to tame nature more.

On January 31, 1929, the Army Corps of Engineers submitted a new plan calling for a 31-foot dike around the lake, along with the deepening of the key drainage canals, the Caloosahatchee and St. Lucie waterways. The corps estimated the cost at $10.7 million, with the state and local interests paying about 62 percent. In most projects such as the proposed dike, regions had split with the feds, paying one-third to Washington's two-thirds. In this plan, 62 percent would be more than $6 million. Florida had now been racked by the great real estate crash and two cataclysmic hurricanes, and finding that kind of money was out of the question.

In May 1929, the finger pointing reached the floor of the Florida House of Representatives. The target: the Internal Improvement Board, responsible for flood safety in the Glades. The House approved, 54 to 16, a bill to give responsibility to a local board. "The I.I. Board has had charge of the Everglades Drainage District for many years, and someone is responsible for the more than 2,000 lives lost," one representative shouted. Having finally met on the issue eight months after the storm, it created the Lake Okeechobee Flood Control District, which held its first meeting in September 1929, a year after the storm. Florida hinted it would pay as much as half. But Florida State Representative Herbert Drane suggested the feds pay the larger share, since the money would be used to keep federally controlled water from drowning people who came to Florida from all over the country.

In February 1929, new governor Doyle Carlton had invited the newly elected president, Herbert Hoover, a month away from inauguration, to tour Florida's interior. Florida was one of only four southern states Hoover had carried, and Carlton knew the president, an engineer, had a special interest in flood control. Hoover left his vacation home in Miami Beach and traveled in a twenty-car motorcade around two-thirds of the lake. In his car: Carlton and the ubiquitous F. C. Elliot.

Hoover attended a dinner in Clewiston and spent the night in the Glades. He had seen for himself the damage that prevailed some five months after the storm: houses standing twisted or half-destroyed, piles of wood that had been homes, highways still strewn with debris, fields still full of junk or simply too torn up to farm.

The anniversary of the storm passed with no new threat on the horizon. But nine days later, on September 25, 1929, weather officials were saying a powerful storm was moving through the Bahamas, aiming at Miami. That sick feeling started all over again. Coastal Palm Beach County nailed up and moved out. Thousands of people called newspaper offices for updates. The approaching storm covered most of the front page of the September 26 *Palm Beach Post,* broken only by a gossip column, a sensational murder trial in Los Angeles, and word that legendary New York Yankees baseball manager Miller Huggins had died.

This time, the lake was low, some $4\frac{1}{2}$ feet lower than it had been in the 1928 storm, but water was moving into it. Several hundred people left the Glades; some to the coast, others on free train rides to Central Florida. South Bay reported only eight people left in town. By the next day, the crisis appeared to have passed. The storm was weakening and seemed headed to the Keys. Hurricane warnings were dropped. But on September 27, weather officials said the storm had strengthened again and was 100 miles southeast of Miami. Finally, on Friday, September 28, the storm was moving through the Keys and out of the picture.

The plan to dike the lake went through more machinations before finally, on July 3, 1930, Hoover signed it into law. It called for Florida to provide $2 million and all land and rights-of-way and Washington to pay the rest, whatever its eventual total.

The federal government had worried about setting a precedent by approving a project designed primarily for flood control. They imagined ponying up for project after project along the length of the Mississippi River or Chesapeake Bay. So, in typical Washington fashion, they did a brilliant end-around. Congress passed, and President Hoover signed, what was essentially a navigation project: a channel along the southern perimeter of the lake. And, by the way, all that dirt dug out has to go somewhere, so, hey! Let's pile it up and make a dike!

The first shovel for the new and improved dike was turned in November 1930, two years after its forerunner had washed away. Among those operating dredges: Belle Glade businessman Lawrence E. Will, who would later write a history of the 1928 storm.

Less than eight years later, in March 1938, a little shy of a decade after the great storm, the Herbert H. Hoover Dike stretched for 85 miles around the north, northwest, south and southwest shores of the big lake. Some 68 miles along the southern shore had been finished in 1936, and another 16 miles by 1938. It was 34 to 38 feet above sea level and rose pyramidically, 10 to 30 feet wide at the top but 125 to 150 feet wide at the base. At the drainage canals, 34-foot-high locks and hurricane gates kept the water in. The state had put in $1.3 million. Washington had dropped $19.1 million—a figure that would rise to $23.4 million by 1942.

The dike would soon be tested. In 1947, back-to-back hurricanes flooded vast stretches of South Florida. Two years later, a major storm slammed into the coast and over the lake. Both times, the dike held. But the disasters did lead to the creation in 1949 of the Central and Southern Florida Flood Control District, forerunner to the South Florida Water Management District.

The 1928 storm's destruction, combined with the hand wringing over the dike and the possibility of future disasters, had failed in one regard. Within a year, Belle Glade's population was five times what it had been in 1928. A December 30, 1928 freeze had killed a crop of beans reaching maturity, but not slowed the return to productivity. And with Lake Okeechobee finally tamed by the new tall dike, the giant growing region between the lake and the growing metropolitan areas of the Atlantic coast began to switch to sugar. In the 1929–30 harvest season, the Glades had 17,000 acres of vegetables and less than 7,000 acres of sugar in cultivation. Sugar acreage doubled in four years, slowed only by marketing quotas. World War II brought a temporary suspension of quotas but a scarcity of manpower. By 1949, some 110,000 acres was in farming; 75,000 was in vegetables, 30,000 in sugarcane, and the rest in pasture and minor crops.

In March 1955, one of the largest pump stations in the world came on line at 20 Mile Bend. It was designed to pull storm flows from a 230-square-mile area along the West Palm Beach Canal, running 20 miles from Lake Okeechobee, and dump the water into the conservation areas that would serve as giant reservoirs for South Florida's exploding population.

At the ceremony were five current and former governors. One was John Wellborn Martin, now seventy, who as Florida's governor had had two catastrophic hurricanes land on his head like twin grand pianos. Another man present, now seventy-six, can be seen in a photograph, his hair and mustache now white, sitting with his arms folded just to the right of the podium: F. C. Elliot, the chief engineer who had steered the drainage of the Glades and the creation of the giant flood-control and water-supply machine, the man who had so bluntly warned that an undiked lake was a monster waiting to bring death.

While most of the dike was in place by the late 1930s, it was not dedicated formally until January 12, 1961. It was named for Herbert Hoover, who had approved the project more than three decades earlier. Hoover was keynote speaker at the ceremony. Before heading toward the lake, the eighty-six-year-old, then the oldest living ex-president, stopped in Palm Beach to visit president-elect John F. Kennedy, forty-three, the youngest man ever elected to the White House.

The next day, about 5,000 people gathered under rainy skies at the foot of a towering lake levee in Clewiston. They included survivors and relatives of victims of the 1926 and 1928 storms. The dignitaries were on a platform erected next to Hurricane Gate 2. Farris Bryant, inaugurated as governor only nine days earlier, told Hoover the true monument to him was not the bronze plaque unveiled at the event "but in the cities and people that have grown around the lake." Former Governor Doyle Carlton, now seventy-three, recalled that day more than three decades earlier in February 1929, when he and Hoover had inspected the still-shattered region and the president-elect Hoover had said, "I'm going to help you with this thing."

"Controlling the water in Lake Okeechobee is like having an Ever-glades panther by the tail," U.S. Army Corps of Engineers district engineer Paul T. Troxler said in an interview published the day of the dedication. "It's not a question of how to let go, but rather a problem of finding the bridle and saddle that best fit the beast."

Hoover died at ninety about four and a half years later, in October 1964. He had outlived young President Kennedy by nearly a year. Doyle Carlton died in 1972.

On August 27, 1964, Hurricane Cleo struck Miami with top sustained winds of about 115 mph and moved up the coast and slightly inland. Later, inland, Cleo's top sustained winds of 70 to 75 mph put it barely at hurricane strength. But in a scenario frighteningly similar to the 1928 storm, it passed near Lake Okeechobee, bringing winds down from the north that pressed the lake's water against the southern shore. The Army Corps of Engineers said the big lake fluctuated 6 to 7 feet between the north and south ends. But the dike held.

In the mid-1960s, the engineers had returned at Congress's command, increasing the dike's height and building the remaining portion on the lake's northwest corner. Now the dike encircled the big lake for 140 miles.

Not everyone likes it. Before the area east and south of Lake Okeechobee was drained for farming, water had flowed naturally from the lake through the Everglades and into Florida Bay, at the very end of the peninsula. The water was filtered as it went. Now clean, it recharged aquifers and supplied enough pressure to keep salt water from leaching into them from the adjacent seas. This flow supplied oxygen and nutrients to Everglades plants and fish, indirectly benefiting migrating birds and land animals who fed on them. Environmental scholars say the draining of the area and the building of the dike blocked that flow. On top of that, filtering swamps were replaced by fields of sugarcane loaded with fertilizer that washed through the swamp, polluting the flow all the way to Florida Bay. Environmental researchers suggest that we may never know the extent of these changes.

The dike's northwest stretch has proven the most controversial. The shore there is both higher and less populated than the south shore, and the building of that part of the dike wiped out at least 120 square miles of marsh, destroying habitat for wading birds and fish. A federal study in 1960 said the portion wasn't necessary and officials of Glades County, where that part stands, had told the flood-control district of the potential damage to wildlife breeding grounds. In 1993, a group of South Florida scientists renewed the call to tear out the northwest dike. Besides undoing environmental damage, removing the dike would actually increase the lake's capacity, they said.

In 1996, University of Miami planner Dan Williams brought back an idea last discussed at a congressional hearing in 1929. He suggested removing a 1- to 2-mile section of the dike near Belle Glade, leaving a low ridge that the lake could spill over during high water. That would restore the natural "sheet flow" of water to the end of the peninsula, a flow that had been good enough for eons before man decided to tamper with it. At the edge of the lake, Williams said, a park could offer a place for the water to flow on its way to replenishing mucky soils and organic farms. To pay for the work, crews could excavate the dike and sell the fill. Williams's pitch was universally dismissed. Growers said it would be disastrous for agriculture. The U.S. Army Corps of Engineers said it wouldn't work. And, of course, people next to the gap in the dike would be in danger of a repeat of 1928. This time, they'd have advance warning and be able to evacuate, but of course their property would be destroyed.

Over the years, the dike has withstood storms of varying strengths. But what of a monster hurricane, repeating the disaster of 1928? In 1993, federal and state researchers and emergency managers in the five counties around Lake Okeechobee did a study that concluded the dike would hold, hurricane forecaster Brian Jarvinen said. Researchers studied 4,500 different combinations. They studied scenarios in which imaginary storms passed through the region and slammed into the lake at various strengths and forward speeds, at different spots, and from different angles and direction, and with lake levels at various heights. Scenarios also included the 1926 and 1928 storms.

"Incredibly, even at the high lake elevations, no over-topping occurred at any of the levees," Jarvinen said.

Of course, a dike overflow or total collapse is only a theoretical danger. Another already exists: the dike leaks.

It's called "piping." The big dike is made of dirt and rock. When the lake is high, water finds its way through the dike, sometimes eroding the soil as it goes. Eventually a waterway is formed that accelerates the erosion. That raises the most horrifying specter of all: a breach of the dike.

Two failures in the 1970s had small consequences but put a nasty scare into the U.S. Army Corps of Engineers. In 1974, a breach occurred on a stretch of dike that extends for about 6½ miles from the lake along the Kissimmee River. Because the lake was low, water actually flowed into it from a canal. Five years later, the reservoir dike at a Florida Power & Light plant east of the lake breached, causing extensive flooding. Heavy rains in 1995 and 1998 sent the lake level past 18½ feet above sea level and caused major leaks.

The Army Corps of Engineers considers the dike at dangerous levels for failure at about 21 feet; its highest recorded level was 18.9 feet in 1949. Engineers have said that while there was little chance of it, they cannot guarantee there won't be a major failure, unleashing a wall of water onto the 40,000 people living around the lake that would make the 1928 surge look like an overturned wheelbarrow. One panel of engineers from as far away as Michigan and the Netherlands concluded that "a very serious risk of catastrophic failure" was real and reasonable. The problems so far have shown up only on the lake's east side, from around Okeechobee down to Belle Glade, and west to Moore Haven.

Emergency managers are planning for the worst. As part of a 2002 statewide drill, every county started with the same imaginary hurricane, patterned after Hurricane King in October 1950. Managers were then free to come up with consequences as intense, varied, and widespread as they chose. And they created a doozy. The pretend-storm had brought the lake's surface to 18 feet above sea level, and the great dike around it had one really big leak. Water poured through the gash. Engineers were unable to keep up with it. Already, a stretch of lakeshore from Pahokee to Belle Glade was chest-deep in lake water. Some residents got out by car as the water rose, others in personal boats, and emergency officials were sending high-wheel vehicles and airboats for the rest. Five days after the imaginary storm, the scenario suggested, four feet of water would still stand as far east as 20 Mile Bend.

The Army Corps of Engineers has suggested an ambitious project to shore up the dike, starting with the shoring up of the 22 miles of levee from Port Mayaca to Belle Glade, where dike failures in the 1928 storm caused the most deaths. The overall price tag: $180 million.

Not everyone has pursued the idea of dikes and other forms of protection from the power of storms. Some push prevention. Long before 1928, and up to today, meteorologists have received suggestions about how to stop or deflect hurricanes. None has proven effective. The 1928 storm brought out every kind of entrepreneur, huckster, amateur meteorologist, and nut case certain he knew how to prevent future tragedies. Their letters to C. F. Marvin, chief of The U.S. Weather Bureau, most of them within weeks of the 1928 hurricane, speak volumes about how much forecasters and the general public knew about hurricanes—and how little.

A Mr. W. J. Anson suggested breaking up storms with giant explosives fired from battleships or land. A Mr. H. P. Tate, in Smackover, Arkansas, suggested dropping bombs into storms from airplanes. Captain H. P. Fransen of Panama's U.S. Canal Zone proposed sailing ships to the spot where a storm was reported forming and firing projectiles into its vortex. C. J. Reed of Orlando also suggested explosives, adding, "I will ask that you please do not give my name or address to any publicity sources." Sorry, Mr. Reed.

In each case, the U.S. Weather Bureau replied diplomatically that such attacks would be worthless. "All the energy in a million dollars worth of explosive is not one part in a thousand of that in a great storm," Marvin wrote Tate.

Professor William Franklin of Rollins College in Winter Park, near Orlando, suggested creating a storm that would knock out the conditions that feed the hurricane, similar to starting a backfire to burn out a wildfire. His idea was to use gunpowder in a high steel cone 300 to 400 feet high and 100 feet across to fire 34 tons of compressed air up into the atmosphere. Mr. Franklin didn't say just how such a cone would be transported to the middle of the ocean. Marvin said he didn't believe that would have any effect. His staff estimated 34 tons, or 500,000 cubic feet, of air would form a column 10 feet by 10 feet and a mile high. It will never be known if Franklin had answers to Marvin's challenges. The same month his letter landed on Marvin's desk, the car his wife was driving went off a bluff in Wilmington, North Carolina, killing the couple.

Some apparently had ideas so fabulous they were reluctant to reveal them until after Washington had ponied up. "I can guarantee this work and can interest you as I am a famous storm breaker," Frederick Heaton of East Omaha, Nebraska, wrote. "Would work by the month. What would be your best proposition, including transportation?" G. H. Dalton of Chicago wrote on a postcard that he had a plan to prevent large loss of life; he wanted to know to which agency to submit it "relative to getting paid for it if adopted." And Cecil N. Cooley of Indianapolis asked Marvin to "send your local representative."

Other inquiries were even more far-fetched. Tire salesman C. H. Sutton of Tazewell, Tennessee, wrote only, "Did the radio broadcasting stations, in your belief, cause the Florida storm." No, Marvin replied

"Did The U.S. Weather Bureau predict in August this year, immediately following the August hurricane, that there would be another hurricane following within 30 days?" Longfield Smith of Southern Automobile Insurance Exchange wrote from Lake Wales on October 3. "Is it possible to predict 15 or 30 days in advance the formation of a tropical windstorm?" Marvin responded that the bureau made no such prediction and that no one can do so accurately.

Henry Anderson, manager of the insurance department at Paramount Pictures, which had several properties in Florida, reminded Marvin he had assured Anderson after the 1926 storm that there were no weather conditions suggesting a greater chance of future storms. Anderson asked diplomatically if Marvin still felt that way. Marvin replied in effect that it all came down to averages and luck and that before Florida became populated, storms large and small passed without notice.

Then there is the August 7, 1929 letter from D. H. Lewis of Takoma Park, Maryland. He'd received a correspondence from an acquaintance in Lake Worth. There was "much talk there about the arrival of another storm similar to the one that swept the coast of that section before. She lost heavily in that and I shall be pleased to have you advise me of any information you have as to the probability of another such storm in the future."

Marvin told Lewis to forward to his battered friend that, sadly, until storms form and begin their movement, the weather bureau "issues no predictions regarding occurrences of hurricanes at a particular place." Three-fourths of a century later, with all their technology, forecasters still can't offer us that peace of mind.

How to stop hurricanes, and how to stop them from killing, were top priorities after the 1928 hurricane. Its black victims were not. In West Palm Beach, in the black neighborhood along Tamarind Avenue, a giant hole was dug and filled and covered up. The grass grew over it and soon things returned to normal. After a while, people outside the neighborhood forgot that anything dramatic lay beneath the street.

1891–1960

"Their Eyes Were Watching God"

As winds howled in the Glades on September 16, 1928, black migrant workers huddled, wept and prayed, and while they stared into the darkness, "their eyes were watching God," Zora Neale Hurston wrote.

Hurston wasn't at Lake Okeechobee, or even in Florida, when the winds took the lives of so many black men, women, and children. Much of her narrative of that night is based on actual accounts of the storm she collected later. Many of the people she spoke with are also described in this work. But she immortalized the hurricane just as she captured the lives and humanity of mid-twentieth-century black Americans.

During her life, Hurston had spotty success in the literary world. She died in obscurity, but there has been a resurgence of interest in her writing after her death in 1960, and she has finally taken her place among America's influential black writers.

She had been in the Caribbean in the summer of 1928 and arrived in New Orleans that August, and probably was there when the hurricane struck South Florida. She stayed in New Orleans through the winter, returned to South Florida, and then, in October 1929, went to the

Bahamas. She was there when a strong hurricane struck the islands. Inspired partly by that experience and partly by the end of a romantic relationship, she later wrote *Their Eyes Were Watching God* in Haiti. In her autobiography, *Dust Tracks on the Road,* she said *Their Eyes* "was dammed up in me." She wrote it in seven weeks. It was published in 1937.

The story takes some liberties. For example, it described winds of an unrealistic 200 mph, and it perpetuates the legend of the Seminoles fleeing the storm before everyone else because they saw sawgrass blooming. Otherwise, Hurston does give an accurate account of the storm's slow but steady assault and its aftermath.

Her protagonist, Janie Crawford, born of a rape, is abandoned by her mother and raised by her grandmother, Nanny. At seventeen, she has an arranged marriage to a nearby farmer who is prosperous but much older and unexciting to Janie. When Nanny dies a short time later, Janie is alone. Charismatic Joe Starks, a traveling man with a knack for making a buck, shows up, and Janie leaves the older farmer to follow Starks to the all-black Central Florida town of Eatonville. He becomes mayor of the town, owner of the town's general store, and one of Eatonville's most influential businessmen.

Many of the townspeople become jealous of the couple's success. At the same time, Joe, much older than his wife, is jealous of her youth and beauty and wants her to hide it. He also doesn't want her to take an important role in the store. The continuing tension climaxes with Joe striking Janie and driving her from the store. Soon after, Joe falls ill and dies. Liberated, but all alone again, Janie continues to operate Joe's business. Now about forty, she meets Tea Cake, only twenty-five, who has come into the store to buy cigarettes. She goes with him to Jacksonville, and eventually to the Glades. It is a rich land and laborers find prosperity.

Their good life ends dramatically when a great hurricane descends on Lake Okeechobee and the growing region around it. As the storm's power grows, Janie and Tea Cake quickly gather money and insurance papers and make their way through their front yard in water already up to their waists. Flotsam floats around them in the waters pouring from the lake. The two swim until they reach high ground, then start walking. Tea Cake grows tired and they lie down to rest. Jane tries to grab a piece of tar-paper roofing to place over Tea Cake as a blanket, but the wind picks up the roofing and lifts her up, throwing her into the water. In desperation, she grabs the tail of a cow swimming by. A dog is on the cow's shoulders. When it tries to attack Janie, Tea Cake opens his knife and grabs the dog, but his exhaustion gives the animal the upper hand. Though he is able to kill it, it has bitten him on the face.

The couple struggle through the winds and walk for hours. Finally the storm dies down and they arrive at the coast. Tea Cake wants to turn around and return to the Glades, but he must find work to raise money. Two armed white men draft him to help bury the dead. Tea Cake takes part in helping load bodies into the mass grave.

Janie and Tea Cake eventually get back to the Glades, where there is work clearing the broken homes and other wreckage. But the dog Tea Cake had killed exacts its vengeance even in death. Tea Cake has rabies. As the disease ravages his brain, the madness takes the form of paranoia and suspicion of his wife. He points a pistol at her and pulls the trigger once. Janie raises a rifle, more to scare him. Tea Cake aims again, and the two fire simultaneously. Tea Cake is killed. Janie is charged with her husband's murder, but the shooting is declared justified. She buries Tea Cake.

Their Eyes Were Watching God did not draw great attention to the legacy of the 1928 hurricane. Perhaps because it came out nearly a decade later, after the 1935 Labor Day storm and others had created all new stories of horror. Perhaps because, as with many news events, people move on to the next one. And perhaps because, while the storm was the mechanism that formed the climax of the book, it was the characters, not the weather, that people remembered.

Hurston's characters can be seen as typical victims of the storm and the social conditions of their times. They were black in Florida in the 1920s. They were poor. They were oppressed. Instead, Hurston showed them as people who took what an unfair life gave them and enjoyed it despite that—especially Janie, at first weak but later strong and independent. Because of that, many of Hurston's literary colleagues didn't like the book; they preferred the characters to be more pitiable.

Meanwhile, Zora had herself moved on to new accomplishments.

Florida: A Guide to the Most Southernmost State quotes an old-timer who says of one storm that it "blowed a crooked road straight." It's quite possible Hurston herself collected that old adage. She had served as general editor of the book published in 1939 as part of a series of state guides assembled by the Works Progress Administration, a Depression-era government program. She and others used the project to gather tales and folklore from across the countryside, providing a glimpse into the colorful world that lay down each country lane. It was that fanciful world from which she herself had sprung.

Hurston had said she was born in Eatonville, about 10 miles north of Orlando. Scholars now conclude she was born in Macon County, Alabama, in January 1891 and moved to Eatonville three years later.

Eatonville claimed to be America's first incorporated black municipality. In 1887, black residents of adjacent Maitland, most of them freed slaves, had decided they wanted their own town. They bought 112 acres and named the place for Josiah Eaton, a local landowner who had helped with the purchase. They sold 44-by-100-foot lots for $35 to $50. The initial population was 300; a century later it would be 3,000.

Zora Neale Hurston was the sixth of nine children of John Hurston, a tenant farmer who came to Eatonville when Zora was a toddler and moonlighted as pastor of a Baptist church in town. At a time when black women were doubly invisible—as both blacks and women—her mother urged her to "jump at de sun," a phrase she recalled in *Dust Tracks on the Road*.

When she was a child, her mother died and her father remarried quickly. She had a turbulent relationship with her stepmother and eventually began to get passed among relatives. One bright spot of her youth was the time spent on the "lying porch," the porch of Joe Clarke's store, where the men of the town passed around tall tales. Clarke would be the inspiration for Joe Starks, Janie's second husband.

When Hurston was about fifteen, she found work as a wardrobe girl in a traveling Gilbert and Sullivan troupe. She left the show in Baltimore, where she earned a high school diploma from Morgan Academy. Then she went to Howard University, the famed black college. There she began writing.

In 1921, when she was about thirty, she published her first short story. She lied to her publishers and the public about her age, saying she was only twenty, which made her a literary prodigy. Four years later, she left a job as a manicurist in Washington and moved to New York to pursue a career in writing. The city was experiencing the Harlem Renaissance, and she was to be part of the historic surge in black literary achievement.

Hurston got a scholarship to Barnard College, the women's campus of Columbia University. She majored in anthropology and earned a degree in 1928. Her early stories won her quick acclaim but not much money, and she later worked as a live-in secretary to novelist Fannie Hurst. They had a close relationship and Hurst had no time for the era's racial mores; once, when they were barred from eating in a segregated Vermont restaurant, the quick-thinking Hurst introduced Hurston as an African princess.

During her time in New York, Hurston edited an avant-garde magazine and worked with other writers on several plays. She got a fellowship to travel through the South and collect black folklore. Her first book, *Of Mules and Men,* published in 1935, is considered the first such compilation of its kind. Her interest in anthropology took her to Jamaica, Haiti, the Bahamas, and New Orleans, where she gathered more tales. She published a second collection, *Tell My Horse,* in 1938.

Her first novel, *Jonah's Gourd Vine,* had come out in 1934. It was based loosely on her parent's lives in Eatonville. *Moses, Man of the Mountain,* which followed *Their Eyes* in 1939, was a combination of bible and folk tales. Her autobiography, *Dust Tracks on a Road,* was published in 1942. Again, white critics liked her work while blacks accused her of trying to ingratiate herself with whites.

Hurston visited Eatonville often, but she had made some enemies in the town. She would sometimes portray townspeople in her books, often transparently and often in a less-than-positive way.

Later, in a bizarre twist, Hurston became a rare breed: a black political conservative. In 1946, she worked for the Republican opponent of black Congressman Adam Clayton Powell, Jr.

She opposed integration and called black intellectuals "the niggerati," earning the praise of white racists and pushing her farther away from her people. Soon she had lost any potential audience and could find few outlets for her work. She even opposed the *Brown v. Board of Education* U.S. Supreme Court ruling that integrated public schools, arguing in essays that blacks didn't have to sit beside whites in order to learn.

Her last novel, *Seraph on the Suwannee,* the only one whose main characters were white, was published in 1948, and even her strongest supporters have little to say about it. She also worked on a novel about King Herod, but couldn't find a publisher for it.

In 1950, a *Miami Herald* reporter found her working as a maid in the upscale Rivo Island neighborhood. Hurston told the writer she had hit a creative block and was doing the domestic work "to shift gears." Later, she would be a librarian at Patrick Air Force Base, near present-day Kennedy Space Center; a columnist for the black weekly *Fort Pierce Chronicle,* and a substitute teacher. She lived in a rent-free room in a tiny house owned by a doctor. Her furniture was donated or was nothing more than fruit boxes.

In October 1959, Hurston suffered a stroke. She died in January 1960 in a segregated nursing home in Fort Pierce with no money to her name. Friends and some publishing colleagues scraped enough money together to pay for a funeral. There wasn't enough left over for a headstone.

In 1973, the writer Alice Walker paid to have a marker placed at her grave. Giving an incorrect birthdate, it reads:

ZORA NEALE HURSTON
A GENIUS OF THE SOUTH
1901–1960
NOVELIST, FOLKLORIST
ANTHROPOLOGIST

Two years later, in 1975, Walker wrote an article for *Ms.* magazine about Hurston's life and work. Robert Hemenway, now chancellor of the University of Kansas, spent seven years interviewing people about Hurston and published her literary biography in 1978. Her posthumous comeback had begun.

In her life, Hurston never made much money. The most she ever earned from a book was $943.75. But years after her death, all four of her books were back in print. Eatonville's Zora Neale Hurston Center was opened in 1987. And every year since 1990, as many as 75,000 people have come to Eatonville to attend the Zora Neale Hurston Festival of the Arts and Humanities. In 1996, the Library of America published a two-volume set of her works. Doubleday later paid nearly $150,000 for a volume of her letters. And Quincy Jones and Oprah Winfrey bought the film rights to *Their Eyes Were Watching God*.

In *Their Eyes,* Hurston describes how Tea Cake and other black workers labored to bury the hurricane dead in two giant pits. White supervisors made sure the laborers checked each of the swollen, discolored bodies as carefully as possible to make sure whites went in the correct pit and blacks in the other.

It was part of a piece of fiction, but it rang all too true.

The Dead

1928–2003

> **"The exact number . . . will never be known."**

How many really died on September 16, 1928?

The National Hurricane Center and the almanac and encyclopedia people use the storm's official death toll of 1,836. Few historians and scholars believe it. Even as government and relief leaders were issuing their final figures soon after the storm, they were conceding the numbers were low.

"The exact number (of deaths) in and around Lake Okeechobee caused by this hurricane will never be known," Stewart G. Thompson, director of the state's Bureau of Vital Statistics, wrote in the October 28, 1928 *Health Notes,* the newsletter of the Florida State Board of Health. "Most of the deaths were among the negro laborers who entered the Everglades for the planting season which had opened a short time previously. Since a large percentage of these negroes were from Nassau, which is outside of the state, it was not possible in a great many instances to identify the bodies."

Palm Beach County Red Cross chairman Howard Selby, in a September 26 radio address broadcast in Washington and New York, placed the estimate at 2,300. He said 1,500 were confirmed dead and buried and many others had been buried in fields and outlying areas.

Lawrence E. Will, author of *Okeechobee Hurricane and the Hoover Dike,* wrote the State Board of Health and the Red Cross in 1958, saying he had always accepted a figure of 2,500. Will said the mayor of Belle Glade at the time had told him 1,850 bodies had been taken from Belle Glade alone. There is nothing in Will's files to indicate a response.

If you just add up the number in the graves, the number is already past 1,836. The mass grave for blacks on Tamarind Avenue: 674. Wood-lawn: 69. In a trench dug into a canal bank at Miami Locks: 22 to 800. Ortona: 28. Sebring: 22. And that mass grave at Port Mayaca, on the northeast shore; a marker says 1,600 are buried there. News reports suggested additional burials of blacks at Loxahatchee, at the western edge of the coastal communities. If such a cemetery was established, historical contacts would say in 2002 that they never heard of it, although it may be there, back in the brush somewhere. It's not hard to imagine a small burial site for dead black migrant workers in a rural area being established and then forgotten as quickly.

Now, dear reader, the author is left in the awkward position of arguing the official death toll is too low, while at the same time challenging the number of people allegedly interred in the various mass graves.

The figures for Tamarind and Woodlawn are not in dispute. Authorities counted the bodies as they were buried. Joseph Orsenigo, chairman of the Belle Glade Museum Board and Glades Historical Society, is highly skeptical of the figure of 800 for Miami Locks, west of Clewiston. He said 22 might be more accurate.

As for Port Mayaca, there is good reason to doubt the information on the marker that stands atop the grave that reads: "To the 1,600 pioneers in this mass burial who gave their lives so that the Glades might be as we know it today." The plot is about the size of two parking spaces. Let's say you dug a trench 12 feet long and 24 feet wide. Assume that a body takes up 6 feet by 2 feet by 2 feet. You could make two rows, each of 12 bodies: 24 bodies, for each layer. In order to fit 1,600 bodies, divide 1,600 by 24, and you'd get about 67 layers, each 2 feet deep. That's 134 feet deep. This is low-lying Florida. It's hard to believe anyone would be able to dig a 134-foot-deep hole. That also presumes that they knew in advance how big a hole they would need and that they laid the bodies in perfect rows and layers. Both are doubtful.

Some writings suggest no one is buried at Port Mayaca, and the marker is instead a monument to all storm deaths, which would of course be an incorrect total. Other writings say bodies were burned first and their ashes placed in the hole. But pioneers say bodies were definitely buried there intact. The most likely scenario is that the cemetery managers at the time simply picked a nice, large, round number and that's what they went with. No records survive to solve the mystery.

"Who kept an accurate tally sheet?" Joseph Orsenigo wrote in February 2002. "It was a mass burial."

Today, at Port Mayaca, brightly colored flowers surround a koi pond. Water flows gently into it down a series of rocks. It is a dramatic and ironic counterpoint to what an angry rush of water did on September 16, 1928. The future of the plot, and the quiet rural cemetery around it, was guaranteed by Vinson Henderson. The vegetable hauler, born in Georgia, lived most of his life in Pahokee. In the 1930s, faced with the problem of moving vegetables over the muddy or flooded roads of the Glades, he modified a Model A Ford into a light truck; the brokerage and trucking business that followed expanded to Central Florida and to South Carolina, where Henderson died in 1995. In 1993, he had donated $125,000 to build a mausoleum in memory of his wife, Louise. After his death, it was learned he had bequeathed $1 million to the cemetery where he is also buried, as well as its almost-unfathomable link to the great hurricane of 1928.

At the Florida Agricultural Extension Service Everglades station in Belle Glade, the water from the 1928 storm finally subsided after several weeks, again exposing the farm fields where the researchers grew and studied crops. The station continued its work, as it does today, still standing at the edge of what are now sweeping fields of sugarcane. Outside the station, the pole planted in 1924 that measures how much of the rich muck is blowing away still stands. The muck now measures three feet, down from nine feet in just three-quarters of a century—and still counting.

The conditions under which farm workers labored in the Glades at the time of the storm, and still do, has been a black eye for South Florida for decades. In 1960, CBS broke new ground in television and devastated the image of Palm Beach County with its historic documentary, *Harvest of Shame*. It ran on the night after Thanksgiving, when Americans were still sitting fat and full and nibbling on leftover turkey and pumpkin pie probably sweetened by Florida sugar.

"Never before in the dismal history of migratory farm labor in the United States has there been such widespread personal knowledge as there is today of the shocking conditions under which the migrants live and work," the *New York Times* wrote in an editorial nine days after the broadcast. Documenting the daily existence and movement of workers from Belle Glade to orchards and fields around the country, the program displayed the low wages, poor housing, and grueling work and contrasted it with the good life enjoyed by the farm owners. Edward R. Murrow, the crusading CBS reporter who had helped bring down U.S. Senator Joseph McCarthy and his anti-Communist witch hunts in the mid-1950s, described the farm fields of the Glades as "the sweatshop of the soil." The documentary was hailed by activists, pilloried by farming interests, and denounced as inaccurate and unfair by Florida U.S. Senator Spessard Holland. But activists contend conditions are still a disgrace in the twenty-first century.

In the years directly following the storm, South Florida suffered through the Great Depression. Then its economy was saved by the same thing that lifted the rest of the country: war. In 1940, Florida hosted eight military facilities—hospitals, airfields, bases. By 1943, it was 142.

The war also did in the *August Leonhardt,* the ship that had had survived the 1928 hurricane between the Bahamas and the Florida coast. On November 4, 1940, the British submarine *Sealion* would spot the German freighter, aground off Anholt, Norway, and finish her off with a torpedo.

World War II brought enemy submarines right to Florida's beaches, but it also helped spark one of the greatest population explosions in American history. From 1940 to 1950, the state's population increased by 50 percent, from 2 million to 3 million. It would be 7 million by 1970. By the turn of the century, it would be more than 15 million.

And as if to shatter the optimistic idea that Nature spreads out disasters in the interest of fair play, in a brief span of nine years, three storms—in 1926, 1928, and 1935—would strike 300 miles apart in South Florida. They would kill at least 2,500 people, by official tallies, and perhaps as many as 4,000 people, and set records for destruction surpassed only by Andrew.

The 1935 "Labor Day" storm would be the last nail in the coffin of the Great Depression.

Having built the palatial Whitehall on Palm Beach for his bride in 1902, Henry Flagler had one last accomplishment in mind before his long life came to an end: the monumental task of building a 128-mile-long railroad through the sea to link the mainland with the isolated island of Key West. The railroad, at the time one of America's largest privately financed engineering projects, cost Flagler $20 million, two-fifths of his total Florida investment. Detractors called it "Flagler's Folly." But after seven years of work by 3,000 to 4,000 men, the railroad had come to Key West. On that glorious day in January 1912, a stooped and weak Flagler made a triumphant entrance. What the *Miami Herald* called the eighth wonder of the world would last less than a generation.

After World War I, many veterans became embittered that their nation had forgotten them. That frustration boiled over in 1932, when about 15,000 camped out in Washington to demand a bonus that had been promised them in 1924. President Herbert Hoover ordered in troops, who violently ran the veterans out of the capital, led by a young Douglas MacArthur, who would later lead American troops in the Pacific in World War II.

As the Depression solidified its grip, veterans demanded dignity and a job. Like many, they were rescued by new President Franklin Roosevelt and his recovery projects. Civilian Conservation Corps camps were set up where more than 700 veterans worked building new bridges and causeways down the Keys, alongside the railroad, to accommodate the heir to Mr. Flagler's world: the automobile.

Soon word came that a storm was coming. Railroad officials made plans to send a rescue train south to evacuate the workers, but because it was Labor Day weekend, they had trouble rounding up crews. In this mad race against time, a drawbridge over the Miami River held up the train for ten minutes, and the engineer stopped in Homestead for fifteen minutes to switch to the engine to the back, to allow for a quick return. In the upper Keys, a loose cable alongside the track hooked the locomotive. Releasing that took more than an hour. The time they needed to load the workers and get them out of the storm was quickly running out. As the train approached Islamorada, waves were already washing over the tracks. The train overran its planned stopping point in the blinding rain and hurricane-force winds and had to back up. The road workers got only five minutes to try to board. Then a 20-foot wave washed over them.

The storm was the most powerful ever to strike North America and, with Camille and Andrew, one of only three Category Five storms on record. In a 10-mile stretch from Tavernier to Key Vaca, nothing was left standing. One of the first doctors to get to the scene found 39 men dead in a window where a wave had left them. A man sat against a broken wall with a piece of two-by-four run completely through him, under his ribs, out over the kidneys. He refused the shot of morphine the doctor offered him, before he pulled it out. The man said matter-of-factly that he believed when it was pulled out, he would die. He asked for two beers, drank them, and said, "Now pull." The doctor pulled, and the man died.

In all, the Labor Day storm killed at least 577 people. But some bodies were never found. At least 288 of the dead were those Civilian Conservation Corps highway workers. Also dead was Mr. Flagler's railroad, much of it washed away. Officials had planned a second chain of bridges for a motor highway to meet the booming motoring craze. But there was an urgency to reconnect the Keys to the mainland, and many of the railroad beds were too damaged to salvage. So instead work proceeded apace to complete the Overseas Highway. Now there was an artery for cars, just in time for the car to establish its dominance. That accelerated the tourism industry in the Keys. Few had the heart to rebuild the railroad, and no one ever did.

The same year of the Labor Day hurricane, the weather service finally created a hurricane prediction center in Jacksonville. It came three years after Alexander J. Mitchell, who had headed the Jacksonville weather office for decades, retired. Mitchell died in Jacksonville in 1937.

The march of hurricanes did not abate.

On September 3, 1933, a hurricane with 125 mph winds struck between Jupiter and Fort Pierce, causing minimal damage to central Palm Beach County but extensive damage on the Treasure Coast. A hurricane in July 1934 crossed the northern part of the Florida peninsula, killing eleven in Florida and Texas. In 1944, another hurricane crossed the peninsula from the Gulf Coast to the northeast corner and killed eighteen. A September 15, 1945 storm started a fire that destroyed a strategic World War II blimp base in southern Miami–Dade County, wiping out 368 military and civilian aircraft and 28 blimps. The site now hosts Miami's Metrozoo.

And Palm Beach County got not one, but two hurricanes, plus a tropical storm, all within an amazing five-week period in 1947. The storms poured massive rains on top of an already remarkable rainy season. For up to six months during and after the storms, floodwater covered 3 million acres—some 4,700 square miles—in twelve counties from Kissimmee to Florida Bay. South Florida is one of the wettest spots in North America, averaging five feet of rain per year. In 1947, nearly six feet fell in just 4½ months, and the total for the year was eight-and-a-half feet. The year started with an unusually rainy dry season and by July the sprawling fields of the interior were already flooded.

"There had been wet years in the Everglades before," Lamar Johnson, a flood-control district engineer from the 1920s to the 1970s, wrote in his 1974 book, *Beyond the Fourth Generation*, "but not since the area had become so populated, the property values so great, or the tools with which to battle the flood in such poor condition."

The September 1947 storm, the fifth of the season, actually had a name, albeit unofficial: "George." While it would be three more years before hurricane forecasters began naming storms formally, the National Weather Service's Miami office, following a military tradition begun during World War II, had begun giving storms names privately. "George" had top winds at 155 mph as it came ashore around midday on September 17 between Pompano Beach and Delray Beach. That made it a Category Four storm and the nineteenth most powerful on record to strike the U.S. mainland. Palm Beach temporarily lost virtually all its beach and large stretches of State Road A1A were washed away as far south as the Boynton Inlet. Boca Raton Army Air Field, now Boca Raton Municipal Airport and Florida Atlantic University, reported initial damage estimates of $4.5 million and later said that figure would rise. The storm then rolled across the peninsula at about 10 mph—Andrew had raced across at 18 mph—before crossing the Gulf of Mexico. In that crawl across Florida's interior, it dropped 6 to 8 inches of water over the Glades. Cattle stood in floodwater up to their bellies. Waves lapped over Conners Highway, and four feet of water pressed on dikes near Belle Glade. The storm went on to strike the upper Gulf Coast, and would eventually account for 51 deaths, 17 of them in Florida.

Despite the storm's tremendous power, forecasters received high praise for providing plenty of warning in time for people to shore up their homes or get out of the way. Some two days before it struck, the Miami office had already issued hurricane warnings for Florida's southeast coast. Unlike their 1928 counterparts, they were willing to err on the side of caution rather than brashly predict a complete miss and be disastrously wrong.

Then a tropical storm brushed the Gulf Coast on September 22, dropping still more heavy rains across the peninsula. Before the fields could drain, along came the October storm. The storm came ashore at Cape Sable at the peninsula's southwest corner, and angled across the Everglades, feeding on all that still-standing water. Had it dropped but a few inches of rain on top of an already-soaked South Florida, the results would have been catastrophic. But it proved to be even wetter than the September hurricane. Miami's National Weather Service office in Miami counted 1.3 inches of rain in ten minutes. The water plant in Hialeah recorded 6 inches in a little over an hour before its gauge overflowed. Totals of up to 15 inches were recorded over the Lake Okeechobee farming region. By the time the second storm had passed, floodwaters covered the peninsula.The water would finally subside. Total damage, if figured in today's dollars, would approach $1 billion.

Two more hurricanes struck in 1948, killing at least three people. Another flood inundated 3 million acres and caused another $50 million in damage. The U.S. Army Corps of Engineers asked Congress to authorize $208 million for the Central and Southern Florida Flood Control Project, a system of water-control reservoirs and canals that would cover 16,000 miles. The project began in 1948. The following year, it evolved into the Central and Southern Florida Water Management District, later renamed the South Florida Water Management District.

An August 26, 1949 hurricane struck the Palm Beach County coast and interior. It caused $1 million damage at Palm Beach International Airport in West Palm Beach, destroying or damaging 37 planes. But the Lake Okeechobee dike and the flood control system, only in their infancy, reduced the potential damage.

Soon the Water Management District wasn't just about where the water was going, but also whether there was enough and whether it was safe to drink. The agency became one of the most powerful government entities in Florida. In the meantime, nearly 7 million people had poured into South Florida, even more than optimistic projections had foreseen. And while storms did threaten Florida, none were on the magnitude of the great tempests of 1926, 1928, and 1935.

In the 1950s, forecasters began naming storms after the military phonetic alphabet; Able, Baker, Charlie. After just two years, they dumped that unwieldy system, and in 1953, the weather service went with female names. They reasoned people might pay more attention to a storm if they envisioned it as a tangible entity, a character, rather than just a bundle of wind. But the use of only women's names eventually was rejected as sexist and forecasters finally went to both male and female names in 1979.

A September 1950 storm, still unnamed, killed two. In October 1950, King, the first named storm, killed four. Flossy, in September 1956, struck Louisiana and north Florida, leaving fifteen dead. Donna, in August and September 1960, went from Florida to New England, causing fifty deaths. In 1964, Hurricane Cleo churned up the coast from the Keys to Georgia, causing $200 million in damage to Florida, $50 million of that in Palm Beach County alone. Just a few weeks later, Dora killed five in northeastern Florida and southern Georgia. And in October 1964, Isbell crossed the Everglades from the west. Several tornadoes were sparked by storm; one demolished twenty-two mobile homes in Briny Breezes, on the coast near Boynton Beach. One man died while putting up an awning at his Lake Worth home.

In 1965, Hurricane Betsy's outer edge, with wind gusts up to 60 mph, caused scattered damage to Palm Beach County as it passed through the Florida Keys and on to Louisiana. It killed seventy-five.

In 1972, Agnes marched from Florida to New York, leaving 122 dead. Three years later, Eloise hit the Florida Panhandle and eastern Alabama, killing four. Then, in 1979, came Hurricane David, the last hurricane considered to have struck Palm Beach County. Officially, David is considered a glancing blow. But it still did $30 million in damage in the county, collapsing the roof of the Palm Beach Jai-Alai fronton and knocking over a radio tower. It moved up the eastern seaboard, then came ashore in Savannah, caused mudslides in the Shenandoah Valley, and was still a nasty storm in Ontario in Canada. Along the way, it killed nineteen people, five in Florida. And it had left more than 1,000 dead in the Caribbean.

For the most part, though, the second half of the twentieth century was a quiet time in Florida. Many scares, but nothing significant. At the same time, the population explosion continued. Hurricanes? People didn't pay much attention.

Fast-forward to October 1995. People were glued to their televisions, watching the O. J. Simpson verdict. Over on the Weather Channel, forecasters were begging residents of Florida's Panhandle to put O. J. aside for the time being. A storm had turned monstrous overnight and was rushing toward the Panhandle. Hurricane Opal leveled the Panhandle and much of the Southeast, killing nineteen.

South Florida residents could only shake their heads in sympathy. They had had their ordeal already. It was called Andrew.

If you visit southern Dade County, you'll see that the birds have returned. The trees have grown back. The walls are back up. Unless you look closely, you might never know. But the people remember. They can't get Andrew out of their heads that easily. Many of the homes and buildings that had been blown away have been rebuilt. But many of the families and businesses that gave them life never came back. The outside walls ripped from an apartment building, exposing its rooms like a dollhouse, are replaced. But the people who lived there may never feel safe again. The two-story church from which Andrew tore away an entire wall, bringing wind and rain into God's own house, is as good as new and back in operation. But people still wrestle with the question: Why?

People got plenty of warning, but even then, forecasters said on the afternoon of Friday, August 21, 2½ days before Andrew struck, that the storm was disorganized and wandering and they should go about their normal business. The next morning, the storm had reorganized and was on a beeline for Miami. Even then, forecasters still kept up hurricane warnings for a 230-mile stretch of Florida's east coast from Vero Beach to Key West.

Because of the uncertainty, and despite the fact that Andrew—remarkably—killed only fifteen people, emergency managers fear that everyone will flee next time a major hurricane threatens, and one million people in Palm Beach County will collide with two million racing up from the larger population areas to the south, causing a monstrous traffic jam in which motorists are still sitting in their cars at the Florida's Turnpike Lantana tollbooth when the giant winds envelop them. South Floridians see that calendar move inexorably toward summer, watch the satellite pictures of white fluffs of cotton crawling across the blue ocean, feel that tightly wound spring in their bellies, and wonder: Will I be next?

The National Hurricane Center moved to South Florida in 1943. In 1992, it was in an office building at Coral Gables, its instruments on the roof, when Andrew struck. The storm blew away almost every device. In May 1995, the center moved into a twenty-first-century facility on the campus of Florida International University, west of Miami.

Compared to the hurricane-forecasting technology of today, forecasters in 1928 didn't do much more than wet a finger and hold it into the wind. Forecasters now enjoy access to satellites and survey dozens of computer models. They fly in a $50 million jet, dropping instrument packages from 8½ miles up that send data faster than the human eye can follow. They employ everything from special radios to the Internet to warn people of danger. The geographic range of possible landfalls established when a storm is five days from striking is now about as wide as forecasters thirty years ago could set for a storm that was three days from hitting land.

But now, ironically, people have come to expect exactness. They see the dotted line that forecasters use to show the most probable track, and they think that's the *only* possible track. But what they should be paying more attention to is the "cone of probability" that surrounds the line and grows wider the farther out the forecast. Even now, the average geographical range for a storm twenty-four hours from landfall is about 90 miles. That's the equivalent of forecasting that a storm will make landfall at Fort Lauderdale, only to see it hit Fort Pierce to the north or Islamorada to the south. Or, say, forecasting a storm will strike Atlantic City, New Jersey, and having it slam into Manhattan or rake Maryland's eastern shore. Or making the call that the storm will hit Mobile, Alabama, and having it come ashore as far east as Fort Walton Beach, in the western Florida Panhandle, or as far west as New Orleans. And about 50 million people—more than one in seven Americans—now live on the Atlantic and Gulf coasts, the prime target areas for a hurricane.

"It scares the bejeebers out of me to see the development on the coast and know these people have not experienced the core of a hurricane," National Hurricane Center Director Max Mayfield said in May 2002. "A lot of people have what I call 'hurricane amnesia.' "

While Mayfield had weather counterparts in 1928, there were no emergency managers to coordinate preparations for—and recovery after—a major storm. The military and service agencies such as the Red Cross took it on themselves to bring help and recovery. When local, state, and federal governments finally did establish emergency-management agencies in Florida and elsewhere, it was in response not to hurricanes, but to the greater threat of nuclear attack.

Early managers had come from military backgrounds. For decades, Palm Beach County's emergency center was a quonset hut near the airport that dated back to its military operations in World War II. Finally, in 1998, the county opened a $6.2 million, 35,000-square-foot state-of-the art fortress in suburban West Palm Beach designed specifically to deal with severe weather, fire or explosion, a terrorist attack, or some other disaster. It had hookups for television live shots, Internet links, and giant screen televisions, along with backup generators. If necessary, a giant metal grate could slam down across its front door to protect it from a storm's powerful winds. For its first few years of existence, the center handled a few hurricane scares, then the famed ballot recount in the 2000 presidential election, then the response to the anthrax attack on the headquarters of the tabloid *National Enquirer* in nearby Boca Raton. But no actual hurricanes.

Hurricane Camille had been America's last catastrophic killer, causing at least 256 deaths in 1969. Agnes, three years later, killed 122; it is the last hurricane to kill more than 50 people in the United States. In the three decades since then, tropical storm Alberto killed 30 and tropical storm Allison 44, both due to heavy flooding. Increasing awareness and preparation, better building codes and the advent of mass communications have dropped average hurricane deaths from thousands per year at the beginning of the twentieth century to 100 a year now. But property damage has risen sharply. In a 1998 study, researchers— adjusting for inflation, population growth, and increased property values—determined the 1926 storm, should it follow the same path today, would be the costliest on record, with an estimated $80 billion in damage, dwarfing Andrew.

In the twentieth century, major hurricanes—with top winds of 111 mph or more—accounted for about 25 percent of all tropical storms, but have wreaked 85 percent of damages over the years. The Florida peninsula was hit by major storms seven times between 1944 and 1950. It was struck by only three in the nearly half-century that followed. In that time, the state's total population rose from 2 million to 15 million. In the twelve counties that make up peninsular South Florida from Lake Okeechobee south, the population went from just 584,233 to 5.7 million. Many people built many houses in many places they shouldn't have: on the beach, in low-lying swamps that were filled in, in areas without adequate drainage. William Gray, the Colorado State University professor who is uncanny in his hurricane predictions, points to a return to the climate conditions of 1931–1965, when eleven major storms struck the peninsula. He points to the way Florida juts out into the ocean, almost daring a storm to strike it. He says it has the greatest potential for catastrophic economic losses in America because of its large population and great wealth. And he points to the sheer law of averages.

"Florida," he says, "is just a sitting duck."

How Florida deals with hurricanes is another issue altogether.

America's fourth-most-populous state, with so many of America's problems and so many that are unique to it, is full of people who are from somewhere else—and it seems they have been there for only ten minutes. Most of them have never been through a hurricane. Just in the ten years following Hurricane Andrew in 1992, the population of the six counties from Fort Pierce to Key West grew from 4.5 million to 5.5 million. Even those who have grown up in the state are still hurricane novices. Andrew was the only major storm in Florida in decades, and struck such a concentrated area that, as people living just outside the Miami area viewed the images of destruction, they might as well have been watching something that happened in Texas.

It's rare for a storm—especially a powerful one—to actually strike South Florida, and there's much to compete for people's attention. As a result, residents, whether transplants or natives, just don't pay heed to the warnings. They don't shutter their homes and, when the storm is threatening, they line up in the parking lots of home-improvement centers and fistfights erupt as they struggle for panels of plywood to cover their windows.

Could another 1928 disaster happen? The easy answer is no. Now, in the twenty-first century, we receive days of warning that a storm may be coming our way. We can brace our homes or run like hell. A giant dike surrounds the lake. Could a hurricane still bring great loss of life? Sure.

And where would we put the dead?

The Grave

September 1928–September 2003: Seventy-five years

"Forgive us, O Lord."

Then they dug a hole.

In September 1928, in steaming hot South Florida, some 2,000 bodies lay decomposing, along with uncountable carcasses of snakes, chickens, cows, pigs, and every other animal, not to mention rotting vegetation. Most of the corpses were in standing water. The result was a medical crisis.

That's what faced health managers in September 1928. While it's easy to condemn institutional racism for the less-than-decent way they solved the problem, the immediate health emergency was real and had to be handled promptly.

Some bodies had to be fished out of the standing water with boat hooks. Sometimes they were so deteriorated that there was nothing strong enough to grab onto or the bodies simply fell apart. Often workers had to use nets.

At first, rescue workers—some loosely organized, some under the official supervision of the National Guard or local law enforcement—tried to bury people in a prompt but still-dignified manner. Soon the

227

sheer numbers of the dead made that plan impractical. Compounding that problem was the fact that the Glades was still in standing water, and would be for weeks. Where there was high ground, the muck was so saturated that bodies would just pop out of it.

So the rescue supervisors used barges to float bodies toward the coast. Once the barges were at high ground, near land, the bodies could be transferred to trucks to drive them the rest of the way to burial sites.

And, of course, the bodies of blacks and whites had to be separated. The whites would go to the city's Woodlawn Cemetery. The blacks would go somewhere else. Some corpses were too deteriorated to determine race, leaving workers with the terrible possibility that a Negro would go into a white grave. But they toiled on.

At Woodlawn, a backhoe dug a trench for the white dead. Inside were placed 69 people, most of them laid in coffins. Over on Tamarind Avenue, at the informal black cemetery, backhoes dug a much longer trench, 75 feet long and 20 feet deep. Inside were placed 674 bodies. None were in coffins.

Bodies of the white dead were placed on display for twelve to twenty-four hours to give loved ones a chance to identify them before they went into the grave at Woodlawn Cemetery. Black bodies pretty much went from the trucks to the trench at Tamarind. If a worker had been able to identify a black victim in the field or en route to Tamarind, it was tagged. Sometimes relatives got a chance to look over—and possibly identify—the black bodies just before they went into the hole, and a name was quickly written on a foot tag. The rest went in unidentified and unclaimed. Lime was sprinkled over the pile of bodies.

It's important to note that no official sat behind his desk and said, "Let's embark on a conscious and conspiratorial effort to treat blacks separately and without dignity." Local cops, weekend National Guardsmen, and everyday citizens who'd volunteered or been drafted into positions of leadership suddenly found themselves in charge of an unprecedented crisis. So they simply followed the critical needs of the moment and the mores of the era. Floridians in the 1920s would never have imagined any other response than to draft blacks for menial work. They'd never have imagined any plan other than to bury white bodies in the white cemetery and the much larger volume of black corpses in the larger trench in the black cemetery.

Clothilda Miller wasn't allowed to come near the mass grave on Tamarind to try to look for her relatives. While she believes some or all of them are in that hole, she has never found out which, if any, went in. She says few others got the opportunity for identification either.

"Nobody was saying, 'This is my sister. This is my brother,' " Clothilda, now Clothilda Orange, recalled in 2001. But, she said, "I presume, I'm sure, they got drowned. I guess I just knew in my heart."

At 3:00 P.M. on Sunday, September 30, recovery workers at the two West Palm Beach mass graves stopped their labor. For one hour, by proclamation of Mayor Vincent Oaksmith, everyone was to stop their labor in honor of the dead. Two separate ceremonies were held. Long before they began, people had begun gathering at the giant trenches about three miles and a world apart.

At Woodlawn, about 5,000 people sang "Jesus, Lover of My Soul." It was the same hymn Lucinda Sears had intoned for strength as she and her family clung to a tree in South Bay at the height of the storm. "Our hearts ache, dear Lord," a minister intoned. A woman swooned. Muffled sobs rose. A band played a funeral march. Three volleys were fired by National Guardsmen from the 124th infantry—Knolton Crosby's outfit. Perhaps Crosby himself fired his gun for the second time in a week, this time ceremonially and at the place where Crosby himself would lie one day. Taps wafted over the mass grave. A band played "Onward, Christian Soldiers" as it marched out of Woodlawn and into the street, ending the ceremony.

At the Tamarind grave for the black victims, 2,000 to 3,000 people came for the service. Clothilda Miller Orange said decades later she may have gone, but wasn't sure. She said her family held no formal service for their dead relatives, although they may have done something at their church.

Mary McCleod Bethune, the black education pioneer who also founded what is now Bethune-Cookman College in Daytona Beach, did attend.

"Our hearts were torn at the sight of the one large mound containing the hundreds of bodies of men, women and children," Bethune wrote later. "Those who had been spared stood with tear-stained cheeks, wringing their hands, because many of them had lost entire families, or many, many members of their families had been taken. The sadness of this scene fell upon us like a pall."

The next morning, schools finally opened. Life's cycle was slowly being renewed.

The inscription over Woodlawn Cemetery—"That which is so universal as death must be a blessing"—has stood for decades. But no such marker pointed to where Clothilda Miller Orange believes her loved ones rest. Over the years, the tract along Tamarind Avenue that held the 1.5-acre mass grave in its northeast corner hosted a slaughterhouse, a dump, an incinerator and a sewage plant. In 1964, 25th Street was moved, and part of it was built over the grave and neighboring graves from a paupers' cemetery. Workers pulled out bones to make way for the road and reburied them at Woodlawn.

For the survivors, life went on.

On Christmas Day 1928, Ruth Shive had her baby, Milton. Many in the Glades came to visit the symbol of rebirth, born on a day that celebrates rebirth, in an area returning from the dead. In 1929, she made about twenty-six pages of handwritten notes about her ordeal; Milton later saved them.

Coot Simpson's widow, Juanita Simpson, eventually remarried, to a man named Jules Nixon. She died in 1963. Marriage records show that Stanford Simpson, Coot's son, married Louisianne Wright in Palm Beach County in February 1941. He later divorced and married Ida Margaret Lea in Maryland. The two lived for four decades in Delaware, then retired in 1984 to Appling County, Georgia, where Stanford had been born. He died of cancer at seventy-eight in April 1997 and was buried at Rachel Baptist Church, the same rural black church whose cemetery held the grave of his father. Stanford and Ida had raised a daughter, Michele. They sent her to Boston College, where she received a bachelor's degree. She later got a master's degree in management at Lesley College, near Boston. She is now director of human resources for the Boston Red Sox, the last major-league baseball team to hire a black player.

Michele Julian knew how her grandfather had died but had never learned anything about Knolton Crosby, the man who killed him. "The really frustrating thing is I can't tell my father what happened to him [Crosby]," she said in 2002.

At some point in the 1930s or early 1940s, Rachel Baptist Church had a fire. The building burned down and its records were destroyed. Coot's grave marker has long since been destroyed by the elements.

Vernon Boots, the fourteen-year-old who rode a floating, bucking house into the side of the U.S. 27 embankment and lost his parents and brother, moved in with his two surviving brothers to the home of his half-brother, Bill Rawle, and Bill's wife and two daughters. Willie and Ray later moved but Vernie stayed until he was married at twenty-seven in 1940. Vernie would later farm and would help build the big dike around the lake in the 1930s and 1940s. He went on to become a designer of farm equipment and eventually retired and moved into an assisted-living facility in Tampa. In a 1988 interview for a story on the storm's sixtieth anniversary, he was asked why he believed he survived when so many had died. He said, "You just have to accept things. It's just good not to question the Lord."

Helen Sherouse, later Helen McCormick, the thirteen-year-old who had lost eighteen of her nineteen relatives, told the story many times in her life. She would say that for the rest of her life, each approaching hurricane filled her with dread. "It leaves you with the feeling that anything can happen at once," she said in 1988, still tearing up sixty years later. "I live with it every day." But, she said, "It wasn't me that saved me. A thirteen-year-old kid couldn't have saved themself. It just wasn't my time, I guess."

In high school, in a fit of catharsis encouraged by her teachers, she wrote her memories of the storm. She later gave them to a friend. But years later, when she wanted to give the notes to the local historical society, the friend could not find them. Helen died at eighty-four in February 2000. In 1988, in an anniversary article, she had said ominously of Palm Beach County, "We haven't had a hurricane here in years. And the next one's going to be terrible."

After Charles and Lucinda Sears climbed down from the tree that had saved their lives, the Red Cross took Lucinda to West Palm Beach.

Nine days later, in a Miami hospital, Lucinda gave birth to Thomas. Another child, Vernita Cox, would later become mayor of South Bay. Lucinda died in September 1977, Charles in April 1986. Daughter Effie said in 2001, "Even if a strong wind comes, I'm afraid of the storm. Even today."

Carmen Salvatore rebuilt the home he had lost and returned to farming. He would say later that, every once in a while, as he worked the land, he'd run across a collection of bones in the muck. Whether these skeletons were new or prehistoric or were, in fact, the remains of 1928 storm victims will never be known.

Carmen spent eight years on the city council and housing authority and represented the Glades on the Palm Beach County School Board, at a time when Pahokee was the county's third-largest town. He later helped found the East Beach Drainage District and was commander of the local American Legion post. In 1976, he was named Pahokee Citizen of the Year. During his first year on the school board, in 1933, he spent a day with Eleanor Roosevelt, who was on a visit to South Florida. Carmen had long spoken out about conditions in the labor camps that housed the migrants who worked the fields. He said they were so crowded they "had children in the yard on clothes hangers." The first lady's touring car met him in South Bay. She opened the door and told him to jump in. Within months, quite possibly through Eleanor Roosevelt's influence, the labor camps broke up, and federal-government crews were building new labor villages.

Carmen retired from farming in the early 1960s, after three bad crop years brought losses totaling more than $100,000. He sold 400 cows and most of his land, paid off his creditors, and got out. Filing for bankruptcy, he would say later, would have meant stealing from creditors who had kept him in business for four decades, even through the Depression.

Into his later years, Carmen suffered a series of ailments but his voice remained strong and his memory sharp.

Halley's comet bypassed earth in 1986. Again it brought cries of catastrophe. But Carmen had survived it in 1910 and had survived a real catastrophe, in 1928, right in his backyard. What could a mere comet do?

The Grave

Carmen, Jr. went on to become a crop-duster pilot, despite his father's efforts to steer him to less perilous work. Late one afternoon in 1959, forty-year-old "Junior," exhausted from a long day of flying, had agreed to make one last run from the Belle Glade municipal airport. Over a field in Pahokee, not far from the family compound, one of his plane's wings caught a power line. The aircraft spun to the ground, igniting a full load of sulfur dust and killing him. His son, Carmen "Skeets" Salvatore, III, was Pahokee's police chief for thirty-one years before retiring in May 2000.

In 1988, Skeet's son Adam Salvatore, then seventeen, had taken part in a project with about 100 high-school students in a gifted-students' program at the Belle Glade campus of Palm Beach Junior College, now Palm Beach Community College. The group produced a half-hour documentary on the great 1928 storm. They called it *The Night 2,000 Died*. The tape had been introduced in May of that year. The students spent a year going through clippings and museum items and videotaped interviews with about a half-dozen survivors, including Adam's great-grandfather, Carmen Salvatore. At times, teacher Pam Campbell said, students were moved to tears.

On September 16, 1988, Carmen and about eight other survivors had joined about 150 people at the mass grave at Port Mayaca. It had been exactly sixty years since the storm. Limping and supported by his great-grandson Adam, he placed a wreath of flowers at the granite marker. Belle Glade police fired an eighteen-gun salute. A color guard lowered the flag. Willie Pyfrom, director of the band at nearby Glades Central High School, played taps. That day, Hurricane Gilbert had struck northern Mexico. In all, Gilbert would kill 327. At one point, in the open ocean, it had been the most powerful storm on record.

In 1992, "Pop" and Ella held an open house to celebrate three-fourths of a century of marriage. Carmen died two years later, in June 1994. He was ninety-eight. Ella died, also at ninety-eight, in December 1999. Daughters Mary Paulette, Iris Hodges, and Lucille Herron, who survived the storm in their parents' arms, still live in Pahokee. Milton, a son born later, lives in Ocala. At last check, there were eight grandchildren, fifteen great-grandchildren, and two great-great-grandchildren.

During the author's recent visit to the Salvatore compound in Pahokee, Skeets walked the property, marking off where the house had been and where his grandfather had fallen into the flooded ditch with his children and his grandmother had pulled them out. He pointed to the house where Iris and Mary still live and the old McClure house several hundred yards to the north along Bacom Point Road where the Salvatores had sought refuge. He noted the small cemetery that had been partially washed out by the storm. He crossed a footbridge to the giant dike and over it to the big lake, so big you cannot see the other side. And he stood beneath the cypress tree that had stood before Carmen Salvatore had moved to Florida, stood when the young doughboy had stepped off a mail boat into his bride's arms, stood against a great storm, stood as Pop and Ella celebrated seventy-five years together, and stands even now.

Eugene McCann, III, born at West Palm Beach's Good Samaritan Hospital at the height of the storm, moved with his family from their home near the hospital in 1934. He followed his grandfather to the West Palm Beach Police Department, where he spent fifteen years as a vice cop, followed by six years as chief investigator for State Attorney Marvin Mounts. He also belonged to the National Guard, and helped transport refugees from their homes to shelters in the middle of the 1949 hurricane. In 1971, McCann left police work and trained to become a Seventh-Day Adventist minister. He spent the next two decades serving congregations across Florida before retiring in 1993 at his last stop, Bushnell, about an hour's drive northeast of Tampa.

The 1928 hurricane and the real estate crash that followed did Harry Kelsey in. In 1931 he left the city he had founded and which bore his name. Eight years later, it changed its name to Lake Park. The arch that greeted visitors turning into the town near Old Dixie Highway was torn down. Kelsey died in 1957. Meanwhile, Kelsey's former business partner, Sir Harry Oakes, had moved to the Bahamas, where he was bludgeoned to death in 1943 in one of the area's most sensational society murders. His son-in-law was charged with the slaying but later acquitted, and the case remains officially unsolved. In 1997, some Lake Park residents floated an idea to restore the name "Kelsey City," but the plan fizzled.

The Grave

Thelma Dey, who had struggled in the water in only a kimono and lost her husband and infant son, recovered slowly from the crushed knee and cuts she suffered. Her two surviving children were placed in an orphanage until she reclaimed them the following year. She later remarried, and her two sons both served in World War II. Son Lewis, named for his father but called Billy by everyone, went on to be a policeman in West Palm Beach and later in Lake Park, where he rose to police chief. Thelma's leg remained stiff for the rest of her life, and in every home she lived in until her death in 1963, she made sure there was one secure room. She wrote down her story of the hurricane and tried many times, without success, to have it published, although excerpts did appear in publications. Her family says the original manuscript is lost. Thelma had gone often to the Ortona cemetery, to place stones on the homemade concrete headstones etched by hand with the names of her first husband and her baby. Years later, in 1998, Thelma's daughter, Jane Dey, was searching the cemetery. She had made many visits in the past but been unable to find the stones, buried in the sand. Jane insists she distinctly heard the voice of her dead grandmother directing her to the spot, where she dug and found the stones.

The son of Floyd Wilder, one of only six survivors in his home, later started a company in Lake Worth with his own three sons. It sells window protection for hurricanes.

Gus Jordahn, the tough guy of Gus's Baths, who had rode out the storm on the island of Palm Beach, went on to serve as a commissioner in both the town of Palm Beach and Palm Beach County. On his fiftiest birthday, "Captain Gus" swam the Intracoastal Waterway from Palm Beach to the mainland and back. Only six years later, in February 1938, he died of pneumonia, less than a decade after he had successfully challenged one of the world's greatest hurricanes head-on. In 1991, a plaque that had been mounted on a Palm Beach seawall to honor the Cowboys of the Sea was smashed to rubble. It fell victim to a powerful wave, not from a hurricane, but a strong fall storm. The marker was replaced a short time later.

Lawrence E. Will, who had shut down his gas station and hid from the storm, became fascinated with local history and traveled all over the

Glades. Will would later become the Glades' "cracker historian," writing in a backwoods dialect that might have sounded genuine—except that Will was born in Wisconsin, was the son of a Harvard-educated scientist who had been a college president, and went to high school in Washington, D.C. Between 1961 and 1968, he wrote six books, all in a folksy backwoods dialect. They include *Okeechobee Hurricane and the Hoover Dike,* the first significant telling of the storm. It came out in 1961, the same year Hoover came to South Florida to dedicate the dike named for him. Will dedicated the book to Hoover. Will spent the last years of his life in West Palm Beach, where he died in December 1977. His books are still in print, and the museum attached to the county library in Belle Glade bears his name.

Former Florida Governor John Wellborn Martin died in Jacksonville in February 1958. He was seventy-six. That same year, longtime state engineer F. C. Elliot retired after forty-six years of service. He was eighty. He died five years later.

Charles Seabrook would stay on at the Jupiter Lighthouse until 1947 and died some time in the 1950s. For decades, the story of how the equipment to turn the giant light broke down, how Seabrook became ill, and how his sixteen-year-old son, Franklin, continued to turn the giant light by hand was accepted as fact. But then Ray Swanson, the son of assistant keeper Ralph Swanson, challenged the long-held story, arguing his father, not the boy, turned the mechanism. Swanson claimed Franklin Seabrook, trying to obtain a college scholarship, either invented or at least encouraged the story. "Old man Seabrook always thought his son was up there," Swanson said.

Franklin Seabrook never did go to college; he captained numerous privately owned yachts and was only forty-nine when he died of heart failure in 1961. "I've never heard anyone ever even question the story," his daughter, Janet Rosenkrance, a Jupiter-area bookkeeper, said in 2001. "All the years the story was told, neither he nor his father ever said anything differently. It's unfortunate Mr. Swanson picks now to deny the story when there's no one left to support it."

Perhaps Seabrook's wife was the culprit; "Maybe he told his son to go up and she kept him from going up and never told Seabrook that the son didn't go," lighthouse director Carol Dickenson said.

"It doesn't make sense that the keeper would send his son up there when he had two other people on the base," argues Charles Milhauser, a retired professor who is also a guide and wrote the tour manual that guides use for reference. "It was their job. If they had the duty that day or night, no matter what the weather or risk to their lives they had to do it or they'd be fired."

Aggravating the problem is the fact that neither the museum, the National Archives, nor any other agency has the original keeper's logs dating back to 1928.

The Coast Guard, which had taken over management of the light-houses when the U.S. Lighthouse Service was shut down in 1939, let all keepers stay on until they retired. A succession of Coast Guard lighthouse keepers followed until 1987, when the light became fully automated. Except for a lightning strike here and there and some electrical problems in the late 1980s, it shone nonstop until October 1999, when the historic light tower underwent a six-month, $856,000 renovation. The lenses, hand-ground in France more than a century and a half earlier, were taken down by the Coast Guard and recalled and reinstalled. 500 gallons of imported paint restored an earlier brick-red color to the exterior. The light was rekindled in April 2000 and continues to sweep the seas off the Florida coast.

After the 1928 storm, a cousin had taken in Clothilda Miller and her family in until the Red Cross rebuilt their home. For the rest of her life, she donated to the organization in gratitude. She said later she could not remember when things returned to normal or when she went back to work. "You didn't have time to grieve," she said. "Not with the house gone and all. I grew up quick. We took care of each other. We listened to each other. I had to get on with my life."

Soon after the storm, Clothilda dropped out of school and found work washing clothes in the afternoons for several West Palm Beach families. She recalls earning $3 a week. She never had to look for work. It was plentiful, and she got many references. Five years later, on October 4, 1933, Clothilda Miller, then nineteen, was married to clothes salesman Willie Orange at the Palm Beach County Courthouse by County Judge Richard Robbins. The couple divorced about fifty years later, in July 1982, and Willie Orange died at seventy-six on October 31, 1988.

At last count, Clothilda had twelve grandchildren and three great-grandchildren. In 1999, when Hurricane Floyd, as powerful as Andrew and as big across as Hugo, threatened South Florida, a grandson from Orlando came down with a suitcase to pack her things and get her out. She would not leave. She trusted her concrete-block home to keep her safe.

During her life, Clothilda Miller Orange had never gone out to the Glades, to the place where she believed her parents died. "Never interested," she said. "Not that I couldn't go. I didn't want to go. What am I going to the Glades for?" Then she said, looking into the distance, "That's history. You have to pick up and move on."

She had gone a few times to that unmarked spot off 25th and Tamarind. Her parents are probably down there. But who knows? "I love my parents, but I didn't want to go," she said.

Like Clothilda, few in the black neighborhood forgot about the grave. But it had no fence to set it off, no marker, no sign proclaiming that so many lay there.

In 1983 the city swapped the land to Union Missionary Baptist Church for other land the church owned. Church officials later said the city never told them the property held a mass grave. In 1987, still unaware of what was under the soil, the church sold the property to the father of local pest-control executive Jim Kolkana for about $175,000. Because of its grim legacy, the tract's appraised value might have been as little as $1,000.

In the early 1990s, the movement to mark the mass grave moved into gear. In 1992, activists cried desecration when crews used backhoes to try to find the site's boundaries. The crews soon realized that city maps of the area were off. And in October 1991, about seventy people had conducted a ceremony that included Yoruba rituals from Nigeria designed to capture the spirits of the dead and release them to the afterlife. One of those attending was Robert Hazard.

Hazard had grown up in New England and had never heard about the 1928 storm until around 1975, the year he moved to Florida. He was at a Kwanzaa party and heard an old woman talk about the storm and the grave and the years of neglect. It made him angry and determined to do something. Hazard knew firsthand that segregation was not exclusive to the South. At seven, he'd been banned from playing in the Worcester, Massachusetts, Little League.

Hazard, currently an administrator at a West Palm Beach charter school, began compiling a list of those in the grave by combing newspaper reports from 1928 that gave daily listings of dead, separated by race, of course. He presumed all of those on the black list to be in the grave. But he also knew the list was far from complete.

And he got an idea. He envisioned a 14-acre project: a $6 million garden, monument, and memorial and educational center. Exhibits would detail the history of local blacks and the migrant workers who toiled in the fields, complementing the many proud histories of white Glades pioneers with the stories of the black, Caribbean and Hispanic workers who toiled alongside them. Displays would tell of the 1928 storm and its victims. They would explain hurricanes and how to prepare for them and provide updated weather reports. A volunteer program based at the center would run lectures. It would also serve as a community center. A garden would encourage picnics or play or reflection.

Hazard created the Storm of '28 Memorial Garden Coalition. But he didn't raise any significant amount of money and had difficulties with staffing and expertise and maintaining momentum. An early partner, Bennie L. Herring, II, left and has focused on educational programs. In 2002, Herring and Fred Barch, a program planner in the Palm Beach County School District, designed a curriculum about the storm that won an award from the Florida Governor's Hurricane Conference.

The city ordered up some plans as well. One called for spending about $50,000 for a black granite memorial, perhaps with a gate or arch leading into a pavilion, surrounded by wildflowers.

West Palm Beach mayor Joel Daves began negotiating with the Kolkanas, the pest-control family that owned the land. Talks slowed, and an attempt to obtain a state grant to buy the land failed when the application was found to be faulty. Hazard, Herring, and other activists wondered publicly and loudly if the city would be moving faster were 674 white people buried under the street. The city commission finally voted to seize the land outright from the Kolkanas. The city employed its power of eminent domain, which lets government buy land at an appraised value without the owner's consent.

In December 2000, the city commission approved $180,000 to buy the property outright and lease it to the coalition for ninety-nine years. Plans called for a four-foot-high decorative fence and landscaping.

About a year later, in January 2002, for the first time in three-fourths of a century, the grave holding the remains of nearly 700 people was recognized officially. A walkway lined by logs and covered with fresh bark mulch now led from 25th Street to the black sign with white lettering that identified the site and told the story of the storm and the mass grave.

"Forgive us, O Lord, for the times when we allowed hate, or just prejudice, or situations that we grew up with, to shield from our eyes, and especially our hearts, the reality of your love for us and the reality that we are all alike," said Bishop Anthony J. O'Connell of the Diocese of Palm Beach.

Soon after that ceremony, Hazard got a surprise ally: the local state attorney, Barry Krischer. Krischer had moved to the county from Brooklyn in 1973. Remarkably, despite recent publicity, he had not heard of the grave until reading about the marker ceremony. Krischer's office had recently applied for a grant to preserve the papers of William Holland, Sr., a local black lawyer who had marched alongside the Reverend Dr. Martin Luther King, Jr., in the 1960s. Holland had started the local desegregation movement in 1956, when he sued to force an all-white school to enroll his five-year-old son in a West Palm Beach school. Krischer suggested the storm museum also be a repository for the history of Palm Beach County blacks. It would house Holland's large collection and those of others. A local architecture firm was approved to design the building as a pro bono project. The local power company was asked to donate about half of a 5-acre piece it still owned on a corner of the tract that includes the grave. Soon Krischer had obtained $325,000 in state money. And in September 2002, the National Park Service approved the city's request and placed the site on the National Register of Historic Places.

Over the years, more ceremonies have been held. On a Friday morning in March 2002, King Nana Kwame Akuoko Sarpong, a chief from

Ghana, in West Africa, stooped and poured water from a crystal vase onto the mass grave, calling for peaceful rest for the souls of the dead.

In the 1970s, Ruth Wedgworth, whose husband owned a large Glades produce firm, got the idea of a memorial to hurricane victims and survivors. It would go in front of the Palm Beach County Library branch in Belle Glade. Hungarian-born sculptor Ferenc Varga of Delray Beach got a $30,000 commission to create it. Bert Roemer, a local contractor, donated a chunk of concrete, and Varga made a relief that was mounted on it April 13, 1976. It showed farmers, animals, homes, and telephone poles caught up in waves. On Memorial Day in 1976, the town held a festival for the U.S. Bicentennial. The parade grand marshal was Lawrence Will, the Glades' "cracker historian." A wing of the county library was dedicated as the Lawrence Will Museum. And the 8½ ton, 6½ foot bronze statue was dedicated. A man, a woman and a boy are running. The woman carries an infant in her arms. As they look over their shoulders, they raise their arms in a feeble attempt to ward off an unseen wall of water.

And back in West Palm Beach, the Storm of '28 Memorial Garden Coalition was, as of this writing, planning commemorative events for the storm's seventy-fifth anniversary, in September 2003. Plans included a symbolic motorcade or procession of empty coffins, from the Glades into West Palm Beach and directly to the mass grave. The coffins would represent the faceless dead of the storm of 1928.

The group was also trying to raise $500,000 for the first phase of the memorial and educational center at the site of the mass grave on Tamarind. An architect's drawing shows the building in the center of a walkway lined with trees, flowers, and benches. The walk is in the classic cyclone shape of a hurricane. In the rendition, the colors are bright, as if bathed in sunshine on a beautiful day.

There are no black clouds.

Storm at a Glance

Chronology: September 1928

Mon 10	Morning	First evidence of storm, 600 miles east of Barbados
	8 P.M.	First warning issued, for Martinique
Tue 11	3 P.M.	Winds shift at Barbados, indicating storm's approach
Wed 12	Noon	Landfall, Pointe à Pitre, Guadeloupe.
	Evening	Landfall, St. Kitts and Montseratt
Thu 13	11 a.m.	Landfall, St. Croix
	Evening	Landfall, Porto Rico
Fri 14	Morning	Storm off northeast cost of Haiti
Sat 15	Midnight	Landfall, Turk Island
		Warnings issued for Florida coast
Sun 16	2 A.M.	Storm passes north of Nassau
	10:30 A.M.	Hurricane flags hoisted from Miami to Daytona Beach
	About 6 P.M.	Eye makes landfall near Palm Beach
	9:15 P.M.	Eye passes over Canal Point
	10 P.M.	Lowest air pressure recorded in West Palm Beach
	10:45 P.M.	Highest winds recorded in Canal Point; estimated 160 mph
Mon 17	7 A.M.	Storm passes near Bartow, east of Tampa
	1 A.M.	Storm passes west of Jacksonville
Tue 18	Late P.M.	Storm crosses into North Carolina
Wed 19		Remnants merge with extratropical storm north of Parry Sound, Canada

The Hurricane in Numbers

Highest Florida winds (estimated) 160 mph. Fifth most powerful U.S. landfalling storm

Florida rainfall: almost 10 inches from 8 A.M. Sept. 15 to 4 P.M. Sept. 17; 18.42 inches Sept. 15–22

Deaths

Guadeloupe	600–1,200
Grand Turk	18
Nassau	3
Martinique	3
Porto Rico	312–1,600
Total Caribbean	**1,224–2,824+**
Florida	Official: 1,836 (pending increase to 2,500 under review in summer of 2003)
Philadelphia area	7
New Jersey coast	3
Maryland	1
Total Americans killed	**2,300–4,000**
Total death toll	**3,000–7,000**

Florida Health Department Death Totals

Belle Glade	611
South Bay	247
Pahokee	153
Miami Locks	99
Chosen	23
West Palm Beach	11
Prosperity Farms	5
Jupiter	4
Fort Lauderdale	2

Storm at a Glance

Kelsey City (Lake Park)	2
Bartow	1
Boca Raton	1
Canal Point	1
Deerfield Beach	1
Pelican Lake	1
Orange City	1
Stuart area	1
Unknown locations	669*

*would include 25 reported dead at Okeechobee

TOTAL   **1,833**

Florida damage and Red Cross relief

Affected area	112,200 people in 20 counties
Buildings destroyed or damaged	32,400
Damage	$75 million (in 1920s dollars)
Livestock killed	1,278
Poultry lost	47,389
Families given aid	30,325
Volunteers assisting	3,390

The Legacy of the 1928 Hurricane

The mass grave in West Palm Beach is at the corner of Tamarind Avenue and 25th Street, about two miles northwest of downtown. Write Storm of '28 Memorial Garden Coalition, 1607 W. 40 St., West Palm Beach 33407. Call (561) 881-8298. Web page: **www.evergladesvillage.net/storm28/**

The 1928 storm monument in Belle Glade is in front of the Palm Beach County library, 530 S. Main St., 33430. Call (561) 996-3453. Open 10–8 Monday through Wednesday, 10–5 Thursday through Saturday. The Lawrence E. Will Museum, owned by the city of Belle Glade, is in an annex to the county library. Founded in 1976, it displays artifacts, memorabilia, photographic, and written records about the Glades growing region. A panel display recounts the 1928 storm. Access to Lawrence E. papers and area newspapers dating to 1294 is by permission. Contact museum board: (561) 996-0100, ext. 601. Library web page: **www.pbclibrary.org/branch-bg.htm**

Port Mayaca Cemetery is the easternmost of two cemeteries on the south side of State Road 76, about two miles east of U.S. 441/98 at Lake Okeechobee. Write U.S. Highway 441, Pahokee 33476. Call (561) 924-2362

The Jupiter Inlet Lighthouse is open for tours, weather permitting, from 10 A.M. to 4 P.M. Sunday through Wednesday; last tour leaves 3:15 P.M. Admission: $5. Visitors must be at least four feet tall. The DuBois house is open 1 to 4 P.M. Wednesdays and Sundays. No admission charge. Call (561) 747-8380. Florida History Center and Museum is open 10 A.M. to 5 P.M Tuesday through Friday and 1 to 5 P.M. weekends. 805 North U.S. Highway One, Jupiter 33477. Call (561) 747-6639.

Palm Beach County Historical Society is in the historic Paramount Theatre building, at 139 North County Road, Suite 25, Palm Beach 33480. Research by permission. Call (561) 832-4164. Fax: (561) 832-7965. E-mail: **historicalsocietypbc@yahoo.com**

Florida Historical Society is at the Alma Clyde Field Library of Florida History, 435 Brevard Avenue, Historic Cocoa Village, 32922. Call (321) 690-1971 or (321) 690-0099. Web page: **www.florida-historical-soc.org/**

Lord, Somebody Got Drowned

The source of this poem and song is unclear. An October 24, 1928 *Palm Beach Post* story gives no author, saying only that it was found in the files of the American Red Cross. Examinations of those files at the National Archives in 2001 and 2002 did not uncover it. The 1928 story says the "negro spiritual" is "typical of the songs the negro has always woven around catastrophe." It says the song was first performed at a religious service three days earlier, on Sunday, October 21, and predicts it would "travel by 'grapevine' from community to community until it will be heard wherever negroes are to be found in this country."

> On the sixteenth day of September, in the year of 1928, God started to riding early and He rode to very late.
> In the storm, oh in the storm, Lord somebody got drowned. Got drowned, Lord, in the storm!
> He rode out on the ocean, chained the lightning to His wheel. Stepped on the land at West Palm Beach, and the wicked hearts did yield.
> Over in the town of Pahokee, families rushed out the door. And somebody's poor mother has never been seen no more. Some mothers looked at their children, and as they looked they began to cry. Cried, oh my Lord, have mercy, if you don't we all must die!

The Legacy of the 1928 Hurricane

Schoolhouses, halls and theatres, in the storm, they was all blown down. In the city of West Palm Beach, only two churches left in town.

I'll tell you, you wicked people, what you had better all do. Go down and get the Holy Ghost, and live a good life, too.

Out around Lake Okeechobee, all scattered on the ground. The last account of the dead folks, there was twenty-two hundred found.

South Bay, Belle Glade and Pahokee, they tell me they all went down. And in the little town of Chosen, they say everybody got drowned.

Some folks are still missing, and ain't been found, they say. But this we know, they will come forth on the Resurrection Day.

When Gabriel sounds the trumpet and the dead begin to rise. I'll meet those saints from Chosen, up in the heavenly skies.

In the storm, oh in the storm, Lord somebody got drowned. Got drowned, Lord, in the storm!

Source: *Palm Beach Post,* October 24, 1928

Read More About It:

Lawrence E. Will, *Okeechobee Hurricane and the Hoover Dike,* Great Outdoors Publishing, 1961. For decades, *Hurricane* was the only book-length account of the storm.

Eric L. Gross, *Somebody Got Drowned Lord,* planned for publication by University Press of Florida. Adapted from Gross's 1995 doctoral dissertation at Florida State University. A comprehensive analysis of the politics surrounding the disaster, especially the settlement of the Glades and the building of the dike.

Robert Mykle, *Killer 'Cane, the Deadly Hurricane of 1928* (2001, Cooper Square Press). Mykle, a travel and adventure writer and a part-time resident of Palm Beach County, interviewed dozens of survivors.

Zora Neale Hurston, *Their Eyes Were Watching God,* 1937, Harper Perennial, New York. This classic of black literature features as a key plot line the 1928 hurricane and the treatment of its black victims.

Note: Some of the material in *Black Cloud* was previously published in the *Palm Beach Post.*

Acknowledgments

Unlike Academy Award winners, the author will not bore the reader with a lengthy display of gratitude. But it is a fact that this book would never have happened if not for the copious and unconditional assistance of the following agencies and individuals:

Howard Kleinberg

Jeff Gerecke, JCA Literary Agency, and Philip Turner, Keith Wallman and Linda Kosarin of Carroll & Graf. Also: writer John Underwood, for introduction to Jeff.

Palm Beach Post: Managing Editors Tom O'Hara and John Bartosek, Associate Managing Editor Jan Tuckwood, Delray Beach Bureau Chief Elisa Cramer; head librarian Sammy Alzofon and staff researchers Monica Martinez and Dorothy Shea; reporters Doug Kalajian, Bob King, Scott Hiaasen and Mary McLachlin; books editor Scott Eyman.

Archives of *Palm Beach Post, Palm Beach Times, Fort Lauderdale News, Miami Herald, Miami News, New York Times*. Other newspapers as listed in chapter sources.

National Archives, Washington, D.C., and College Park, Md.; Marjorie Carliante (visits April 9–10, 2001 and June 3, 2002)

Library of Congress, Washington, DC

U.S. Coast Guard; historian Robert M. Browning, Jr.

National Hurricane Center, Miami; Director Max Mayfield; Deputy Director Director Ed Rappaport; specialists Brian Jarvinen, Jack Beven; public affairs officer Frank Lepore; technical librarian Bob Britter.

National Oceanic & Atmospheric Administration Hurricane Research Division, Miami; Stanley Goldenberg and Christopher Landsea

National Climatic Data Center, Asheville, N.C.; Sam McCown, Myra Ramsey

Ontario Climate Centre, Downsview, Ontario; Sandy Radecki

South Florida Water Management District, West Palm Beach; Cynthia Plockelman, Reference Librarian

State Library of Florida; Deborah Mekeel, reference services

Florida State Archives, Tallahassee; archivist R. Boyd Murphree.

National Guard Archives; Crystal McNairy. Florida military historian Robert Hawk. Camp Blanding Museum; Greg Parsons, curator

Florida Photographic Collections, Tallahassee; director Joan Morris

Florida Agricultural Extension Service Everglades station, Belle Glade; Kathleen L. Krawchuck, coordinator of academic support services

Storm of '28 Memorial Garden Coalition; Robert Hazard

T.R.U.T.H.S., Inc.; Bennie L. Herring II, executive director

Belle Glade Museum Board/Glades Historical Society, Belle Glade; Joseph R. Orsenigo, chair

Lawrence E. Will Museum, Belle Glade

Palm Beach Community College/Belle Glade,library; Mohamed Mansour, assistant director

Glades Heritage Project; Sandra L. Mercer, coordinator

Port Mayaca Cemetery; Art Ivester, director

Florida Department of Environmental Protection, Tallahassee; Joe Knetsch, historian

Florida Historical Society, Cocoa; Lewis N. Wynne, director; Debra Wynne, archivist

Acknowledgments

Historical Association of Southern Florida, Miami; Becky Smith and Dawn Wells, staff researchers

Historical Society of Palm Beach County; Cheryl Houghtelin, executive director; Debi Murray, Director of Research & Archives; David Waldstein, research assistant. Historical Society of Martin County; Susan Duncan. Museum of the City of Lake Worth; Beverly Mustaine. Delray Beach Historical Society, archivist Dorothy W. Patterson.

United States Magistrate Judge Ann E. Vitunac, West Palm Beach

U.S. Army Corps of Engineers, Jacksonville District; Public Affairs Chief Jacquelyn J. Griffin

Chicago Historical Society; Archie Motley, archivist

AT&T Archives; Betty Sweeney

Clothilda Orange and the families of Thelma Dey and Carmen Salvatore. Families of Coot Simpson and Knolton Crosby. Local historian Dot Tillman, Surrency, Georgia. Appling County, Georgia, Clerk of Court Floyd Hunter

Florida State University library, Special Collections; Deborah Harper Rouse, instructor librarian

University of Central Florida library; Donna Goda

University of Miami library

Bethune-Cookman College library, Daytona Beach; Bobby R. Henderson, director

Florida Atlantic University Special Collections; Craig A. Tuttle, archivist

Palm Beach County library; Michael E. Parcell.

Broward County library

Miami-Dade County, Florida Collection; Sam Boldrick

Hendry County Library, Clewiston; Kathy Veale, assistant director

University of Florida library, Department of Special Collections; James A. Cusick, curator

Palm Beach County School District; Fred Barch, program planner

American Red Cross Archives, Washington, D.C.; Andrew A. Nichols, Records Specialist

American Legion, Indianapolis; Joe Hovish, librarian,.

Bahamas Archives, Nassau; Jolten Johnson, D. Gail Saunders
Bahamas Department of Meteorology, Nassau; Rodger Demeritte, technical officer
Turks & Caicos National Museum; Nigel Sadler, director
British High Commission for Antiqua and Barbuda; Anne Jackson, Information Officer
British Embassy, Washington; James Forbes and Alex Hall Hall, assistants
Montserrat National Trust; Jean White, office manager
Montseratt historian Bill Innanen

And, of course, my wife and children, for their support and patience.

Research for *Black Cloud* was done without the benefit of the editions of the afternoon *Palm Beach Times* for the month of September 1928, which were apparently stolen from the binders at some point. Any reader who has *Times* materials from that period is urged to contact us in care of the publisher or contact the *Palm Beach Post* directly. Also, at least two sets of files from Lawrence Will's files on the 1928 hurricane disappeared from the Lawrence Will Museum some time between the mid 1970s and 1990. Please contact us or the museum if you know where they are.

The title *Black Cloud* was suggested by my dear friend Art Fyvolent on May 17, 2001, over a martini and a bourbon at the "42nd Street" bar in Tampa, Florida. It suggests the dark clouds of a hurricane, the funeral pyres in the Glades, the storm's many black victims, and the dark tragedy of the treatment of those black victims.

September 1928

xii: "The bracelet caught Festus Stallings' eye." Interview with Frank Stallings, February 2002

xiii: "It is a great lake . . ." *Palm Beach Post,* May 18, June 1, 1988; June 18, 1994; December 19, 1999; March 19, September 16, 19, 30, 2000. Interviews with Clothilda Miller, October 19, 2000, October 5, 2001

Chapter 1: Tamarind Avenue

1: "3 A.M. on a February day on 1919 . . ." Interview with Iris Hodges and Mary Paulette, June 10, 2002. Palm Beach Community College gifted students lectures: Carmen Salvatore, October 7, 1987. *Palm Beach Post,* April 4, 1993; June 8, 1994; December 11, 2000

2: "Clothilda Miller slept . . ." Interviews with Clothilda Miller, October 19, 2000, October 5, 2001

3: ". . . now vanished settlement . . ." Belle Glade Chamber of Commerce

3: Not far from Clothilda's . . ." *Chicago Defender,* September 29, 1928

Chapter 2: Big Water

5: "Before everything else . . ." Nelson Manfred Blake, *Land Into Water/Water into Land.* George E. Buker, *Sun, Sand and Water, a History of the Jacksonville District, U.S. Army Corps of Engineers, 1821-1975.* Florida Waters: A Resource Manual from Florida's Water Management Districts. Kathryn Abbey Hannah, *Florida: Land of Change.* U.S. Congress hearings, "Flood Control in Florida and Elsewhere," January 29, 1929

6: "Early European explorers . . ." *Palm Beach Post,* August 9-11, 1928; September 23, 1984; August 15, 2000; May 27, May 30, 2001. Alfred J. and Kathryn A. Hanna, *Lake Okeechobee, Wellspring of the Everglades.* Nelson M. Blake, *Land Into Water—Water Into Land: A History of Water Management in Florida*

7/8: In 1881, state officials . . ." Hamilton Disston biographical sketch, Florida Handbook, 1993-1994. Address by Jacob S. Disston, Jr., January 17,1950. Lamar Johnson, *Beyond the Fourth Generation.* Junius Elmore Dovell, *A History of the Everglades of Florida,* doctoral thesis, University of North Carolina,. 1947. Charlton Tebeau, *A History of Florida.* Eliot Kleinberg, *Weird Florida*

9: "It would be less than a decade . . ." Napoleon Bonaparte Broward biographical sketch, Florida Handbook, 1993-1994. Samuel Proctor, *Napoleon Bonaparte Broward: Florida's Fighting Democrat*

12: "Carmen Salvatore had settled . . ." Interview with Carmen Salvatore, May 17, 1988. Palm Beach Community College gifted students lectures: Carmen Salvatore, October 7, 1987.

15: Blacks were believed to account for . . ." Eric L. Gross, *Somebody Got Drowned, Lord,* doctoral dissertation, Florida State University, 1995. Belle Glade Chamber of Commerce

15: "By 1928, the state's plan . . ." Everglades Drainage District, *Report of Everglades Engineering Board of Review, May 1927* F. C. Elliot, letter to *Everglades News,* reprinted in September 1978 commemorative edition. Minutes of Everglades Drainage District, September 29, 1928

16: F. C. Elliot was a dapper . . ." F. C. Elliot biographical sketch, Florida Handbook, 1952 Edition. F. C. Elliot biographical sketch, *Florida: Historic, Dramatic, Contemporary,* by J. E. Dovell. Eric L. Gross, *Somebody Got Drowned, Lord,* doctoral dissertation, Florida State University, 1995

17: "Lawrence E. Will had come to the Glades . . ." *Palm Beach Post,* May 18, June 1, 1988; June 18, 1994; December 19, 1999; March 19, September 29, September 30, 2000.

17: William Henry and Mattie Mae Boots . . ." Vernon Boots, "The Story of My Family," memoir, courtesy Joseph Orsenigo, Lawrence E. Will Museum, Belle Glade "Two extremely wet rainy seasons in a row . . ." Patsy West, "The Disastrous 1928 Lake Okeechobee Hurricane," *Update,* Historical Association of Southern Florida, August 1975.

Chapter 3: Black Cloud

19: "The world's great Atlantic hurricanes . . ." *Fort Lauderdale Sun-Sentinel, Sunshine Magazine,* September 12, September 19, 1999. *National Geographic,* July 2001

21: "The storm moves off Cape Verde . . ." "Cape Verde," CIA World Factbook 2000 (Internet)

21: "For centuries, storms were more the province . . ." "The Deadliest Atlantic Tropical Cyclones, 1492-1997," National Hurricane Center. Leonard G. Pardue, *September Remember: The Story of Hurricanes,'* 1977. David Waldstein, "Hurricanes and History," Historical Society of Palm Beach County

21: "In the 1930s . . ." *WPA Guide to Florida*

22: "Christopher Columbus ran into a hurricane . . ." Jay Barnes, *Florida's Hurricane History*. David Waldstein, "Hurricanes and History," Historical Society of Palm Beach County.

23: "While Florida's modern history . . ." Charles Mitchell, "Hurricanes of the South Atlantic and Gulf States, 1879-1928," U.S. Weather Bureau

23: "If the region that would later . . ." *Our Century,* by the staff of *The Palm Beach Post*

24: "The first possible hurricane . . ." *Our Century,* by the staff of *The Palm Beach Post*.

24: "A 1903 storm did extensive damage . . ." *Weekly Lake Worth News,* September 12, 1903.*Tropical Sun,* September 16, 1903. "Deadliest, Costliest and Most Intensive United States Hurricanes of this Century," National Oceanic and Atmospheric Administration, 1997

25: "On October 17, 1906 . . ." Fred A. Hopwood, *The Golden Age of Steamboating on the Indian River.* Jay Barnes, *Florida's Hurricane History.* David Waldstein, "Hurricanes and History," Historical Society of Palm Beach County.Charles Mitchell, "Hurricanes of the South Atlantic and Gulf States, 1879-1928," U.S. Weather Bureau. "Deadliest, Costliest and Most Intensive United States Hurricanes of this Century," National Oceanic and Atmospheric Administration, 1997

25: "But none of these early twentieth century storms . . ." "Deadliest, Costliest and Most Intensive United States Hurricanes of this Century," National Oceanic and Atmospheric Administration, 1997. National Hurricane Center. National Oceanic and Atmospheric Administration, Hurricane Research Division. National Weather Service hurricane synopses. *Palm Beach Evening Times,* October 18, 1926. Interview with Rusty Pfost, meteorologist in charge, National Weather Service Miami office, Friday, December 14, 2001. L. F. Reardon, *The Great 1926 Hurricane and Disaster.* Weather Bureau correspondence, National Archives. *Palm Beach Post,* August 9-11, 1928; September 23, 1984; August 15, 2000; May 27, May 30, 2001

30: "But the storm hadn't limited its damage to the southeast coast." Lawrence Will, *Okeechobee Hurricane and the Hoover Dike. Palm Beach Post,* May 30, 2001.

31: "It didn't take long for the criticism to start flying . . ." Eric L. Gross, *Somebody Got Drowned, Lord,* doctoral dissertation, Florida State University, 1995.

31: "One agency had not waited for politics after the 1926 storm . . ." American Red Cross records, 1928 hurricane, National Archives

31: "Just up the road from West Palm Beach . . ." *Palm Beach Post,* August 9-11, 1928; September 23, 1984; August 15, 2000; May 27, May 30, 2001. Charles Branch, unpublished manuscript; courtesy Lake Park Historical Society

32: "The 1928 season started busily." *Palm Beach Post,* August 9-11, September 12,1928. Jay Barnes, *Florida's Hurricane History.*

Chapter 4: The Islands

35: "On Thursday, September 13 . . ." Charles Branch, unpublished manuscript; courtesy Lake Park Historical Society

35: "The Leeward Islands, fifteen large ones and many tiny ones . . ." Gustavo A. Antonini, "Leeward Islands," World Book Online Americas Edition
36: "On the morning of September 10 . . ." Fernando Bayron-Toro, "Porto Rico," World Book Online Americas Edition
37: "Its neighbor, Martinique . . ." State Department records, National Archives
38: "At Pointe à Pitre . . ." National Weather Bureau correspondence file; American Red Cross records, 1928 hurricane; National Archives
39: "For the most part, scientists see no link . . ." James F. Lander and Lowell S. Whiteside, *Caribbean Tsunamis: An Initial History,* University of Colorado
40: "Among those killed . . ." *New York Times,* September 18-23, 1928
40: "On September 20, eight days after the storm . . ." State Department records, National Weather Bureau correspondence file, National Archives
42: "Montseratt is a tiny, bean-shaped, British-controlled island . . ." National Weather Service synopsis of 1928 hurricane. "A Condensed History of Montserrat," compiled by William G. Iannanen, 1998 (Internet)
43: "Back in West Palm Beach . . ." Palm Beach Post, September 1928
43: "At least thirteen died in neighboring Nevis . . ." R. Spencer Byron, "I Remember When: The Hurricanes of 1924 and 1928," Nevis Historical and Conservation Society, 1988. Kathleen Manchester, "Historic Heritage of St. Kitts," 1971 *London Times,* September 1928
44: "Late on Thursday, September 13, the merchant ship *Matura.*" National Weather Service synopsis of 1928 hurricane. *New York Times,* September 18-23, 1928
Map calculations are from the "How Far Is It" web page sponsored by Indo.com, the Indonesian Internet company

Chapter 5: Porto Rico

47: "Porto Rico is a rectangular island . . ." Fernando Bayron-Toro, "Porto Rico," World Book Online Americas Edition
48: "On Tuesday morning, September 11, Oliver Fassig . . ." National Weather Service synopsis of 1928 hurricane. National Weather Bureau correspondence file, National Archives
49: "At 4 A.M., the lights went out at Catano . . ." National Weather Service synopsis of 1928 hurricane. National Weather Bureau correspondence file, National Archives. *London Times,* September 1928. *Miami Daily News,* September 15, 1928. *Miami Herald,* September 13, 1928. *New York Times,* September 16-17, 1928. *The Times,* San Juan, September 18, 1928. *Lighthouse Service Bulletin,* November 1, 1928
52: "the *Palm Beach Post,* which had played the storm downpage . . ." *Palm Beach Post,* September, 13-18, 1928. American Red Cross, *The West Indies Hurricane Disaster,* September, 1928
52: "On the morning of Friday, September 14 . . ." National Weather Service synopsis of 1928 hurricane. National Weather Bureau correspondence file, National Archives. *London Times,* September 1928. *Miami Daily News,* September 15, 1928. *Miami Herald,* September 13, 1928. *New York Times,* September 16-17, 1928. *The Times,* San Juan, September 18, 1928. Elizabeth K. Van Deusen, "Porto Rico,

Ravaged by Storm, Takes Up Task of Reconstruction," *New York Herald Tribune,* October 7, 1928; "The Porto Rican Hurricane," *American Review of Reviews,* November 1928. U.S. Senate proceedings, "Report of the Central Survey Committee appointed by Governor Horace M. Towner of Porto Rico, Relative to the Losses Arising from the Hurricane of September 13, 1928," December 5, 1928.
55: "By Thursday afternoon, September 14 . . ." Gary Brana-Shute, "Dominican Republic," World Book Online Americas Edition. National Weather Service synopsis of 1928 hurricane. National Weather Bureau correspondence file, National Archives.

Chapter 6: Bearing Down
57: "On Friday, September 14, West Palm Beach residents . . ." *Palm Beach Post,* September 14-15, 1928. National Weather Service synopsis of 1928 hurricane. National Weather Bureau correspondence file, National Archives.
57: "Out in the Atlantic, the Turks and Caicos . . ." Gerald R. Showalter, "Turks and Caicos Islands," World Book Online Americas Edition. William Richardson Tatem, Hurricane Relief Officer, Turks and Caicos Islands, *Report on the Hurricanes of 1926 and 1928.* National Weather Bureau correspondence file, National Archives. W. E. Sadler, *Turks Islands Landfall,* 1980
60: "Mitchell's advisory from Jacksonville . . ." National Weather Service synopsis of 1928 hurricane. National Weather Bureau correspondence file, National Archives.
60: "But on Friday evening, the *Post* . . ." Charles Branch, unpublished manuscript; courtesy Lake Park Historical Society. *Palm Beach Post,* September 13-14, 15, 21, 1928.
62: "Noah Kellum Williams, a dairy farmer . . ." Noah Kellum Williams, "Life in Palm Beach County, Florida, 1918-1928, Part II: The Real Estate Boom and the Hurricane of 1928," from *Grandpop's Book,* edited by Charlton W. Tebeau. Portions courtesy Vera Williams, Cocoa, Fla. Other portions reprinted in *Tequesta,* journal of the Historical Association of Southern Florida, 1984
62: "As the barometer fell . . ." *Palm Beach Post,* September 13-14, 15, 1928
62: "In Nassau, ships scrambled . . ." Victoria Mosely Moss, "Reminiscing: The Terrible Storms of '26 and '29," *Nassau Tribune,* June 18, 1987. Nassau Department of Meteorology observations, September 16, 1928. *Nassau Guardian,* September 15, September 19, September 22, 1928. *Nassau Tribune,* September 15, September 19, 1928. September 1928 marine weather reports, National Climatic Data Center, Asheville. N.C. *New York Times,* September 18, 1928. National Weather Service synopsis of 1928 hurricane. National Weather Bureau correspondence file, National Archives. State Department records, National Archives
67: "But at 6 P.M. in Kelsey City . . ." Charles Branch, unpublished manuscript; courtesy Lake Park Historical Society

Chapter 7: West Palm Beach
69: "About 1 A.M. Sunday . . ." "Premonition Becomes Grim Reality," James Knott, "Brown Wrapper," *Palm Beach Post,* October 7, 1979
69: " 'Storm Moving Nearer Coast . . ." *Palm Beach Post,* September 18-30, 1928.

National Weather Service synopsis of 1928 hurricane. National Weather Bureau correspondence file, National Archives.

72: "In the black section of town . . ." Interviews with Clothilda Miller, October 19, 2000, October 5, 2001

72: "Beryl Lewis, a writer . . ." *Palm Beach Post,* September 1978. West Palm Beach City Directory, 1928 edition. West Palm Beach Police blotter, September 16, 1928

73: "Shortly after lunch, Tom Rickards . . ." 1928 letters to Kate Rickards from Sheriff Robert C. Baker, March 30, September 27; from Tom Rickards, October 3; from T. M. Rickards Jr., date unknown; all courtesy T. M. Rickards Jr.

73: "Determined not to be caught unprepared . . ." American Red Cross, *The West Indies Hurricane Disaster,* September, 1928. American Red Cross files, 1928 hurricane, National Archives

74: "Ruth Stewart, wife of a West Palm Beach dentist . . ." Letter by Ruth Stewart, September 1928, published in *Palm Beach Post,* November 24, 1988; courtesy Jay Stewart.

74: "About 3 P.M., the power failed . . ." *Palm Beach Post,* September 18-30. . West Palm Beach Police blotter, September 16, 1928

75: "Dick Wilson, a bank director . . ." Biography of Dick Wilson (undated); Historical Society of Palm Beach County

76: "In Jupiter, Bessie DuBois . . ." Bessie DuBois, personal memoir, portions of which appeared in *The Loxahatchee Lament,* 1977, and in the September 2, 1984, installment of Judge James R. Knott's "Brown Wrapper" historical supplement to the Sunday *Palm Beach Post.* Full text courtesy John R. DuBois III.

77: "National Hurricane Center forecaster . . ." Brian Jarvinen, National Hurricane Center; interviews and correspondence, June 27, 2002

77: "Late in the afternoon, as the full force of the storm . . ." Letter from Milburn A. Bishop to his wife Myrtle, September 18, 1928; courtesy of Kevin Beatty

77: About a mile to the north . . ." Interview with Eugene McCann, Bushnell, Fla., May 24, 2002

80: "Just down the road in Lake Worth . . ." Letter from Bo Wright, September 30, 1928; courtesy of his granddaughter, Renee B. Gordon, Palm Beach Gardens

80: "Charles Ruggles, the West Palm Beach Engineer . . ." Letter from Charles Ruggles, September 27, 1928, in National Weather Bureau files, National Archives

81: "The storm was probably about as big across . . ." Brian Jarvinen, National Hurricane Center; interviews and correspondence, June 27, 2002 The Weather Notebook, Mount Washington Observatory.

83: "In West Palm Beach's black section . . ." Interviews with Clothilda Miller, October 19, 2000, October 5, 2001

83: "The Palm Beach Yacht Club lost its pier . . ." The Official Record," newsletter of U.S. Department of Agriculture; September 26, October 3, October 10, October 17, 1928. *Fort Lauderdale Daily News,* September 14-15, 1928. *New York Times,* September 18-20, 1928. *Pioneers in Paradise,* by Jan Tuckwood and Eliot Kleinberg and the staff of the *Palm Beach Post. Palm Beach Daily News,* February 11, 1938; February 10, 1946. *Palm Beach Post,* September 18-30, 1928; June 11, 1933; February 11-12, 1938; October 30, 1994; September 27, 1998; April 17, 2000.

Endnotes

Chapter 8: The Outer Bands

87: "Bessie Wilson DuBois had come to the beautiful Jupiter Inlet . . ." Bessie DuBois, personal memoir, portions of which appeared in *The Loxahatchee Lament,* 1977, and in the September 2, 1984, installment of Judge James R. Knott's "Brown Wrapper" historical supplement to the Sunday *Palm Beach Post.* Full text courtesy John R. DuBois III. *Palm Beach Post,* May 28, 1989; September 27, 1998; September 16, 2001

88: "Dairy farmer Noah Kellum Williams . . ." Noah Kellum Williams, "Life in Palm Beach County, Florida, 1918-1928, Part II: The Real Estate Boom and the Hurricane of 1928," from *Grandpop's Book,* edited by Charlton W. Tebeau. Portions courtesy Vera Williams, Cocoa, Fla. Other portions reprinted in *Tequesta,* journal of the Historical Association of Southern Florida, 1984. "The Hurricane of '28," *Jupiter Courier,* Roger Buckwalter, Editorial editor (Internet). "Hurricane memoirs," Brown Wrapper, *Palm Beach Post*

91: "What happened next?" *Palm Beach Post,* September 16, 2001

92: In Boynton Beach, about 30 miles to the south . . ." Boynton Beach Schoolhouse Museum. Interviews with Lorraine Lewerenz Vicki, Aileen Lewerenz Warner, Marie Shepard; June 19, 2002.

93: "But the southern end of the eye wall was still further south . . ." Delray Beach Fire Department, Delray Beach Historical Society. *Fort Lauderdale Daily News,* September 19, 1928. *Miami Herald,* September 17, 1928. *Miami Daily News,* September 17, 1928

Chapter 9: The Glades

95: "On Sunday morning . . ." Vernon Boots, "The Story of My Family," memoir, courtesy Joseph Orsenigo, Lawrence E. Will Museum, Belle Glade. Interviews by Palm Beach Community College gifted students for "The Night 2,000 Died:" Carmen Salvatore, Edith VanLandingham, Gertrude Van Horn, Helen Sherouse McCormick, Vernita Cox, Vernie Boots. Palm Beach Community College gifted students lectures, 1987-1988: Jabo Tryon, Vernie Boots, Geraldine Grimes, Helen Sherouse McCormick, Carmen Salvatore, Marvin Unwin. C.A. "Mutt" Thomas, "The Story of My Family and Other Historical Information on Lake Okeechobee, Ritta Island and the Lake Harbor Area," with Ruth Irvin, June 20, 1978; courtesy Belle Glade Historical Society. Jeff Klinkenberg, "A storm of memories," *St. Petersburg Times,* July 12, 1992

98: "A pumping station near Pahokee . . ." Nixon Smiley, "The Night the Lake Became an Ocean," *TROPIC* Magazine, *Miami Herald,* September, 15, 1968

99: "State Engineer F. C. Elliot later reported . . ." F. C. Elliot, Chief Engineer, Biennial Report, 1927-1928, to Board of Commissioners of Everglades Drainage District; "Effects of the September Hurricane upon Lake Okeechobee," "Florida Engineer and Contractor," October 1928.

National Archives. National Weather Service. *Palm Beach Post,* September 21-28, 1928

101: "At 6 P.M., Lawrence E. Will had finished filling . . ." Lawrence Will, *Okeechobee Storm and the Hoover Dike*

102: On Kreamer Island . . ." "First Hand Accounts of the 1928 Hurricane," James Knott, "Brown Wrapper," *Palm Beach Post,* December 10. 1978

102: "Helen Sherouse was 13." Interview with Helen McCormick, May 17, 1988. *Palm Beach Post*; June 1, September 17, 1988; September 27, 1998

103: "Ruth Ellen Shive Carpenter had traveled . . ." Ruth Ellen Shive Carpenter, "A Time of Stress," memoir, written 1929, courtesy Milton O. Carpenter and Historical Society of Palm Beach County

104: "Floyd Wilder was ten . . ." "The Story of My family: Experiences of my family in the South Bay area in early days and an account of the hurricanes of 1926, 1928," by Floyd Oliver Wilder, written by Ruth S. Irvin. Text courtesy Wilder family. Portions published in *Tampa Bay History,* Spring/Summer 1983. Wilder died at 64 in 1982.

106: "Frede Aunapu was a dragline operator . . ." Nixon Smiley, "The Night the Lake Became an Ocean," *TROPIC* Magazine, *Miami Herald,* September, 15, 1968

107: "At 8:18 P.M., the anemometer at the University of Florida's . . ." F. C. Elliot, Chief Engineer, "Effects of the September Hurricane upon Lake Okeechobee." American Red Cross, *The West Indies Hurricane Disaster,* September, 1928. Associated Press, "1928 Fla. Hurricane USA's second deadliest," September 21, 2000

108: "Storms usually lose punch . . ." Brian Jarvinen, National Hurricane Center; interviews and correspondence, June 27, 2002

108: "Carmen Salvatore had no idea . . ." Interview with Carmen Salvatore, May 17, 1988. Interview with Mary Paulette and Iris Hodges, June 10, 2002

110: "If it had been daylight the people on the north shore would have seen the water receding . . ." Brian Jarvinen, National Hurricane Center; interviews and correspondence, June 27, 2002. Kyle S. VanLandingham and Alma Hetherington, *History of Okeechobee County*

110: "Charles Sears, Jr., and Effie Sears Ransom had been born . . ." Interviews with Effie Sears, May 31, 2001, and Charles Sears, Jr., June 1, 2001, Fort Lauderdale. Charles Wesley, *Jesus, Lover of My Soul, Hymns and Sacred Poems,* 1740

Chapter 10: In the Morning

113: "At dawn, Tom Rickards and his family . . ." Letters written in 1928 to Kate Rickards from Sheriff Robert C. Baker, March 30, September 27; from Helen Rickards, September 23; from Tom Rickards, October 3; from T. M. Rickards Jr., date unknown; all courtesy T. M. Rickards Jr.

113: "Clothilda Miller and her siblings . . ." Interviews with Clothilda Miller, October 19, 2000, October 5, 2001

113: "In Jupiter, a bleary-eyed and disheveled . . ." Bessie DuBois, personal memoir, portions of which appeared in *The Loxahatchee Lament,* 1977, and the September 2, 1984, installment of Judge James R. Knott's "Brown Wrapper" historical supplement to the Sunday *Palm Beach Post.* Full text courtesy John R. DuBois III.

114: "Why wasn't there more of a storm surge along the coast?" *Palm Beach Post,* September 18-30, 1928; September 15, 1977; June 1, 1988; December 7, 1991

115: "Noah Williams and his party . . ." Noah Kellum Williams, "Life in Palm Beach County, Florida, 1918-1928, Part II: The Real Estate Boom and the Hurricane of 1928," from *Grandpop's Book,* edited by Charlton W. Tebeau. Portions courtesy Vera Williams, Cocoa, Fla. Other portions reprinted in *Tequesta,* journal of the Historical Association of Southern Florida, 1984

116: "On Monday morning, a woman was brought to Fort Lauderdale's . . ." *Miami Herald,* September 19, 1928

116: "In Pahokee, Carmen Salvatore surveyed . . ." Interview with Carmen Salvatore, May 17, 1988

117: "Charles Sears Sr., still in the tree . . ." Interviews with Effie Sears, May 31, 2001, and Charles Sears, Jr., June 1, 2001, Fort Lauderdale.

117: "Frede Aunapu, crushed inside a pile of swirling trees . . ." Nixon Smiley, "The Night the Lake Became an Ocean," *TROPIC* Magazine, *Miami Herald,* September, 15, 1968

117: "Ruth Shive, praying for her unborn baby." Ruth Ellen Shive Carpenter, "A Time of Stress," memoir, written 1929, courtesy Milton O. Carpenter and Historical Society of Palm Beach County

118: "Helen Sherouse had huddled . . ." Interview with Helen McCormick, May 17, 1988. Palm Beach Post; June 1, September 17, 1988; September 27, 1998

118: "Floyd Wilder found his siblings . . ." "The Story of My family: Experiences of my family in the South Bay area in early days and an account of the hurricanes of 1926, 1928," by Floyd Oliver Wilder, written by Ruth S. Irvin. Text courtesy Wilder family. Portions published in "Tampa Bay History," Spring/Summer 1983.

119: "Mutt and his father returned . . ." C. A. "Mutt" Thomas, "The Story of My Family and Other Historical Information on Lake Okeechobee, Ritta Island and the Lake Harbor Area," with Ruth Irvin, June 20, 1978; courtesy Belle Glade Historical Society

120: "The experimental station near Belle Glade was surrounded . . ." National Weather Bureau files, National Archives. F. C. Elliot, Chief Engineer, "Effects of the September Hurricane upon Lake Okeechobee." American Red Cross, *The West Indies Hurricane Disaster, September, 1928.* Red Cross 1928 storm files, National Archives

120: "In New York, Harry Kelsey opened . . ." Charles Branch, unpublished manuscript; courtesy Lake Park Historical Society

123: "The U.S. Weather Bureau advisory for the morning . . ." National Weather Bureau files, National Archives.

123: "Weather officials continued to track the hurricane . . ." *New York Times,* September 17-18, 1928. *Tampa Times,* September 27, 1928. *Times* (London), September 1928

127: "Frank Stallings's family had been the first . . ." Interview with Frank Stallings, February 2002

Chapter 11: Help

129: "About 6:30 A.M. Monday . . ." *Palm Beach Post,* December 7, 1991

130: "On Monday, the head of the Florida National Guard . . ." Florida National Guard Records. Governor John W. Martin biography, Florida Handbook

130: "On Tuesday, Martin and the state's comptroller . . ." Minutes of Everglades Drainage District Board, September 18-19, 1928

131: "The president of the United States also had not waited." *Palm Beach Post,*

September 18-30, 1928. *Miami Daily News,* September 19-28, 1928. *Miami Herald,* September, 18-20, 1928. *New York Times,* September 17-23, 1928. *Okeechobee News,* September 28, October 12, 1928. *Palm Beach Independent,* September 18, 1928. *Clewiston News,* September 21, 1928. *Fort Lauderdale Daily News,* September 19-28, 1928. *Tampa Morning Tribune,* September 19, 1928. American Red Cross records, 1928 hurricane, National Archives. American Red Cross, *The West Indies Hurricane Disaster,* September, 1928." *Catholic Yearbook,* 1929

133: *Post* composing room manager Bo Wright wrote his mother . . ." Letter from Bo Wright, September 30, 1928; courtesy of his granddaughter, Renee B. Gordon, Palm Beach Gardens

133: "The American Legion conference set for Sunday morning . . ." American Legion Correspondence, February 14, 1929

134: Telephone officials reported 32,000 accounts out of service . . ." *Western Electric News,* "Tropical Twister Lays Waste Florida Telephones," November 1928. Information supplied by Sid Poe, BellSouth spokesman, June 22, 2001

135: "The Palm Beach County Commission met . . ." Palm Beach County Commission minutes

136: "In Lake Worth, federal lawman Clarence H. Parks.." *Palm Beach Post,* June 4, 2000

Chapter 12: The Interior

139: "Why did so many die?" Palm Beach Post, June 1, 1999. Erik Larsen, *Isaac's Storm.* Brian Jarvinen, National Hurricane Center; interviews and correspondence, June 27, 2002. NOAA Hurricane Research Division

141: "On Monday morning, Glades resident Chester Young . . ." Chester Young, first-person account, reprinted in commemorative edition of *Everglades News,* 1978.

142: "Dr. William J. Buck . . ." "First Hand Accounts of the 1928 Hurricane," James Knott, "Brown Wrapper," *Palm Beach Post,* December 10. 1978

143: "Frank B. Willits and Noel McAlister, who had been . . ." "Premonition Becomes Grim Reality," James Knott, "Brown Wrapper," *Palm Beach Post,* October 7, 1979

143: "On Monday, West Palm Beach blacks . . ." Interviews with Clothilda Miller, October 19, 2000, October 5, 2001

145: "When the Coast Guard had arrived in West Palm Beach . . ." Florida National Guard Records

146: "About 11 A.M. on Monday, a team from the Florida Board of Health . . ." Florida Health Notes, State Board of Health, October-November 1928

149: "Frank Stallings and his father Festus had been driving straight through.." Interview with Frank Stallings, February 2002

150: "Around that time, Thomas Richard Brown, a National Guard colonel . . ." Letter from Colonel Thomas Richard Brown to his father, Clark Brown, September 18, 1928; courtesy Mary Sowell Baldwin, North Palm Beach

151: "On September 25, a weary woman struggled up the stairs . . ." *Moore Haven News,* September 21, 1928. *Palm Beach Post,* September 18-30, 1928. Letter from Thelma Jane Dey, Polk County, Fla., May 10, 2002

153: "One of the most compelling first-person accounts . . ." American Red Cross, *The West Indies Hurricane Disaster, September, 1928*. American Red Cross 1928 Hurricane files, National Archives

153: The story of Pelican Bay . . ." *New York Times,* September 17-23, 1928. *Okeechobee News,* September 28, October 12, 1928. *Palm Beach Independent,* September 18, 1928. *Hendry County News,* La Belle, Fla., September 20, 1928. *Miami Daily News,* September 19-28, 1928, May 12, 1929. *Miami Herald,* September, 18-20, 1928. *Moore Haven News,* September 21, 1928. *Palm Beach Post,* September 18-30, 1928. *Lighthouse Service Bulletin,* October 1928. Bill McGoun, "Levee, Lives no Match for Hurricane in 1928," "Yesterdays," *Palm Beach Post,* September 23, 1984. Patsy West, "The Disastrous 1928 Lake Okeechobee Hurricane," *Update,* Historical Association of Southern Florida, August 1975.

Chapter 13: Cleaning up and Rebuilding

157: "On Wednesday afternoon, September 19 . . ." *Palm Beach Post,* September 18-30, 1928.

158: "Coroner Tom Rickards and his family . . ." Letter to Kate Rickards from Helen Rickards, September 23, 1928; courtesy T. M. Rickards Jr.

159: "Willie Rawls, 14, of West Palm Beach . . ." Bill McGoun, "Levee, Lives no Match for Hurricane in 1928," "Yesterdays," *Palm Beach Post,* September 23, 1984

159: "The *Palm Beach Independent* was a rag . . ." *Palm Beach Independent,* September 21, September 28, 1928

161: " "What a joy it is to hear the birds again . . ." *Delray Beach News,* September 21, September 28, October 6, 1928

163: "On September 27, Palm Beach County Red Cross Chairman . . ." American Red Cross, *The West Indies Hurricane Disaster, September, 1928*. American Red Cross files on 1928 hurricane, National Archives. *Palm Beach Times,* November 20, November 22, 1928

163: "Tampa banker L.A. Bize wrote state newspapers just days after . . ." *Tampa Morning Tribune,* September 19, 1928

166: "On November 20, the Red Cross came under fire . . ." XX: "Our people are experiencing the worst treatment . . ." *Chicago Defender,* September 22, October 6, November 3, 1928

168: "While the correspondent was heavy on vitriol . . ." NAACP, report of the acting secretary for November (1928) Meeting of the Board; from NAACP papers

Chapter 14: Black and White

169: "On October 30, 1928, Colin Herrie the Red Cross' recovery coordinator . . ." American Red Cross files on 1928 hurricane, National Archives. *Palm Beach Post,* September 18-30, 1928. *Clewiston News,* September 21, 1928

175: "The Chicago-based Associated Negro Press . . ." "Declare Reports of Red Cross Unfairness in Florida Are Unfounded," Associated Negro Press release, November 1928, courtesy Chicago Historical Society

177: "On December 21, John D. Cremer, associate director . . ."John D. Cremer,

April 3, 1929 memorandum, in Red Cross files on 1928 hurricane, National Archives
178: "Statewide, the storm ruined . . ." *Okeechobee News,* September 28, 1928
179: "Nearly a month after the storm . . ." National Weather Bureau files, National Archives
179: "On October 23, Florida National Guard . . ." Florida National Guard archives
181: "Monday, September 24, eight days after the storm . . ." Lawrence E. Will, *Okeechobee Hurricane and the Hoover Dike*

Chapter 15: Coot Simpson

183: "When the Negro Workers Relief Committee had issued . . ." American Red Cross files, National Archives
183: "Who was Coot Simpson?" Florida and Georgia death certificates, Palm Beach County court records, U.S. Military and Florida National Guard records. Interview with Michele Julian, Boston, June 26, 2001 and February 2002. Interview with Wayman Wilcox, February 2002.
184: "He was a world apart . . ." National Guard records, Florida State archives. February 2002 interviews with Fred Scurlock, Okeechobee, Fla.; Cassie Mae Brooks, Titusville, Fla.
186: "An Associated Press brief that ran . . ." *Miami Herald,* September 24, 1928. *Palm Beach Post,* September 24-25, 1928;
187: " 'Negroes ordered to load bodies at Pahokee' . . ." Letter to Kate Rickards from T. M. Rickards Jr., 1928; exact date unknown; courtesy T. M. Rickards, Jr.
189: "On January 20, 1947, Crosby, then living at 712 Evernia . . ." *Palm Beach Post,* January 21, 1947

Chapter 16: The Dike

191: "Ten days after the hurricane . . ." Charles Branch, unpublished manuscript; courtesy Lake Park Historical Society
191: "The top of the front page of the *Okeechobee News* . . ." *Okeechobee News,* October 12, 1928
191: "The local American Legion . . ." F. C. Elliot, Chief Engineer, Biennial Report, 1927-1928, to Board of Commissioners of Everglades Drainage District; text of address to Rotary Club luncheon, Clearwater, March 13, 19
192: "In an October 24, 1928 note to Washington . . ." Weather Service Correspondence File, National Archives
193: "F. C. Elliot couldn't agree more." F. C. Elliot, Chief Engineer, Biennial Report, 1927-1928, to Board of Commissioners of Everglades Drainage District; text of address to Rotary Club luncheon, Clearwater, March 13, 1929
193: "In November, the Everglades Drainage District . . ." Minutes of Everglades Drainage District board, November 13, December 6, 1928
194: "'They built us a wall of dirt . . .'" *New York Times,* September 19, 1928
194: "On September 24, less than a week after the storm . . ." *Palm Beach Post,* September 18-30, 1928

194: "Within two weeks of the storm . . ." U.S. Congress hearings, "Flood Control in Florida and Elsewhere," January 29, 1929.U.S. Senate proceedings, "Emergency Relief for Storm Sufferers of Southeastern United States," Senate Committee on Agriculture and Forestry, December 19, 1928. *Clewiston News,* September 28, 1928

195: "On January 31, 1929, the Corps of Engineers submitted a new plan . . ." Elliot, F.C., Chief Engineer, Biennial Report, 1927-1928, to Board of Commissioners of Everglades Drainage District; text of address to Rotary Club luncheon, Clearwater, March 13, 1929. "Florida Everglades," United States Geological Survey Circular 1182

195: "In February 1929, new governor Doyle Carlton . . ." *Palm Beach Post,* February 16-17, 1929. Lawrence Will, *Okeechobee Hurricane and the Hoover Dike.* Nelson Manfred Blake, *Land Into Water/Water into Land*

196: "The anniversary of the storm passed . . ." *Palm Beach Post,* September 26-29, 1929;

196: The federal government had worried . . ." Okeechobee Flood Control District Report to Board of Commissioners, Activities of 1929-1943

197: "The dike would soon be tested . . ." Jay Barnes, *Florida's Hurricane History.* *Palm Beach Post,* September 18-October 1, 1928; February 16-17, 1929; May 18, September 17, 1988; November 18, 1990; April 4, 1993; June 1.

198: "While most of the dike was in place . . ." Ellis W. Hawley, "Hoover, Herbert Clark," World Book Online Americas Edition. *Palm Beach Post,* January 12-13, 1961. *Clewiston News,* January 12, 1961

199: "Not everyone likes the dike." *Palm Beach Post,* June 1, 1999; February 27, 2000; September 12, September 29, December 11, 2000; May 30, July 3, September 16, 2001; January 28, January 29, February 2, May 7, May 24, May 25, 2002. Steven M. Davis and John C. Ogden, editors, *Everglades: the Ecosystem and its Restoration.* Mark Derr, *Some Kind of Paradise.* "Lake Okeechobee and the Herbert Hoover Dike: A Summary of the Engineering Evaluation of Seepage and Stability Problems at the Herbert Hoover Dike," U.S. Army Corps of Engineers, September 2000

Chapter 18: Zora

205: "As winds howled . . ." Zora Neale Hurston, *Their Eyes were Watching God.* *Palm Beach Post,* February 25, 1997, December 19, 1999 *Bloom's Notes: Zora Neale Hurston's "Their Eyes Were Watching God."* edited by Harold Bloom.

205: "She had been in the Caribbean . . ." Zora Neale Hurston, *Dust Tracks on A Road*

206: "The story take some liberties . . ." *New Essays on* Their Eyes Were Watching God, edited by Michael Awkward

208: Hurston had said she was born . . ." Robert E. Hemenway, *Zora Neale Hurston: A Literary Biography.* Zora Neale Hurston, *Folklore, Memoirs and Other Writings.* Library of America. *Zora in Florida,* edited by Steve Glassman and Kathryn Lee Seidel. *Palm Beach Post,* December 19, 1999

Chapter 19: The Dead

213: "How many really died?" American Red Cross, *The West Indies Hurricane Disaster, September, 1928*. World Almanac and Book of Facts, 1999 edition. National Hurricane Center. NOAA Hurricane Research Division. Brian Jarvinen, National Hurricane Center; interviews and correspondence, June 27, 2002. Charlton Tebeau, *A History of Florida*, "Boom-Bust-Hurricane Twenties," pp. 388-389

215: " 'Who kept an accurate tally sheet?' " Correspondence from Joseph Orsenigo, Belle Glade Historical Society, February 8, 2002

215: "The future of the plot . . ." *Palm Beach Post*, December 1, 1993, June 6, 2002

217: "The 1935 'Labor Day' storm would be . . ." Rodman Bethel, *Flagler's Folly: The Railroad That Went to Sea and Was Blown Away*. Jay Barnes, *Florida's Hurricane History*. National Hurricane Center, "Deadliest Hurricanes in the United States"

219: " 'There had been wet years in the Everglades before . . .' " Lamar Johnson, *Beyond the Fourth Generation*

221: "In the 1950s, forecasters . . ." Jay Barnes, *Florida's Hurricane History*. National Hurricane Center, "Deadliest Hurricanes in the United States"

222: "If you visit southern Dade County . . ." *Palm Beach Post*, August 24, 1997

223: "Compared to the hurricane forecasting technology of today . . ." *Palm Beach Post*, December 1, 1993, June 6, 2002

224: "Hurricane Camille had been America's . . ." Jay Barnes, *Florida's Hurricane History*. National Hurricane Center, "Deadliest Hurricanes in the United States"

225: "In the twentieth century, major hurricanes . . ." *Palm Beach Post*, June 1, 1997. U.S. Senator Bob Graham, D-Florida, address at first commencement of Florida Gulf Coast University, Fort Myers; May 3, 1998. Text courtesy Graham staff.

Chapter 19: The Grave

227: "In September 1928 . . ." *Palm Beach Post*, September 18-October 1, 1928; February 16-17, 1929. *Palm Beach Times*, February 16, 1929; *Clewiston News*, September 28, 1928. *Glades County Democrat*, September 28, 1928. *Miami Daily News*, May 12, 1929. *Moore Haven News*, September 21, 1928. American Red Cross, *The West Indies Hurricane Disaster, September, 1928*

229: "Clothilda Miller wasn't allowed . . ." Interviews with Clothilda Miller, October 19, 2000, October 5, 2001

229: "At 3 P.M. on Sunday . . ." *Palm Beach Post, Palm Beach Times*, October 1, 1928

230: "Coot Simpson's widow . . ." Interview with Michele Julian, Boston. July 17, 2002. *Chicago Defender*, September 29, 1928

231: "Vernon Boots, the fourteen-year-old . . ." Interview with Vernon Boots, May 17, 1988

231: "Helen Sherouse, later Helen McCormick . . ." Interview with Helen McCormick. May 17, 1988

231: "After Charles and Lucinda Sears . . ." Interviews with Effie Sears, May 31, 2001, and Charles Sears, Jr., June 1, 2001, Fort Lauderdale.

232: "Carmen Salvatore rebuilt the home . . ." . . ." Interview with Carmen Salvatore, May 17, 1988 Palm Beach Community College gifted students lectures: Carmen Salvatore, October 7, 1987. *Palm Beach Post,* April 4, 1993, June 18, 1994

234: "Eugene McCann III, born at West Palm Beach's . . ." Interview with Eugene McCann, Bushnell, Fla., May 24, 2002

XX: "The 1928 hurricane and the real estate crash that followed . . ." "*Our Century,* by the staff of *The Palm Beach Post*

235: "Thelma Dey, who had struggled in the water . . ." *Moore Haven News,* September 21, 1928. *Glades County Democrat,* September 28, 1928. Letter from Thelma Jane Dey, Polk County, Fla., May 10, 2002

235: "Gus Jordahn, the tough guy . . ." *Palm Beach Post,* March 6, 2002

XX: "Lawrence Will, who had shut down his gas station . . ." *Palm Beach Post,* December 19, 1999

236: "John Wellborn Martin died . . ." Florida Handbook. *Miami Daily News,* May 12, 1929, March 20, 1955; November 9, 1963

236: "Charles Seabrook would stay on . . ." *Palm Beach Post,* September 16, 2001.

237: "After the 1928 storm a cousin had taken in Clothilda Miller . . ." Interviews with Clothilda Miller, October 19, 2000, October 5, 2001

238: "In 1983, the city swapped the land . . ." *Palm Beach Post,* December 11, 2000, January 29, 2002. Roy-Fisher Associates, "Burial Memorial for the Victims of the 1928 Hurricane," report for city of West Palm Beach, undated

240: "Soon after that ceremony . . ." *Fort Lauderdale Sun-Sentinel,* February 28, 2002

241: "In the 1970s, Ruth Wedgworth . . ." *Palm Beach Post,* December 15, 1975; April 14, April 15, June 1, 1976.

241: "And back in West Palm Beach . . ." Robert Hazard, "Storm of '28 Memorial Garden Coalition" (web page)

The Storm at a Glance:

National Weather Service, National Hurricane Center, American Red Cross, individual islands

Index

271

Index

Index

Index

Index

Orsenigo, Joseph, 214, 215
Ortona, Fla., 30, 119, 145, 151, 152, 214, 235
Overseas Highway, 218

Pahokee, Fla., 1, 2, 12-14, 18, 61, 98, 108, 116-18, 138, 145, 148, 155, 162, 187, 201, 215, 232, 233, 234
   1928 hurricane, 116-18, 138, 145, 148, 155, 162, 187, 244
Palm Beach Community College, 233
Palm Beach County, xiv-xv, 12, 23, 87, 216, 224, 230, 231, 235, 240
   1928 hurricane, 60, 82, 147, 153, 162, 163, 178, 180, 213-14, 243
   post-1928 hurricanes, 196, 219, 221, 222
Palm Beach County Commission, 135
Palm Beach County Courthouse, 73, 75, 79, 113, 165, 187, 237
Palm Beach County Historical Society, 248
Palm Beach County Library, 241, 247
Palm Beach County Loan Farm Fund, 178
Palm Beach County School Board, 232
Palm Beach County School District, 239
Palm Beach, Fla., 1, 3, 24, 114, 217, 219
   1928 hurricane, 82, 83-85, 120, 129, 135, 137, 235
   1928 hurricane relief, 129, 132, 159, 160
Palm Beach High School, 83
Palm Beach Independent, 159-60, 167
Palm Beach International Airport, 221
Palm Beach Junior College, 233
Palm Beach Lakes Boulevard, West Palm Beach, Fla., 78
Palm Beach Mercantile Company, West Palm Beach, Fla., 70
Palm Beach Post, 33, 132, 161, 187, 196, 248
   employees, 72, 80, 146, 163
   offices, 70, 81, 136, 151
   1928 hurricane, damages and relief, 133, 152, 155, 158
   1928 hurricane, forecasts, 43, 52, 60, 69-70, 74
Palm Beach Times, 32, 133, 175
Palm Beach Yacht Club, 83
Paradise Island, 64
Paramount News, 74
Paramount Pictures, 203
Parks, Clarence H., 136
Parry Sound, Ontario, Canada, 126, 243
Pass Christian, Miss., 139-40
Patrick Air Force Base, 210
Paulette, Mary Salvatore, 109, 233, 234
Paxton, Susannah, 176
Payne, W. A., 163
Pearl Harbor, Hawaii, 130
Peebles, Herbert Walter, 42
Pelican Bay, 153-54
Pelican Lake, Fla., 154, 245
Pensacola, Fla., 22, 30, 155
Pennsylvania, 125

Pennsylvania Hotel, West Palm Beach, Fla., 134, 156
Perla neighborhood, San Juan, Porto Rico, 54
Perth Amboy, N.J., 126
Philadelphia, Pa., 126, 137, 163, 244
Pickens, William, 176-77
"Picture City," 26
Pierson, Nat, 162
Pioneer Services Station, Belle Glade, 101
Pittsburgh, Pa., 126
Plymouth, Montserrat, 42
Point Pleasant, N.J., 126
Pointe à Pitre, Guadeloupe, 38, 40, 243
Points, J. Frank, 65
Polk County, Fla., 178
Pompano Beach, Fla., 76, 135, 149, 153, 165, 179, 219
Ponce, Porto Rico, 50
Port Mayaca, Fla., 11, 99, 202
   mass grave for hurricane victims, 147, 214-15, 233, 247
Port of Palm Beach, 162
Porto Rico (Puerto Rico), xiv, 22, 42, 43, 44, 46, 47-56, 73, 123, 131,163, 243, 244
Portugal, 21
Powell, Adam Clayton, Jr., 209
Prohibition, 14, 66, 136, 145
Prosperity Farms, Fla., 244
Puerto Plata, Dominican Republic, 56
Puerto Rico. See Porto Rico
Punta Gorda, Fla., 72, 121
Punta Rassa, Fla., 75
Pyfrom, Willie, 233

racial prejudice, xiv, 14-15, 37-38, 41, 62, 71, 120, 155, 158-60, 165, 186, 190, 194, 207, 227, 240
   Red Cross accused of racial prejudice, 167-77
   segregated burial of hurricane victims, 141, 148, 204, 211, 227-30
   segregation, 2-3, 149, 210, 239
Rachel Baptist Church, Surrency, Ga., 188, 230, 231
railroads, 6, 10, 11, 14, 25, 26, 92, 135, 181, 217-18
Randall, H. E., 120
Ransom, Effie Sears, 110
Raus family, 148
Rawle, Bill, 119, 231
Rawls, Willie, 159
Reardon, L.F., 28
Red Cross. See American Red Cross; French Red Cross; Junior Red Cross
Reddick, C. L., 142
Redding, Horace, 14, 117
Reed, C. J., 202
Reineck, Walter S., 37-38
Reno, Janet, 28
Rice, Estelle, 51
Rich, Claude, 130

279

Index

Index

About the Author

Eliot Kleinberg, a Florida native, has written six books, all focusing on Florida.

The son of noted South Florida journalist and historian Howard Kleinberg, he has spent a quarter-century in both broadcast and print news, including more than fifteen years at the *Palm Beach Post* in West Palm Beach, where he has covered such major events as Hurricane Andrew, the 1996 ValuJet plane crash, the 2000 presidential election recount, the September 11 hijackers' Florida movements, the Boca Raton anthrax attack, and the Catholic church's local sexual abuse scandals. He also writes extensively about Florida and Floridiana and has a column on local history.

He is a member of the Florida, South Florida, and Palm Beach County historical societies.

He lives at Casa Floridiana in Boca Raton, Fla. with his wife, bank executive Debra Vogel, and teenage sons Robert and Henry.